Cricket In The Park

Cricket In The Park

The Life and Times of Lord Sheffield
1832–1909

By Roger Packham

Methuen

First published in Great Britain in 2009 by
Methuen
8 Artillery Row
London
SW1P 1RZ

www.methuen.co.uk

1 3 5 7 9 10 8 6 4 2

Typeset by SX Composing DTP

Printed and bound in Great Britain by the Cromwell Press Group, Trowbridge

The author has asserted his moral rights.

A CIP catalogue record for this book is available from the British Library

ISBN 978 0 413 77693 8

Contents

Foreword   vii

Acknowledgements   ix

Introduction   xi

1   The Holroyds of Sheffield Park   1

2   Sheffield Park: A Lord's Ground   15

3   Lord Sheffield: Sussex President   29

4   Australians in the Park   46

5   The Prince in the Park   75

6   Other Grand Matches at Sheffield Park   83

7   Music and Dining in the Park   104

8   On Tour in Australia 1891–92   116

9   The Sheffield Shield   128

10   Parties in the Park   134

11   Scandal in the Park 1886–1889   153

12   The Vicar's Daughter   165

13   Disputes in the Park   175

14   Travels with Lord Sheffield   196

15   Trials in the Park 1880–91   209

16	Club Cricket 1845–1909	222
17	Soldiers in the Park	240
18	Death of Lord Sheffield	250
19	Sheffield Park 1909–2009	257
	Chronology	264
	Appendices	266
	Bibliography	287

Foreword
By The Rt Hon
Sir John Major KG CH

There are few historians of cricket with a knowledge to match that of Roger Packham, nor anyone I know with a greater love of the game.

Roger has a gift of bringing the past alive and setting it before the reader as if it were contemporary. Events and characters from long ago spring to life under his pen.

Lord Sheffield is one such man, who made his mark upon cricket in both England and Australia. His story, and that of his cricket ground, occupies an intriguing niche in the history of one of our national games, and I am delighted that Roger has turned his eye to this important, but neglected, subject.

It is not only lives of individuals that tell a story: so does the life of a place, and this is assuredly true of Sheffield Park. Sussex was one of the early cradles of cricket, long before Sheffield Park staged its first game in 1845, but Lord Sheffield and his new ground played a prominent part, as cricket grew from a minority interest to a national obsession in Victorian England.

Roger Packham takes us through these great events, including memorable matches against the Australians that were full of controversy and drama. There are also legendary tales: 'Sorry, Doc', said Ernest Jones, as he nearly decapitated W. G. Grace with a ball that passed through his beard – 'it slipped'.

Many of the most famous names in cricket stalk these pages. They are part of the folklore of cricket but, more specifically, so is the history of Sheffield Park and its remarkable owner, the third Earl, who will be remembered for as long as cricket is played.

John Major
London
April 2009

Acknowledgements

My sincere thanks are due to so many people in helping with this story of Lord Sheffield and his historic cricket ground.

I am forever indebted to staff at Methuen for having faith in the project and the patience to await the final text. I am also extremely grateful to Sir John Major for speedily contributing a splendid foreword.

Nicholas Sharp has allowed the use of some remarkable photographs from his unrivalled collection and has kindly read through the typescript. Nicholas has suggested many improvements and even persuaded his wife Brenda to read it critically. Brian Tester has been involved with the project from the early stages and has long been a knowledgeable student of Sheffield Park history, purchasing some fine photographs from the Sheffield Park sale in 1971. Brian has investigated many historic themes and provided some invaluable references. David Bonser exceeded the bounds of friendship by transferring my archaic typescript into a presentable format and I can never adequately repay a debt of gratitude.

Rob Boddie, the honorary librarian at Sussex County Cricket Club has made some of the club's precious records available to me including early minute books and photographs and he has supported the project with his unbounded enthusiasm. The public libraries at Brighton, Caterham (Mrs Jan Campbell), Colindale and Croydon have been friendly and efficient.

It has been a pleasure to work with the National Trust staff at Sheffield Park Garden for over three years. The property manager, Sue Medway, entrusted me with William Moore's diary for 1896 and she and her assistant, Ashley Brown, have provided invaluable encouragement and information. Daphne Strachan found time from her busy post to provide the vital introduction to Methuen and has been kindly checking on my tardy progress at regular intervals. Daphne's support has been invaluable.

Hylda and Derek Rawlings of the Danehill Parish Historical Society kindly opened their impressive archive to me and allowed some invaluable copies to be made. It was a privilege to view Miss Attenborough's scrapbook of so many events at Sheffield Park.

Additionally, the following have provided welcome information and illustrations:

David Rayvern Allen
David Boorman
Tim Carder
Daphne Collard
Andy Collier
David Cooper
Guy Curry
Norman Epps
Eton College
Mike Felmore
David Frith
Brian Gregory
Bernard Hall
John Hawkins

Roger Heavens
Geoff Isted
Juraj Hrk (photography)
Tony Laughton
Roger Mann
Rodney Packham
Philip Paine
Malcolm Pearce
Dave Robbins
Chris Saunders
Tony Turk
Peter Wigan
The late Simon Wright

Introduction

When Lord Sheffield died on 21 April 1909 a remarkable chapter in cricketing history came to an end. Here was a gentleman who had created a magnificent cricket ground on his own estate in East Sussex and then entertained famous cricketers in international matches. W. G. Grace, perhaps the most famous of all cricketers, was often Lord Sheffield's captain and the visiting teams included Australians, South Africans and Parsees.

The Australians came to Sheffield Park on five occasions between 1884 and 1896 and Lord Sheffield was always keen to foster cricket links with that country. He arranged and financed the England tour to Australia in 1891–92 when he accompanied the team with W. G. Grace as his captain. He also donated the money for the iconic Sheffield Shield – still played for by the Australian states and due to make an appearance at Sheffield Park on 28 June 2009.

The matches at Sheffield Park provided an opportunity for the public to watch famous cricketers in delightful surroundings. Most of the matches were played in May when the landscaped gardens were an added attraction. The arrival of the railway at Sheffield Park in 1882 ensured that large crowds attended the matches and Lord Sheffield never charged admission money.

The apogee of cricket at this famous but forgotten ground was on 11 May 1896 when over 25,000 people arrived to see the splendid gardens, the Prince of Wales, the Australians, W. G. Grace and the cream of Sussex society.

In setting out the story of cricket at Sheffield Park I have tried to concentrate on the social history behind Lord Sheffield's matches. His life was extraordinary: exceedingly shy and paranoid about having his photograph taken, his generosity in promoting cricket and beautifying the Sheffield Park estate was astounding. Sussex County Cricket Club depended heavily on his purse during his three spells as the Club's president and it is quite probable that without Lord Sheffield's generosity Sussex county cricket would have been reduced to a very humble status.

I have briefly mentioned Lord Sheffield's private life in chapter 1. There is little that can be verified apart from his surprising adoption of the daughter of the Vicar of Fletching but I have tried to dispel some of the other myths associated with Lord Sheffield: he was certainly not a misogynist. I have also tried to show that he was a cricketer of above average ability and historians have neglected his appearance in first-class cricket.

The official history of Sussex CCC is in error over the date of Lord Sheffield's first presidency (by 18 years) and other histories mistakenly refer to a schoolboy friendship with the Prince of Wales even though the Prince was nine years younger. The Sheffield Arms, a local public house, is often credited with having accommodated the famous visiting cricketers but there is no evidence for this. Most reports describe Lord Sheffield's generosity in putting up the tourists in Brighton hotels and in 1886 the Parsees were quartered at a neighbouring farmhouse. The two distinctive pavilions on the cricket ground have been wrongly identified and dates given in cricket histories for the opening of the ground are also in error.

My main source of reference has been the *Sussex Agricultural Express* and I would like to pay tribute to the anonymous reporter whose eye for detail and appreciation of the glorious setting at Sheffield Park make his contributions a pleasure to read.

The National Trust and the Armadillos Cricket Club are to be congratulated on restoring the famous old ground from a wilderness to enable the return of country house cricket at Sheffield Park in the centenary year of Lord Sheffield's death. The celebration match on 28 June is the culmination of much hard work and it is reassuring to think that visitors to Sheffield Park Garden can now picture the magnificent setting where Grace, Murdoch, Fry and Ranji so enlivened the scene in cricket's golden age.

Roger Packham
Caterham May 2009

1

The Holroyds of Sheffield Park

The sleepy village of Fletching in East Sussex, with its timeless high street of historic buildings, has as its dominant neighbour the sizeable estate of Sheffield Park. Until 1909 this was home to the earls of Sheffield, whose family name was Holroyd. Mentioned in the Domesday Book, the house has a long history and there are records going back to the reign of Edward I.

John Baker Holroyd

The Holroyd family's connection with Sheffield Park began in 1769 when John Baker Holroyd (1735–1821) purchased the estate from Earl De La Warr for £30,000. The new owner then engaged the services of the fashionable architect James Wyatt to remodel the great house and he also commissioned the renowned 'Capability' Brown to transform the extensive pleasure grounds around it. Brown's work was added to later by that of Humphry Repton, another celebrated landscape gardener.

The legacies of these two men can be enjoyed by the general public today as the garden at Sheffield Park, extending to more than 100 acres, was bought by the National Trust in 1954 and, with its magnificent trees, shrubs and lakes, has become one of its most popular sites.

The main house has been converted to a number of apartments so is no longer open to the public. However the exterior can be seen from some parts of the garden and is an imposing sight.

John Baker Holroyd was a successful soldier and politician with interests in trade and finance. He became a Member of Parliament

The house at Sheffield Park was remodelled for John Baker Holroyd in the Gothic style by James Wyatt in 1776–7 and again in c.1780–90. (R. Packham)

in 1780 and gained a reputation as an authority on farming. In 1803 he was appointed President of the Board of Agriculture. He is best remembered though for his great friendship with the historian Edward Gibbon, who wrote several chapters of *The Decline and Fall of the Roman Empire* in the library at Sheffield Park. When Gibbon died in 1794 his body was brought from London to be buried in the Holroyd family mausoleum in Fletching Church.

In 1781 Holroyd was created an Irish peer as Baron Sheffield of Roscommon. A barony of the United Kingdom was added in 1802 and in 1816, at the age of 81, he became the first Earl Sheffield. On his death five years later the estate passed to his son George (1802–76), who became the second earl at 19 years of age. George married Lady Harriet Lascelles and, after losing a boy in infancy, the happy couple produced a son and heir in 1832, Henry North Holroyd, a baby brother for Susan. The family was completed in 1834 with the birth of a second son, Douglas Edward Holroyd.

Henry North Holroyd

Henry North Holroyd was born on 18 January 1832 at 58 Portland Place, the family's elegant town house, near Regent's Park in London. The future third earl took the courtesy title of Viscount Pevensey and that is how he was known until he succeeded his father in 1876.

It is not clear how much time the young Henry spent at the family's London home and how much at Sheffield Park. Nor is it known how he was educated prior to being sent to Eton a few days before his 12th birthday in January 1844. But it was at Eton that the young man's lifelong love of cricket was nurtured and this was confirmed in an interview he gave in 1893 when he told a reporter:

> To state the cause of my interest in cricket I must go back to my school days. My first real match was, I think, in 1845 but I have always been an enthusiast in cricket. I played myself for about thirty years in small matches in Sussex and also in several of the contests of the 'Gentlemen of Sussex' against those of other counties. In those days there were many matches between the gentlemen of different counties.

Young Pevensey's 'first real match' mentioned above was almost certainly the one played at Sheffield Park in August 1845 where an indulgent father had laid out the first cricket ground on the estate and arranged a competitive match to take place during his son's school holidays.

Henry's time at Eton was spent in William Adolphus Carter's house where he remained until December 1848. He didn't gain selection for the Eton XI in their annual matches against Harrow and Winchester at Lord's but he was clearly athletically inclined because he was a member of the Field Eleven and the Oppidan Wall – Eton's two versions of football. Many years later Henry arranged for important football matches, both rugby and soccer, to be played in Sheffield Park.

Henry's younger brother Douglas followed him to Eton in September 1847 and remained there until July 1851 before taking up a place at Christ Church College, Oxford. Douglas shared his elder brother's love of cricket and we can be sure the pair of them attended Eton's matches at Lord's in support of their school friends.

The Young Diplomat

On leaving Eton in 1848 Henry, perhaps unexpectedly, did not go on to university. He clearly had other interests to pursue. This suggests a desire for travel and action because for a couple of years he served with the Army in India. Then in 1851, when still only 19 years of age, he accompanied Sir Stratford Canning to the British Embassy at Constantinople to act as his private secretary. The following year he became attaché to the British Legation at Copenhagen but in 1853, with the outbreak of war in the Crimea, at first between Turkey and Russia, he returned to Constantinople where he held a key position until 1856. Some of these experiences remained with him and as an elderly gentleman he returned to the Crimea in 1895 – an unhappy occasion.

Young Henry's five years in the diplomatic service were alleviated by return visits home and on 18 January 1853 he celebrated his 21st birthday at the Sheffield Arms, Fletching, a local public house:

> About five o'clock the tenantry, by Lord Sheffield's invitation, sat down to a sumptuous dinner at the Sheffield Arms. The room was decorated for the occasion with banners, laurels and other characteristic embellishments. At the back of the chair was a large flag, with the arms and quarterings of the family, which was the more interesting from being the needlework and design of the Countess of Sheffield. Over the mantel-piece was the initial 'P', at the foot of which was inscribed, 'Loyal to his Queen, true to his country,' the whole worked in laurel leaves upon a pink ground. Opposite the chair were the arms and supporters of the Sheffield family, and in each recess were the military banners of the late Earl of Sheffield. On the arrival of the company, they were conducted to the reception-room, where they all most cordially expressed their congratulations to Lord Pevensey on the auspicious occasion.

As befitted the occasion, Henry, Viscount Pevensey occupied the chair and among the guests were his brother Douglas; brother-in-law E. V. Harcourt; Sir T. M. Wilson Bart, a neighbouring landowner and W. E. Baxter, the noted Lewes printer and publisher. Amidst

The future third Lord Sheffield celebrates his 21st birthday at the Sheffield Arms, Fletching in 1853. The 'P' for Pevensey was worked in laurel leaves. (*Illustrated London News*)

many toasts Henry, in an eloquent address, thanked the company and concluded:

> I wished much to inaugurate my appearance on the threshold of manhood, by raising my voice, humble as it is, to advocate principles of loyalty and firmness, to exhort you to the defence of your country, to aim a blow at your deadliest enemy, democracy; and to cement those amicable relations which ought to exist between landlord and tenant, and which I fancy do exist, or we should not be associated together this evening.

The Cricketing Diplomat 1851–56

Viscount Pevensey enjoyed further holidays at home during his time in the diplomatic service and in September 1854 he made his only appearance in a first-class match when he represented XVI of Sussex against the professional United All England XI at the Dripping Pan, Lewes. The keen young cricketer failed to score in either innings but on the following two days he was back in action playing for the Gentlemen of Sussex against the Gentlemen of Surrey on the old County Ground at Hove.

These two matches were by no means his only appearances in a good class of cricket. In 1851, when he first travelled to the Crimea as a 19-year-old, he had played for the Gentlemen of Sussex against the Gentlemen of England in a three-day match at Hove. The Sussex team on that occasion included some well-known cricketers in the history of the county club – Edwin and William Napper, G. W. King and H. M. Curteis. They were to become part of the young aristocrat's life as he became increasingly involved with the affairs of Sussex County Cricket Club.

Matches played by the Gentlemen of Sussex were an integral part of the county's fixture list at this time, satisfying the strong amateur ethos within the county and in 1856, the last year of young Pevensey's diplomatic career, he played 'home' and 'away' games against the Gentlemen of Kent at Hove and Gravesend. His brother Douglas also played in both the games.

The brothers' enthusiasm for the game of cricket was infectious. In June 1855 a new ground was opened at Sheffield Park with a match between the home team and Lewes Priory. Both brothers played in the match and were always available for selection for other matches.

The Cricketing Member of Parliament 1857–65

In March 1857, after resigning from his duties in Constantinople, the 25-year-old Pevensey stood as Conservative candidate for the parliamentary seat of East Sussex following the resignation of Charles H. Frewen, the sitting member. His opponent was J. G. Dodson, a Liberal, whom he defeated by 2,302 votes to 2,234, a majority of 68, and was duly elected to Parliament. Only a month later came the General Election when both Pevensey and Dodson were returned and in 1859 the pair were re-elected without a contest. After eight years as a Member of Parliament, Pevensey decided to stand down before the General Election of 1865.

It is difficult to assess Pevensey's political contribution but he was clearly interested in the provision of further education for the less privileged members of society. In 1858 he and the Bishop of Chichester and other influential persons held a meeting in Brighton for the purpose of establishing local examinations in connection with the University Extension movement.

An abiding memory from this period of Pevensey's life was a very serious accident at Lewes in 1860 involving himself, his brother Douglas and R. A. Blencowe of Chailey. When climbing into a horse-drawn carriage outside the White Hart Hotel the rear of the carriage collapsed and his fellow passengers were thrown into the street. Douglas was very badly concussed and his condition was grave enough to cause his parents to be summoned from Sheffield Park.

Happily Douglas recovered and was able to play cricket that season for the Gentlemen of Sussex and Sheffield Park, on one occasion opening the batting with his brother who was no doubt enjoying a break from constituency duties.

However committed Viscount Pevensey was as a Member of Parliament, there is no doubt that cricket was paramount among his other interests. In 1857, shortly after he entered Parliament, he was elected President of the revived Sussex County Cricket Club, a position he held for 11 years. He would later accept the position for two further terms.

In 1858 Viscount Pevensey, MP and President of the County Club, played alongside his brother for 22 Gentlemen of Sussex against the United All England XI on the old Bopeep Ground at St Leonards. The Gentlemen were allowed the services of a professional bowler, George Hooker, who took 16 out of the 20 wickets to fall. One of his victims was the famous Surrey wicket-keeper Tom Lockyer, who was caught out by Viscount Pevensey.

His last recorded match for the Gentlemen of Sussex was played at Lewes in 1860 against Gentlemen educated at Oxford and Cambridge Universities. On this occasion Douglas was on the opposing side.

Third Lord Sheffield

Having stood down from Parliament in 1865 Henry continued his involvement with Sussex County Cricket Club as president and later patron. He devoted more time to affairs at Sheffield Park and in January 1866 chaired a meeting at the Sheffield Arms to oppose a planned Ouse Valley railway line by backing an alternative scheme.

Ten years later, in April 1876, Henry who was now 44, succeeded to the earldom on the death of his father and became the 3rd Lord Sheffield. A local newspaper outlined his father's sporting interests in the following terms:

> The late Earl was for half a century devoted to hunting, was a strict observer of foxes, a subscriber to the packs he hunted with and attached to stag hunting. Some thirty or forty years since he kept a red deer or two at Sheffield Park and had a few hounds of his own. Lord Sheffield was ever courteous and affable in the field, was a good landlord and a warm friend. Though a Conservative the Earl was not an active politician and was during his long life esteemed and honoured by all with whom he came into contact.

The death of his father marked the start of increased activity in Henry's life. In September 1876 he chaired another meeting of landowners at the old Star Hotel in Lewes for the purpose of preparing a parliamentary bill for a railway between Lewes and East Grinstead. He became financially involved in the project and was appointed chairman of the directors of the Lewes and East Grinstead Railway Company. The railway opened on 1 August 1882 with a station at Sheffield Park – convenient for cricket matches. The route north from Sheffield Park to Horsted Keynes is now a most successful preserved line known as the Bluebell Railway and work is currently in progress to extend it to East Grinstead.

Lord Sheffield's last attendance on the railway steering committee was in May 1879 and coincided with his election as President of the Sussex county club for a second term. He was now a wealthy man, having inherited from his late father, and he set about using some of his wealth for the improvement of Sussex cricket.

At home, he had already begun to transform the garden and cricket ground. It was an enormous undertaking and the work would take ten years to complete. The project provided winter

Bust of Lord Sheffield 1832–1909. (Melbourne Cricket Club)

employment for the estate workers whose efforts created a first class cricket ground in a most magnificent setting that would host the Australian tourists on five separate occasions. On the last of these visits HRH the Prince of Wales, later Edward VII, graced the occasion by attending the first day of the match, 11 May 1896. Needless to say Lord Sheffield was the proudest noble in the land.

Lord Sheffield's Generous Nature
From all that we have seen of Lord Sheffield it is obvious that he was an extremely generous man who was passionate about cricket. His other interests included military matters, yachting and travel. He spent large sums of money on staging spectacular events at Sheffield Park and on transforming Sussex County Cricket Club from an ailing concern to a glamorous team in a golden age. He funded England's entire tour to Australia in 1891–92, paying a colossal fee for the services of W. G. Grace.

His wages bill for professional cricketers, estate workers and his yachting crew made him a considerable employer. He assumed responsibility for many other expenses including hotel accommodation for visiting teams to Sheffield Park. In later life he spent much time himself in expensive hotels, especially in Brighton, Naples and the south of France.

Lord Sheffield was proud to stage the great cricket matches at Sheffield Park regardless of expense. The games attracted large numbers of spectators all of whom were allowed into the ground without charge.

In an interview in 1893 his policy of free admission to the park was discussed:

'Why should I make a charge for admission?' said Lord Sheffield to our representative on Tuesday. 'Even if I had charged a nominal three pence or four pence they would probably have plucked my crocuses and rhododendrons as a recompense. As it is, knowing they are my guests they treat me with courtesy.' And they certainly were orderly. 'There is not a 'welsher' in the crowd' said he. 'They are all cricket lovers.'

Lord Sheffield's generosity extended to handsome donations to professional and amateur cricketers alike. In 1883 he gave £100 to Henry Charlwood's benefit and £50 to William Mycroft's – vast sums at the time. In 1886 he contributed £100 to Sussex player Harry Phillips' benefit.

When in Australia with the England team in 1891–92 he arranged for the purchase of the Sheffield Shield for inter-state competition at a cost of £150. Other donations included £50 to Bobby Abel in recognition of an outstanding innings; £10 to Austin Hospital, Melbourne where William Midwinter's son was an orphan and he subscribed £2 towards a tombstone for Johnny Mullagh, a champion Aboriginal cricketer. At the end of the tour the energetic secretary of the Melbourne Cricket Club, Ben Wardill, who had acted as manager with Alfred Shaw, was presented with a silver bowl, now on display in the museum at Melbourne Cricket Ground.

A handsome gold watch was presented to Sussex captain Robert Ellis in 1881 and in the same year Lord Sheffield commissioned Elkingtons the silversmiths to design and manufacture (for 60 guineas) a silver cup to be awarded to the most successful Sussex batsman of the season.

Members of the Sheffield Park team were not forgotten. John Gilbert received a new bat with an engraved silver plaque for his innings of 250 not out in 1884 and in 1891 the brothers Alfred and William Payne were presented with talent money for scoring 100 and 56 respectively against Horsted Keynes.

When the Sheffield Park Cricket Association was set up by Lord Sheffield in 1907 he presented a silver cup containing 13 sovereigns to the winners. His generosity knew no bounds.

A resident of Lewes, East Sussex possesses a silver rose bowl which bears the inscription:

Presented by the Earl of Sheffield

Hon. Col. of the 1st Royal Engineer Volunteers

Sheffield Park

July 5th 1901

The rose bowl was presented to A. J. Nell on his return from the Boer War.

Lord Sheffield's Complex Character
There were other attractive qualities in Lord Sheffield's character. He had a strong sense of duty appropriate for a gentleman in his privileged position and he had a genuine like of children. However, he was extremely sensitive, irascible and quick to take offence. He would resort to letters, telegrams and newspapers to get his own way. He was notoriously shy about having his photograph taken and very few images of him exist despite his high profile appearances. Alfred Shaw, the famous Nottinghamshire, Sussex and England professional, was an employee of Lord Sheffield for many years and in

1896 he wrote: 'His Lordship is a very good Fellow but he takes a lot of understanding.'

Lord Sheffield's love of cricket induced him to contribute forewords to several books on the game. He also permitted his name to be used in dedications including books by Walter Bettesworth, Alfred Gaston, George Giffen, James Pycroft and Alfred Shaw.

More surprisingly Lord Sheffield allowed his name to be used in advertisements to endorse commercial enterprises. In an advert for the periodical *Cricket: A Weekly Record* in 1892 he wrote:

> I always read with the greatest pleasure your excellent periodical CRICKET, and anything I can do to promote its prosperity I will gladly do. Believe me, yours truly, SHEFFIELD

He also helped to advertise the photographic company of E. Hawkins of Brighton who were regular visitors to Sheffield Park. In 1884 he wrote in an advertisement: 'Sir, The photos arrived safely, they are very good ones indeed and I congratulate you upon your success.' In 1890 he wrote for the same company: 'I hope you will find many customers for such exceedingly good and excellent Photographs.'

In his private life Lord Sheffield was a bachelor. There are persistent and conflicting rumours in Fletching village that he was either gay or emasculated from an experience in Turkey. Another story has it that he fathered one or more natural heirs with descendants still residing locally.

An unpublished manuscript on Sheffield Park claims that Lord Sheffield had a liaison with Mary Ann Vernon who was later invited onto Lord Sheffield's yacht with a four-year-old daughter. There is also a reference to a solicitor's document regarding arrangements for the private education of the child. It has been speculated that it was this 'daughter' who in quite recent years wrote to the Danehill historian Hylda Rawlings from Australia enclosing a letter from Lord Sheffield – frustratingly returned.

Despite extensive enquiries it has not been possible to confirm any of the above conjecture and the only relationship that can be verified is the ageing Lord Sheffield's adoption of Miss Mabel Attenborough as his daughter in 1895, discussed in chapter 12.

Decline of a Family

Lord Sheffield's younger brother and cricketing companion Douglas died in 1882 at the comparatively young age of 47. His death brought great sadness to his family. Douglas is described in *Lillywhite's Guide* (1861) as a very fair bowler and an excellent long-stop. Douglas had studied at Christ Church College, Oxford after he left Eton and was called to the bar of the Inner Temple in 1863, practising for a few years on the Home Circuit and at Sussex Quarter Sessions. An obituary in the *Sussex Agricultural Express* noted:

> He was fond of cricket and played for some seasons with the Gentlemen of Sussex; he was not only an effective batsman but covered a lot of ground in the field. Of late years, owing probably to delicate health his habits became of a more retiring character and he devoted considerable time to study, although he was nearly always to be seen on the beautiful cricket ground at Sheffield Park whenever a match was going on. Since the death of his father, Mr Holroyd has spent most of his time with his brother, the present earl, and his mother, the countess. Everyone living in the district is aware of the strong and abiding affection and sympathy existing between the widowed countess and her sons and laments that death has created a void in the noble family. Last season he was present at nearly every match in Sheffield Park and his friends rejoiced to see that he continued to gain strength. At the end of October (1881) the deceased gentleman accompanied the Earl of Sheffield to Brighton and has since remained at the Royal Crescent Hotel.

Lord Sheffield's mother often attended the cricket matches at Sheffield Park as an elderly lady and was 87 years old at the time of her passing in 1889. Aubrey Harcourt, Lord Sheffield's nephew, is then noted as frequently accompanying his uncle even though his home was in Oxfordshire. He made a solitary appearance in first-class cricket when he played for Lord Sheffield's XI against MCC in

1891, aged 38. That autumn he travelled to Australia with the England cricket team but was obliged to return home early. Harcourt died in Monte Carlo in 1904 aged 51.

The reminiscences of Lord Sheffield would have made fascinating reading and it is disappointing to discover that he published a book in 1895 entitled *Drifting Towards The Breakers!* under the pseudonym of 'A Sussex Peer': it is a political treatise without a hint of autobiography or reminiscence.

In his declining years, Lord Sheffield was often in indifferent health from a heart condition and he regularly spent his winters abroad accompanied by Miss Attenborough. This complex man passed away at Beaulieu in the south of France in 1909 at the age of 77 and his body was brought back to his home.

His death signalled the end of a glorious era at Sheffield Park. The famous cricket matches and other spectacular events soon became distant memories and the cricket ground was allowed to become a wilderness.

In 2009 arrangements are at an advanced stage to commemorate the centenary of the death of this eccentric man. The cricket ground at Sheffield Park was his pride and joy and it has been lovingly restored by the National Trust to be used again for country house cricket. Lord Sheffield would surely give his blessing.

2

Sheffield Park:
A Lord's Ground

There is no evidence to suggest that the 2nd Lord Sheffield had any interest in cricket or that there had been any cricket activity at Sheffield Park prior to the arrival of his son Henry.

This was to change dramatically and while young Henry was at Eton (1844–8) a cricket ground was constructed in the south-east corner of the park known as East Park. The ground was sited on a plateau overlooking the lakes and though it comprised all the basics it would be some years before it became the magnificent playing field where international matches were staged. Nevertheless it served its purpose and the inaugural fixture was played in August 1845 when the 13-year-old Henry was on school holidays. The young viscount naturally featured in the historic game which was reported locally as follows:

FLETCHING v CHAILEY

A match between these parties was played in Sheffield Park on Thursday se'night in which Lord Pevensey made his debut. His noble father, the Earl of Sheffield, gave the players a dinner on the occasion and bumpers of punch went round the table with 'success to cricketing which has found another noble patron, and health and happiness to the house of Sheffield'.

Appropriately the young Henry opened the batting, as Viscount Pevensey, for the Fletching team but was dismissed for a single. He fared better in the second innings when he batted at number eight. The match was of some local importance and the brothers Gilbert playing for Fletching were cricketers of note. The score has survived (see Appendix A) and so has a printed window bill where both teams are shown as having the assistance of some players from Newick, a nearby village.

This inaugural match prompted the following letter from 'A Midland Cricketer' in a local newspaper for 13 September 1845:

Sir

I was much amused by your account of the friendly game of cricket played in Lord Sheffield's park at Fletching and gratified to learn that the young lord is 'coming out' as a cricketer! Why some of the old inhabitants must have been reminded of the days of OLD DOCTOR SHAW and others of the 'olden time' in their matches upon Piltdown common; and who knows but that by the kind patronage of his lordship that the 'olden time' may be revived. It looks well to see a noble lord playing with his neighbours; it begets a kind feeling and reminds me of a celebrated physician at a recent match at Brighton, SUSSEX v KENT, who, in the joy of his heart said, "here are three thousand persons all happy and content," "This", said the Doctor "is much better than fighting but so long as cricket is the national game of England, we may bid defiance to the world!" There is no doubt of this, Mr Editor, for if Prince Joinville should ever attempt the shores of Brighton, the Sussex bowlers will give him such balls that neither the Prince nor any of his eleven will be able to keep their wickets up!

September 9, 1845

After the inaugural match in 1845, the new ground at Sheffield Park became a regular venue for more fixtures. In the years 1846 to 1850, records show that the Fletching team entertained Withyam, Lewes Priory, East Grinstead Victoria, Lindfield and Newick. At this stage there is no reference to a Sheffield Park team, so that was for the future.

A New Ground at Sheffield Park

Ten years after the first game at Sheffield Park, while Henry was working in Constantinople, his father had embarked on an ambitious rebuilding programme for the cricket ground. The work was completed in 1855 and Henry's return for holidays in that year coincided with the reopening of the ground. By this time Henry was quite an accomplished cricketer and his father had indulged him with a considerable outlay on the improvements. The local newspaper reported the first game as follows:

SHEFFIELD PARK (FLETCHING) v PRIORY CLUB (LEWES)
at Sheffield Park

On Friday the 29th June a match of cricket was played in Sheffield Park between the Sheffield Park and Priory Club, being the first match played on the new ground which the Earl of Sheffield has lately had laid down at a considerable expense, some idea of which may be formed from the fact of there having been 4,000 cart-loads of earth moved to raise and level it, the whole thoroughly drained, and the relaying of upwards of 3.5 acres of turf. Not having been completed more than a month, it was not of course in first rate order; however, it proved as good as could have been expected. As will be seen by the score, the Sheffield Park Club proved victorious beating their opponents by 42 runs. The bowling of Viscount Pevensey and fielding of Hon. D. Holroyd were very good as indeed was the fielding generally, several good catches being made, and but very few missed – in fact not one that could be called 'an easy one.' . . . George Brown made but a short score, but his generalship was excellent.

A week later Hadlow Down were the visitors to what was now being referred to as Viscount Pevensey's ground: 'A large concourse of people were assembled on the ground, in anticipation of witnessing a good game and we believe their expectations were fully realised . . . we cannot but do justice in praising the bowling of Viscount Pevensey, D. Gilbert and J. Gilbert on the part of the Sheffield Park Club."

That summer, the Sheffield Park side also played at Warbleton and Hadlow Down but in later seasons Pevensey made sure that most of their fixtures were played on his beloved home turf.

A rare window bill advertising the first match to be played at
Sheffield Park in 1845. (Mrs H. Rawlings)

A Ground Transformed

In 1876 Henry, Viscount Pevensey succeeded to the earldom of
Sheffield on the death of his father. He wasted little time in spending
lavish sums on the beautiful gardens at Sheffield Park including, of
course, the cricket ground. In October of that year it was reported:

> The Earl of Sheffield, the patron of the Sussex County Cricket Club,
> has determined to have a cricket ground, and a good ground too, in

Sheffield Park, and no doubt therefore, we shall continue to hear of superior play from that neighbourhood. Mr C. H. Ellis, the well-known Sussex wicket-keeper, has, at the request of his Lordship, consented to supervise the layout of the ground, and with his large experience there can be no doubt that he will see that the work is done in the best style.

A year later Ellis's work was evident:

'The cricket ground has lately been made still more picturesque; a quantity of timber has been cut down in the Walk Wood, which has thrown the east and south front of his Lordship's mansion open to view from the ground. The game can also be seen now from the pleasure grounds surrounding the mansion.'

Lord Sheffield's landscaping programme occupied the winters from 1876 to 1886 and provided much-needed employment on a grand scale. In 1879 further alterations were recorded:

There has been, for more years than we can venture to say, a cricket ground in Sheffield Park, but it is not going too far to assert that if anyone who knew the ground three years ago were taken there blindfolded on Friday last, and had his organs of vision suddenly released to the exercise of their functions, he must have failed to recognise the place, so vast are the improvements effected within the last year or so. It seemed almost as if an enchanter's power has been brought to bear upon the ground and its belongings – certainly a delightful transformation has been well conceived and cleverly devised. Formerly the ground was of small extent, and so enclosed on each side with undergrowth and trees, the branches of which were so thickly interwoven as to spoil each other's beauty, and to obstruct the view of everything beyond the pitch of the ball, excepting, perhaps the belfry of the mansion in the distance. The ground is situated on a plateau above the eastern bank of the central lake, and it occurred to the noble Earl, when contemplating improvements, that its commanding position might render available, with careful treatment of the too luxurious growth around it, some charming and diversified views. That thorough success has attended his efforts must be acknowledged by everyone who has the least appreciation of sylvan scenery.

The ground has been increased to thrice its former size, by levelling the earth to the north, east and south, and by removing the furze and other undergrowth from the cricket ground down to the eastern bank of the lake. This opened out a fair view of the lake, with its cascade and footbridge, and the splendid trees bordering it, the little valley on the opposite shore, and in the distance the façade of the mansion.

On the other side of the cricket ground from the gently rising hill, vistas of exquisite beauty have been formed. To the right the eye wanders over the undulated woods on the north side of the park to Horsted Keynes, Ashdown Forest forming the skyline; to the left we look down between the trees upon the village of Newick . . . to the east the spire of Fletching Church, now in the course of restoration, is a prominent object, and turning round, the cricket ground and its accessories are commanded . . .

At the present moment workmen are engaged in adding to the pavilion (which occupies a terrace close to the cricket ground), dressing and retiring rooms, with lavatories and everything necessary for the comfort of those who are engaged in the matches, and before another season comes round the space appropriate to the 'manly game' will be still further extended eastwards, by lowering the summit of a bank and filling up a depression below, so that when the new railway is made, and access to Fletching from Lewes, Brighton and East Grinstead, and indeed, from all parts is rendered easy, a more central and suitable place whereon to hold county matches would be hard to find.

The noble owner of Sheffield Park may well be congratulated upon the fact that the work of beautifying his domain has so far been profitable, instead of entailing cost. Between three and four thousand trees have, within the last few years, been felled without the effect of its disappearance having been duly considered by his Lordship, and so luxuriant is the park in timber that none are missed. They were worthless for ornamental landscape purposes, but the commercial value is a very different matter, and we heard that they represented in the timber market the handsome figure of £30,000!

Charles Payne (1832–1909) made the only century
on the original Sheffield Park ground when he was
bowled by Lord Sheffield. (N. J. G. Sharp)

The Old Ground Remembered

The great alterations to the cricket ground at Sheffield Park from
1876 completely obliterated the old ground and years later in 1895
Charles Payne, an old Sussex and Kent professional, was asked if he
had played at Sheffield Park.

> The ground which is used now was not in existence at that time but
> I played on the old ground and once made 106 on it. It was the first
> time a hundred was ever made on it, and it will be the last, for it is
> now built over. Five or six years ago I was umpiring at Sheffield Park
> and Lord Sheffield asked me if I remembered getting a hundred on
> the old ground. Then he asked me who bowled me out, and for the
> life of me I couldn't remember, until he reminded me that he had
> done it himself.

Charles Ellis (1830–1880) the former Sussex wicket-keeper and
lob bowler, who superintended the alterations and improvements
to the cricket ground at Sheffield Park. (N. J. G. Sharp)

After only a year's reconstruction, progress on the ground was quite
satisfactory and in 1877 during a match between Sheffield Park and
Lewes Priory a presentation of a stick was made to Lord Sheffield by
Charles Ellis, the superintendent of the alterations and improvements "which have made the Earl of Sheffield's cricket ground one
of the best in the south of England". The top of the stick, which was
made from a branch of gorse from the ground, was capped with
silver engraved with his Lordship's crest.

Charles Ellis was one of the many professional Sussex cricketers
who by hard work and initiative made a success of their lives. Others
included the Lillywhites, Box and Wisden. In Ellis's case, apart from

Pavilion in Cricket Ground, Sheffield Park.

Lord Sheffield's private pavilion at Sheffield Park cricket ground was completed in 1883. It is shown here on an Edwardian postcard. (Mrs H. Rawlings)

his work with Lord Sheffield, he was at different times coach to Brighton and Hurstpierpoint Colleges, a cricket outfitter, secretary and caterer to Lewes Priory Cricket Club, publican at Lewes and Brighton, wood engraver, miller and carpenter. His county cricket career with Sussex had been successful and although he was a regular wicket-keeper his lob bowling once claimed 15 Surrey wickets at the old Brunswick ground in 1863.

A match was played for his benefit at Lewes in 1865 involving the United South of England Eleven and he received another benefit at Hove in the Sussex v Surrey match of 1869.

Tragically Charles Ellis's association with Lord Sheffield came to an abrupt end on 17 January 1880 when he passed away at his home, "The Battle of Waterloo", Rock Mews, Brighton, aged only 49. Nevertheless Ellis had taken Lord Sheffield's plans for his magnificent cricket ground towards completion and in the year of his passing the first trial matches took place at Sheffield Park to discover and develop new talent for the County Club.

Lord Sheffield's pavilion of ornamental ironwork was constructed by the Phoenix Ironwork Co. of Lewes and completed in 1883. This view featured in that company's catalogue of 1903. (Mrs J. Middleton)

Pavilions of Splendour

Improvements to the ground continued after Ellis's demise. A report in 1882 described the filling in of the depression in the northern portion of the ground when 16,000 tons of earth were utilised. In addition, a large reservoir with a capacity of 100,000 gallons had been constructed to supply water for new gardens, stables and the cricket ground.

By this time first-class cricket had arrived at Sheffield Park. In 1881 Lord Sheffield's XI entertained Alfred Shaw's XI and in July 1883, the Earl's team was due to take on W. G. Grace's XI. Before that match took place a contemporary newspaper report described in some detail the improvements to the accommodation on the ground:

> . . . behind the pavilion have been erected a number of rooms, one
> for the accommodation of Mrs Coomber (catering), others as
> dressing rooms for professionals and amateurs, and each has been

fitted up with every convenience. To the right, the erection of the noble Lord's private pavilion, a really picturesque and pleasing structure, has been completed. It is surrounded by a wide garden (with iron border fencing), planted with choice shrubs and plants. The building itself is of dark-stained timber, and outside is a verandah, supported on open ironwork, with wooden pillars, the iron roof resting on ornamental iron arches. There is a very ornamental fence (coloured in light blue) running round the verandah. The whole of the front of the pavilion is fitted with windows, and smaller ones are inserted to the sides and back. Shrubs and evergreens are being carefully trained over the woodwork.

The front entrance is by a flight of iron steps and through folding doors. Inside the first apartment is a magnificently furnished library, or drawing room, which is used and intended for the accommodation of the noble Lord and his personal friends, and attached to this is a retiring room (containing a very handsome and costly chimney piece), with lavatories (fitted up in the most elaborate manner with pier-glasses, rich window hangings etc) and other conveniences; water being laid on. The roof of the building is approached by a light ornamental iron spiral staircase, covered in at the top with glass, and, being a lead flat, is used as a vantage ground from which to watch the progress of the games, whilst in addition a view of the beautiful country surrounding the spot is obtained. Round the roof is an open iron fence, and it is ornamental with numerous shrubs. Beneath the pavilion, with an entrance in the rear, is a storeroom for the use of the groundsman.

The Ladies' Pavilion

In the winter of 1885–6 a second magnificent pavilion appeared on the ground and local reports described it in glowing terms as follows:

A charming pavilion for ladies has been erected on the rising ground to the east and immediately in rear of the belt of oaks which fringe this portion of ground. Through an opening in the trees, a fine view is presented, not only of the wickets, but also of the lakes, the

The octagonal ladies' pavilion was completed in time for the 1886 season when the Australians and Parsees both played at Sheffield Park. (N. J. G. Sharp)

cascades, and the mansion in the distance. From the east side of the structure the view of the park is bounded by the well-wooded ridge in which stands the village of Fletching, with the spire of the parish church rising above the trees.

The pavilion is very ornate, is octagonal in form and consists of a principal apartment arranged as a drawing room, with lavatory adjoining under one roof. From the centre rises a spiral staircase, giving access to a cupola opening onto the roof, the margin of which extends beyond the walls of the main structure and being supported by elegant columns at the angles of the octagon, forms a verandah, running round the building.

Between the columns is a fence of trellis ironwork, about two feet six inches high, separating the covered promenade from a pretty parterre, planted with spring flowers. The inner border of the colonade is planted with euonymus of various shades, supported by the walls of the pavilion and protected by a dwarf fence, in keeping with that on the other side of the walk. The promenade on the roof

William Thomas Moore (1847–1923) was Lord Sheffield's excellent groundsman for all the first-class matches at Sheffield Park. (B. Tester)

is also bordered by an ornamental fence. The columns and the rest of the ironwork are of blue and gold, and the walls of stained and varnished wood. On both sides of the entrance, which occupies one face of the octagon, are large vases planted with flowers. The doorway is supported by columns of royal marble, with a background of yellow brocade, and the upper part of the seven windows is also marbled. The windows, which are semi-oval, have a border of stained glass, representing running convuli in white, on pale blue. The interior walls and ceiling are of light oak, with long mirrors at the angles, and large mirrors at the back of the chief apartment. The spiral staircase to the roof is of blue and gold, and stands for flowers of the same colour occupy four of the angles. The furniture is of walnut, the settees and easy chairs being upholstered in velvet and plush of sombre green and gold; hangings of the same tints are suspended from a brass cornice running round the interior. The fittings to hold cloaks and wraps are of mahogany and brass. The lavatories attached to the main apartment are fitted with marble, in which are inserted basins of blue and gold, and a constant service of water is supplied through silver-plated taps. The floor of the interior is covered with mosaic linoleum, and everything is complete, even to an electric bell for summoning attendants. A more pleasant temple as the temporary abiding place of beauty, it would be difficult to imagine. It may be added that this pavilion has been constructed by Mr Fuller of Fletching, from the designs of Mr Jesse Baker, foreman to Mr Cash of Boyce Street, Brighton, who has also effected the decorations. The ironwork is by Mr Packham of Brighton.

The octagonal ladies' pavilion was completed in time for the 1886 season when the Australians and Parsees both played at Sheffield Park.

The spiral staircase of the ladies' pavilion survived the destruction of the building and the lowest section has been housed within the pavilion at Forest Row Cricket Club. Discussions have taken place recently about the possibility of its return to the restored ground at Sheffield Park.

3

Lord Sheffield:
Sussex CCC President

Lord Sheffield's position of influence and generous support of cricket made him a perfect choice as president of Sussex CCC and he occupied that position for three separate terms, totalling a remarkable 31 years. There is no doubt that had it not been for his outstanding contribution the county would not have been able to develop its fixture list and would have been at risk of losing its first-class status or folding completely.

First Term 1857–68
During the 1850s the fortunes of Sussex cricket were at a low ebb and it took a major effort to revive the club from its almost moribund state. The prime mover in this resuscitation was the remarkable Bridger Stent (1820–70) who called a meeting of influential people at the Egremont Hotel, Brighton on 15 July, 1857. Those present arranged for a general meeting at the same venue on 11 August 'which was attended by many of the leading and influential gentlemen of the County, for the purpose of forming a County Cricket Club'. This historic gathering, ignored by cricket historians, was chaired by Viscount Pevensey who was elected President of Sussex County Cricket Club. Although only 25 years of age, he proved to be the perfect choice for not only was he a well-known cricketer and member of the aristocracy but, from 1857, he was also the Member of Parliament for East Sussex.

Henry's tenure as president lasted for eleven years, three years longer than his career as a Member of Parliament (1857–65) but it is difficult to evaluate his contribution to the county club partly

SUSSEX COUNTY CRICKET CLUB.

At a Meeting held at the Egremont Hotel, Brighton, August 11th, 1857, which was attended by many of the leading and influential gentlemen of the County, for the purpose of forming a County Cricket Club,

VISCOUNT PEVENSEY, M.P., in the Chair,

The following Resolutions were unanimously carried :—

That for the support and extension of Cricket in this County, it is desirable to establish a Club, to be called " THE SUSSEX COUNTY CRICKET CLUB."

That His Grace the Duke of Richmond, the Lord Lieutenant of the County, be Patron.

That Viscount Pevensey, M.P., be President.

That H. M. Curteis, Esq., be Vice-President.

That Scott Stonehewer, Esq., be Treasurer.

That Bridger Stent, Esq., be Honorary Secretary.

That, for the purpose of efficiently carrying on the affairs of the Club, fifteen gentlemen be selected to form a working Committee (three to form a quorum), and that they be chosen equally from East and West Sussex and the town of Brighton, the Treasurer and Honorary Secretary to be ex officio members of such Committee, and the Vice-President Chairman.

Fifteen gentlemen were nominated, and a Sub-Committee appointed to draw up a code of rules and bye-laws.

That the thanks of this meeting be presented to Messrs Verrall, Tamplin, Henry Catt, and G. W. King, for their exertions in the maintenance of Cricket in this County during this and past seasons.

(Signed)   PEVENSEY,
                          Chairman.

That the thanks of this Meeting be presented to Viscount Pevensey, for having taken the Chair on this occasion.

BRIDGER STENT,
Hon. Secretary.

The press notice from *The Brighton Examiner*, 18 August 1857, detailing the formation of Sussex CCC at a meeting chaired by Viscount Pevensey. (R. Packham)

because the minute books for this period have not survived. However, the newspaper reports of the annual general meetings suggest that Bridger Stent remained the driving force during those years. At the meeting at the York Hotel in 1862 Stent proposed the acquisition of the lease of Brunswick Ground in Hove on which the club's home fixtures were played. He had already given a commitment on his own responsibility but the meeting supported his proposal. Henry's brother, Douglas, was present at this meeting but there was no offer of assistance from him or his family. Henry did not yet have the resources to be the generous benefactor that he became once he'd succeeded to the earldom.

Second Term 1879–96

When Viscount Pevensey relinquished the presidency of Sussex CCC in 1868 he was succeeded by Herbert Curteis of Windmill Hill near Hailsham. Curteis was an old Westminster schoolboy and land-owner, a more accomplished cricketer than Henry and nine years older. Henry assumed the role of patron. In 1879 Curteis stood down as president after a long tenure of office and though he remained a vice-president, he resigned from the club in 1882 requesting that his name and those of his sons be removed from the list of members.

Henry succeeded Herbert Curteis as president of Sussex CCC and would remain in that office for the next 18 years. It was to be a much more committed term compared with his first because having succeeded to the earldom in 1876 he had inherited a substantial fortune and was thus in a position to help his beloved county in so many practical ways.

The county had left the Brunswick Ground ('The Cricket Ground By The Sea') in 1871 and moved a few hundred yards to the north to the present County Ground at Eaton Road. Performances on the field were poor and the club finished as bottom county in 1877 and 1878 with only a single victory. It was at this point that Henry's involvement and support began to show some positive results:

> At last we are able to record an improvement in Sussex cricket. It is true that on paper the season's results do not present a very imposing appearance, but that a step in advance has been taken, there can be no question. To start with, Lord Sheffield engaged Mycroft to coach the young players of the County, both amateur and professional, at Sheffield Park, and the value of the Derbyshire bowler's teaching was soon made apparent in the improved batting of the team. (*Lillywhite's Companion* 1881)

That season of 1880 was a momentous one because of the Oval Test match between England and Australia, the first to be played in England. The match was a memorable one watched by over 40,000 people on the first two days. W. G. Grace scored 152 and the Australian captain, W. L. Murdoch, countered with 153 not out. 'It was' said the reports 'the most wonderful display of all-round cricket ever seen in England . . . in every sense the match was a complete success . . . in the history of the game no contest has created such world-wide interest.' This famous match, though, could not have taken place without the indulgence of Sussex CCC who agreed to postpone the county's own match with the Australians in order that the Test match could be staged at the Oval. After the season had finished the Surrey treasurer expressed his club's gratitude to Lord Sheffield for his co-operation and his letter enclosed a handsome cheque:

> Great Suffolk Street
> Southwark
> Nov 10, 1880
>
> My Lord,
> As Treasurer of the Surrey County Cricket Club, I have been requested by the Committee to forward to your Lordship, as President of the Sussex County Club, the enclosed cheque for one hundred guineas, in recognition of the kind feeling which induced your Club, for the good of cricket, to make such arrangements as enabled us to play the Australian match, early in last September; and which resulted in such a brilliant success, and was of the greatest advantage, not only to our Club, but I firmly believe, to Cricket also, and which will help to strengthen those friendly feelings already existing between ourselves and our Australian Colonies. I have the honour to remain
> Your Lordship's Obedient Servant
> Mark Cattley

Lord Sheffield's reply was prompt and gracious:

> Sheffield Park
> Nov 12, 1880
>
> Dear Sir,
> As President of the Sussex County Club I beg to tender to yourself and the Surrey Club my heartfelt thanks, not only for the cheque

which is, in itself, a welcome and valuable addition to our funds but for the succeeding handsome and generous spirit which has dictated so liberal a gift.

It will always be most gratifying to the Sussex County Club to remember that their endeavours to meet the views of the Surrey Club and to enable Australia to meet England at the Oval, have met with such a cordial and generous appreciation.

I am confident that the Committee of the Sussex Club will take the earliest opportunity for expressing in the most marked manner in their power the sense of the generous conduct of the Surrey Club. Meanwhile allow me as President to tender to you and through you to the Surrey County Club my own warmest acknowledgement of an act, the liberality of which will not soon be forgotten either by our own County Club, or by the cricketing community of Sussex.

I thoroughly concur with the opinion you have expressed as to the excellent effect of the Australian match itself.

> Believe me,
> Yours truly,
> Sheffield

This successful association with the Australians appealed to Lord Sheffield and undoubtedly influenced his later involvement with cricket in that country. However there was not to be such a warm feeling for the next visit of the Australian cricketers in 1882 when their proposed match against Sussex, arranged for 21–23 August, was cancelled by Henry Perkins, Secretary of MCC, to allow the tourists to play at Taunton.

The heated dispute between Sussex and MCC involved Lord Sheffield and the correspondence between the two parties was later published by Sussex. His Lordship's memorandum to Perkins advised him that the Sussex committee

> if they saw fit, would be fully justified in calling the attention of the MCC Committee to the course pursued by Mr Perkins as being seriously injurious to the general interests of Cricket . . . any breach of an agreement on the part of the Secretary reflects, not only on his

own good faith, but involves the credit of the Marylebone Club itself for due and honourable fulfilment of obligations, a credit which the Committee of the Sussex County Club believe must in future be weakened by this repudiation on the part of Mr Perkins of a distinct obligation which was entered into in full reliance on the good faith of such a functionary as the official representative of the Marylebone Club.

A Generous President

The Sussex CCC minutes show that Lord Sheffield rarely attended committee meetings or the club's annual general meetings but he kept in contact with secretaries George Goldsmith and William Newham over important matters. His biggest contribution to the club was his magnificent financial assistance and his desire to improve the fortunes of the club both on and off the field.

When Lord Sheffield was re-elected to the presidency, the subscription income of the club averaged about £500 per annum of which his own contribution was £25. But in 1881 Lord Sheffield gave the club a guarantee that he would accept responsibility for all expenditure incurred in excess of receipts.

Though very grateful for Lord Sheffield's pledge the club's committee members feared that it might lead to a reduction in ordinary subscriptions. Their fears were unfounded however, for in 1882 subscription income rose to a record £630 – 'thus showing how greatly the cricketing public have appreciated the noble example set them, and how cheerfully they have assisted in strengthening the hands of the Committee in their efforts to raise the standard of cricket in the county!'

The contributions given by Lord Sheffield to balance the books each season were sizeable sums indeed. For the 1880 season he gave £210 (plus his annual subscription of £25); for 1881 the sum was £340; then £370 for 1882; £300 for 1883; £250 for 1884; £250 plus £600 towards the ground purchase scheme in 1885; £250 in 1886 and £250 in 1887. In addition he paid for the private engagement of Alfred Shaw and William Mycroft to coach young cricketers at Sheffield Park and around the county.

This extreme generosity came to an abrupt end at the club's annual general meeting in April 1889 when the club's new secretary, William Newham, read a letter from Lord Sheffield which created quite a stir. It gave details of 'tiresome ruffians' who had been sending letters to Lord Sheffield containing serious threats of assassination. The president's letter appeared in *Cricket – A Weekly Record* and is discussed in a later chapter. The outcome was that Lord Sheffield 'had decided to withdraw all subscriptions from all Sussex public objects until these cowardly brutes are discovered and punished'.

There had been threats to resign at two previous annual meetings but happily these had been averted. This time the financial support was withdrawn and though he remained as president for several more years, Lord Sheffield never again made the same contributions.

He continued, though, to employ Mycroft and Shaw and to arrange further trial matches at Sheffield Park. Most importantly he continued to devote time to improve the club's fortunes.

In 1884 and 1885 he sat on a sub-committee that steered the club towards the purchase of the Hove ground for a price of £13,500. The vendors were the Benett-Stanford family. At the club's annual general meeting for 1886, the purchase was announced to members who were informed that the club had raised £5,000 (£600 from Lord Sheffield) and borrowed £10,000.

The president continued to use his influence to attract well-known and promising cricketers to the club.

In 1884 he selected George Bean, a 20-year-old young professional from Nottinghamshire to become a ground bowler at Hove and his decision, influenced by Alfred Shaw, was a good one. Bean became a successful all-rounder for both Sussex and Sheffield Park and he played three Test matches for England on the Australian tour of 1891–2. At the end of his first season he moved to Sheffield Park, played for Nottinghamshire in 1885 and then represented Sussex with distinction from 1886 to 1898 in over 200 first-class matches.

On another occasion the president facilitated a request from Rev. George Cotterill for his 18-year-old son to play for Sussex. Reverend

Cotterill was a formidable looking master at Brighton College who had played for Sussex in the 1860s and 1870s. His successful letter survives in the club's minute book:

St Bernards Woking
July 19 1886

Dear Lord Sheffield
I have had some intimation that the Sussex Committee might think it worth while to give my boy, now Captain of the Brighton XI, a trial in a County match.

I am writing to say that I have received a similar intimation from the Surrey Committee – my son being qualified to play as you know for either county.

He will be leaving Brighton Coll. this term & will probably live at home until he goes up to Cambridge in Octo. 1887. He will therefore be free to play more cricket than he is ever likely to have a chance of playing again. Both he and I would prefer Sussex to Surrey, but Surrey having been the first to move in the matter I have ventured to ask your Lordship whether the Sussex Committee wish for his services & think it worth while to give him a reasonable trial.

The Surrey Committee under take to pay all expenses. Hoping that your Lordship will pardon me for writing under the circumstances.

Believe me
Yours faithfully
Geo. E. Cotterill

Young Cotterill duly made his Sussex county debut on August 9. There were though, some high profile players that Sussex were keen to employ – but only with the consent of Lord Sheffield. In 1890 efforts were made via Alfred Shaw to engage William Attewell, a dangerous Nottinghamshire and England bowler, who had taken nine Sussex wickets in an innings for 23 in 1886. Negotiations with Attewell came to nothing, but Sussex were more successful in engaging F. W. Marlow from Staffordshire.

W.L.Murdoch

William Lloyd Murdoch, the famous Australian Test captain and Australia's equivalent to W. G. Grace, had been persuaded to come out of retirement to lead the Australians' tour to England in 1890. There is a delightful photograph of these two giants of the game taken at Sheffield Park that year on the occasion of Lord Sheffield's match against the Australians.

In 1891 Murdoch declared his intention to reside in Sussex and the county secretary wrote to other counties, universities and MCC asking permission for Murdoch to play. This was a real coup for Sussex and Lord Sheffield could not contain his excitement. He released the following letters to the *Sussex Daily News*:

> Brighton
> February 16, 1891
> Sir,
> I have Mr Murdoch's permission to send the enclosed letter to you for publication. All those who are interested in Sussex cricket will read its contents with the greatest satisfaction. I myself feel personally much gratified in having the earliest opportunity of announcing such good tidings to Sussex.
>
> Yours &c
SHEFFIELD

A copy of Murdoch's letter was enclosed:

> Kensington
> February 14, 1891
>
> Dear Lord Sheffield,
> I promised to let you know if I ever made up my mind to reside in Sussex, I am now writing to let you know that very shortly I shall be a resident of your county. I need hardly say how very pleased I shall be to represent Sussex in the cricket field as soon as ever I am allowed to do so, which I am afraid cannot be before the season of 1893. Trusting you are well, believe me,
>
> Yours respectfully,
(signed) William L. Murdoch

The newspaper added that 'Sussex cricketers and all supporters of the game throughout the county will cordially welcome Mr Murdoch and will eagerly look forward to the time when he will be able to assist in the Sussex County matches.' Murdoch had to serve a two-year residential qualification before starting his seven years' tenure as Sussex captain.

In 1893, even after the qualification period had been served, there was some doubt whether Murdoch would play. Lord Sheffield kept in touch with the Sussex committee by telegram from Naples and received a reply 'requesting that he could use his influence with Mr Murdoch to induce him to play for Sussex throughout the coming season if possible'.

Murdoch did join Sussex but before he led them out for the first time in 1893, the annual general meeting held that spring received the following from the committee:

> The Committee has much pleasure in being able to report that the Club is at present in a satisfactory state, for it is a subject of sincere congratulation that the number of Members is increasing year by year and has now reached the highest point it has ever attained.

The committee that year was active in further recruiting of players. The Cambridge University Blue, Leslie Gay, was invited to play and C. B. Fry was said to have a birth qualification even though he was born in Croydon. Efforts were then made to secure the services of another famous Australian Test player.

C. T. B. Turner

Charles Turner ('The Terror') was currently touring England with the Australians and in 1893 finished as the leading bowler in first-class cricket with 148 wickets at an average of 14.21. On his previous tours of England he had taken 283 wickets in 1888 (avge 11.68) and 179 wickets in 1890 (avge 14.21). He was still only 30 years of age and the Sussex CCC committee decided that they could offer him £200 p.a. for five years. Two gentlemen on the committee were deputed 'to wait on Lord Sheffield and consult with him and

Alfred Shaw (1842-1907) commenced his Sussex
career at the age of 51. (N. J. G. Sharp)

ascertain his ideas on the matter'. At a meeting in July the committee
was informed that 'As Lord Sheffield appeared disinclined to take
any part in the financial arrangements necessary for the engagement
of Mr Turner the matter was allowed to remain in abeyance.'

Alfred Shaw

Turner was not to be enticed but Sussex still tried to strengthen the
bowling attack. In 1894 it was recognised that Alfred Shaw, Lord
Sheffield's coach and general factotum, even though a portly 51-
year-old, was still a formidable bowler and W. L. Murdoch obtained
Lord Sheffield's consent for Shaw to play for Sussex even though his
last appearance for Nottinghamshire was six years in the past. In
Shaw's second match for his new county he was instrumental in
bowling out his old county for 89, his figures being 7 for 34.
Wisden's review of the Sussex season of 1894 noted:

The famous veteran [Alfred Shaw] bowled with a skill and accuracy which proved him by far the best bowler in the Sussex team. It was, we believe, mainly through the influence of Mr Murdoch that the step (to include him in the eleven) was taken and Lord Sheffield fell in with the proposal in the most sportsmanlike manner, being, as he always has been, anxious to do the very best on behalf of Sussex cricket. The fact that Shaw headed the Sussex bowling averages speaks volumes for the manner in which he has retained his form. Not only on the soft wickets was he very destructive, but many times his accuracy of pitch and the skill with which he varied his pace rendered him difficult to play on even the best of wickets.

Before the start of the following season the Sussex CCC committee received a proposal from Lord Sheffield that the county club should pay Alfred Shaw £150 for his services during the season. The proposal was agreed to on condition that he played the whole season otherwise they would be willing to pay him a fee of £7 10s. for every match he played.

K. S. Ranjitsinhji

At the same committee meeting that considered Lord Sheffield's proposal concerning Alfred Shaw, a letter was read by W. L. Murdoch from K. S. Ranjitsinhji, the young Cambridge University player, informing him that he was willing to play for Sussex if his residential qualification should be thought to be satisfactory. It was quickly resolved that 'In the opinion of this Committee, K. S. Ranjitsinhji is duly qualified by residence to play for Sussex.' 'Ranji' would become the brightest ornament in Cricket's Golden Age.

Ernie Jones

In May 1896 Ernie Jones, the first Australian express bowler, was making his debut tour of England. He had just appeared at Sheffield Park against Lord Sheffield's XI and created a legend that endures to this day by bowling a ball through the famous beard of England's national champion, W. G. Grace. The Sussex minute book for 29 May reveals the following:

The informal proposition to qualify Mr E. Jones of the Australian eleven was discussed. Mr Murdoch informed the committee that he had seen Mr Jones, who was willing to qualify if he were guaranteed £350 a year for 5 years. The Secretary was instructed to ask Mr Murdoch to wire to Mr Jones and ask him if the offer to the S.C.C.C. were still open, and that if so the Committee would be pleased to meet him and arrange terms.

There were later resolutions passed by the committee to the effect that Jones should be qualified for the county; that the club's solicitors should prepare an agreement and that a Guarantee Fund be opened to meet the additional expenditure.

Sussex supporters were to be disappointed. Jones never joined the county.

Sussex CCC Bazaar

In 1894 Lord Sheffield became involved in a successful event to raise funds for the county club. A committee meeting at the County Ground on 23 June was held 'to consider the advisability of holding a Bazaar in the Autumn on behalf of the County Club Funds and to fix an approximate date.' A bazaar committee was set up that included W. L. Murdoch the captain, and in due course the three-day event took place in the Hotel Metropole, Brighton at the beginning of December. It was of course the ladies who made the occasion a success and it was well supported by the public.

The ladies of Sussex by their splendid behaviour on Tuesday, Wednesday and Thursday of this week, and indeed during many preceding weeks of preparation, have placed the County Cricket Club for ever in their debt. That the ladies took an interest in county cricket was never doubted; that their interest is thoroughly practical as well as sentimental has been demonstrated by the gigantic bazaar which they have just organized and carried out at the Clarence Rooms, Brighton, on behalf of the club funds.

This bazaar was no jumble sale: it was officially opened on the first

William Newham (1860–1944) was secretary to Sussex CCC
from 1889 to 1909 as well as being a successful batsman for
the county. (N. J. G. Sharp)

day by Lady Goschen, on the second day by Viscountess Cantelupe
and on the last day by Lady Fletcher. Lord Sheffield was present on
the first day along with many of the county gentry, members of
parliament and cricketers W. L. Murdoch, W. Newham (Sussex
CCC secretary) and W. W. Read (Surrey).

The stallholders were allocated spaces in the octagon room and the
corridor, and entertainments were provided in the large hall by a
ladies' mandolin and guitar band, the Worthing Amateur Banjo Band,
a comedietta and a series of tableaux including one of W. G. Grace.

There was much to interest the cricket folk:

A fine collection of cricket curios, arranged and looked after by Mr
W. L. Murdoch and Mr A. J. Gaston, formed one of the most
interesting features of the bazaar. Lord Sheffield contributed largely
to the collection, which included the celebrated bat used by George
Parr, 'The Lion of the North', in nearly all his innings; other famous
'willows' with which such players as Dr W. G. Grace, W. W. Read
and C. I. Thornton have distinguished themselves; a number of old
prints and engravings illustrative of the game from the earliest times;
numerous photographs and cartoons of the famous cricketers of the
day; and newspapers of 60 years ago, containing accounts of the
cricket matches of the period.

The first day's takings amounted to over £300 and after three
exhausting days the funds of Sussex County Cricket Club were
increased by £750. Some outstanding items from the Bazaar
catalogue are detailed in Appendix E.

Resignation

After eighteen eventful years in his second term as Sussex president,
Lord Sheffield decided to resign. He had presided over a period
during which the cricketing and financial fortunes of the club had
improved dramatically. Lord Sheffield's resignation letter to the
club's secretary Billy Newham has survived.

1897

Dear Newham

I shall be extremely obliged to you if you will kindly express to the
members of the Sussex County Cricket Club, at your meeting
tomorrow, my deep regret at having to sever my connection with
them as President, and my warm gratitude to them for having for so
many years elected me to that post. As you are aware, I have long
entertained a wish to retire from that position, in order to make way
for someone who would give greater attention to the general
management of the affairs of the Club; and a more constant
attendance at the deliberations of the Committee than I am able to
give; and I am confident that the time has come when it is for the best

interest of the Club and County cricket that I should carry out my wish. If, as you suggest to me in your letter, it might be proposed that I should be offered the position of one of the Patrons of the Club, I would send you a reply to such a proposal as soon as I received it. At the same time I would send you a fuller explanation of my reasons for resigning the presidency and withdrawing from further participation in public cricket than I can possibly in the limited space of this letter. I hope you will assure the meeting that of the reminiscences of a longish life, now advancing towards its eventide, I can think of none more happy, more pleasant, or more satisfactory to look back upon than the recollections of the kindness and indulgence of the Sussex County Cricket Club in electing me their President for something more than a quarter of a century.

Yours &c
SHEFFIELD

The 1890s is reckoned to be the start of cricket's golden age and Sussex CCC, with its active president, colourful Australian captain, and Fry and Ranji, made a real contribution to the glamour of the cricket world.

Third Presidency 1904

Following Lord Sheffield's resignation in 1897, he was succeeded by the Duke of Norfolk who served for one year and set a precedent for others. He was followed by Earl Winterton (1898) and the Marquess of Abergavenny (1899). The Duke served again in 1900 then Sir Henry Harben (1901), Lord Brassey (1902) and Lord Leconfield (1903) all held the office for a year. These members of the Sussex nobility and gentry doubtless made their contributions to the club without attempting to emulate Lord Sheffield's involvement and massive contribution.

In the spring of 1904 Lord Sheffield was 72 years old and had scaled down his cricket activities partly as a result of a dispute about the liquor licence at Sheffield Park. When he then assumed the role of president of Sussex County Cricket Club, it must have surprised many in the cricket world. This time, like his recent predecessors, he would serve just one year. The county club's Annual for the new season stated:

> The re-election of the Earl of Sheffield to the Presidency of the Sussex County Cricket Club last March was a signal for general satisfaction and delight throughout the length and breadth of the county. No gentleman has worked more assiduously in the interest of the game in Sussex, both by his personal influence and liberal beneficence than the indulgent Earl, during the time that Sussex cricket was at a low ebb. At one time the Club would have probably dissolved but for Lord Sheffield's timely help. He said: 'Spend what money you like and send the bill to me: I'll pay it' while on another occasion he gave a cheque for £400. Mainly through his zealous and untiring efforts steps were taken which ultimately resulted in the purchase of the ground now occupied by the Club.
>
> Nothing but the highest satisfaction will be experienced at the revival of Lord Sheffield's close association with Sussex County Cricket and his acceptance of the position of President.

In the *Argus* A. J. Gaston showed his delight: 'It is gladness to realise that Lord Sheffield has again honoured the County Club by accepting the post of President, and in a most princely and practical form too by a donation of £100 towards the club funds.'

With Lord Sheffield's donation and another three-day bazaar at the Dome in Brighton (this time he was not involved) the club's deficit was wiped off.

4

Australians in the Park

We have seen in the previous chapter that the first home Test match between England and Australia, played at the Oval in September 1880, took place after Lord Sheffield had agreed to the postponement of Sussex's fixture against the tourists, arranged for the same time.

His gesture certainly led to much goodwill, and when he invited the 1884 Australians to open their tour with a match at Sheffield Park his offer was accepted immediately.

By this time the vastly improved Sheffield Park cricket ground was of proven first-class standard.

His hospitality was famous and he entertained the Australian teams on five occasions: 1884, 1886, 1890, 1893 and 1896. On each occasion it was the first match of the tour thus resembling matches of a later date played at Arundel by touring teams newly arrived in England. The difference though was that Lord Sheffield's matches were no mere one-day 'pipe-openers' and were played in a highly competitive spirit as first-class matches of three days' duration.

The Australian team of 1888 was not entertained at Sheffield Park because Lord Sheffield was being sorely irritated by mischief makers and had closed the park (see chapter 11). With this exception, the Australian matches were grand occasions, involving some huge crowds, spectacular fireworks and culminating in the visit of the Prince of Wales in 1896.

Lord Sheffield's XI v Australians
12–13 May 1884

In 1881 and 1883 Lord Sheffield had staged first-class matches when his team opposed those led respectively by Alfred Shaw and

W. G. Grace (1848-1915) was Lord Sheffield's
captain in six first-class matches at Sheffield Park.
(R. Packham)

W. G. Grace but in 1884 he was able to indulge his competitive streak with a match against the formidable Australians.

The match between Lord Sheffield's XI and the Australians was played on May 12 and 13, 1884. On their previous tour in 1882, the Australians had famously beaten England at the Oval in a match that gave rise to the legend of the Ashes.

In 1884 Sheffield Park had its own railway station. The cricket ground was in excellent order with the newly constructed pavilion on view and his Lordship had assembled a very strong team to represent him, with the venerated W. G. Grace as captain. There was considerable expense in staging the match. The Australians were guests of Lord Sheffield and members of the public were allowed access to the ground free of charge.

A view of the match between Lord Sheffield's XI and the Australians taken from Lord Sheffield's pavilion in 1884.

On the first day the Australians arrived by special train at half-past eleven 'and at that time the weather was simply magnificent. The attendance even thus early must have numbered more than 2,000 and the wide circle continually received reinforcements.'

The local report of the scene on that first day conveys something of the excitement of the occasion and details the preparations that ensured that the event was a great success:

The grand match of cricket, which has been looked forward to with so much interest for some weeks past by all classes in the county, arranged by the Right Hon. the Earl of Sheffield between the Australians and a fairly representative All England Eleven selected by his Lordship himself, commenced yesterday on the charming ground in Sheffield Park. The whole of the arrangements were designed and carried out in a style of princely munificence, which regards not cost, evidently with the view of affording enjoyment to as large a concourse of spectators as could possibly be expected to avail themselves of the privilege of witnessing the match with which the visitors from the other side of the world inaugurate their campaign in the mother country for the present season. The match which commenced yesterday may be regarded as the climax of the efforts which Lord Sheffield has been making for some years past to revive the status of Sussex as a cricketing county.

The cricket ground within the park is in many respects the most picturesque in England, and among those who were present in their thousands yesterday probably few would be found to declare that they had ever seen a fairer sight than was presented by the ground and its surrounding.

Everything had been done by his Lordship not only to facilitate access to the ground from the railway station, but to promote as far as possible the comfort and convenience of his host of visitors. A postern gate had been placed in the park fence close to the railway station, and from this point to the ground a row of pennons 'blazed' the way across the park. The private pavilion with its balconies and central fountain had been redecorated, and its borders planted with brilliant flowers. The clock, pavilion and marquees erected on various points among the trees fringing the ground, were appropriated to refreshments. The fine band of the Royal Artillery was stationed near the pavilion, and performed at intervals during the day; and stands had been erected and seats placed for the accommodation of more than a thousand spectators.

In order that news of the progress of the match might be telegraphed to all parts of the world, where the English language is spoken and interest taken in cricket, special arrangements had been made at the office at Fletching village, a few minutes' walk from the ground. The instruments used are capable of transmitting two hundred words a minute over a single wire. A printing office has also been established on the ground, in charge of Mr Crowhurst, of Brighton.

The utmost care had been taken to render the ground all that could possibly be desired. The turf was as smooth as a billiard table, and with scarcely more nap on it, and difficult, indeed, would it be to find better wickets. Special trains were run by the railway company from nearly every part of their system, and both these and the ordinary trains to Sheffield Park were largely patronised. A very numerous contingent also came by road, and the little village on one side of the park, and the neighbourhood of the Sheffield Arms on the other, presented a gay aspect during the morning. The whole of the arrangements were personally superintended by the noble Earl himself, ably assisted by Mr Nash (the home steward) and Mr John Fuller (the estate builder). Credit is due to Moore, the ground man, for the excellence of the wickets, and, indeed to all concerned in carrying out his Lordship's plans for affording a treat to the lovers of cricket in Sussex, such as has never been enjoyed before.

Lord Sheffield's XI, led by W. G. Grace, was a strong one and included seven 'crack' professionals from Nottinghamshire and Yorkshire as well as three Sussex regulars in Harry Phillips, Jesse Hide and Rev. Frederick Greenfield. The spectators were delighted when 'W. G.' won the toss and opened the batting with Louis Hall at 11.50 a.m. The Australians were given 'a gratifying reception'. Grace was soon given out, leg before wicket, for a single and wickets fell regularly. Lunch was taken with the home side on 83 for 7. When play resumed at 3.10 p.m. only three more runs were added before Lord Sheffield's XI were all out for just 86 from 67 four-ball overs. Giffen and Palmer had bowled unchanged.

The Australians started well in reply with an opening stand of 52 between McDonnell and Alick Bannerman and despite 'W. G.' taking four wickets the visitors finished the day in a strong position at 172 for 4 with Bannerman on 71 and Blackham on 22.

When the Australians resumed their innings on the second morning, 32 runs were added before Bannerman became Grace's fifth victim at 204 for 5. He was caught at short mid-on for an excellent innings of 94. The visitors then collapsed to 212 all out (W. G. Grace 6 for 72) and the Australian lead was restricted to 126.

In their second innings, Lord Sheffield's XI were 26 for 2 at lunch but 'W. G.' ('the Leviathan') was still there and batting well in front of over 9,000 people. Shrewsbury failed and despite a modest stand between 'W. G.' and William Barnes, in which Grace hit Palmer 'clean out of the ropes' for 4, the home team only managed 120 to lose by an innings and six runs.

Lord Sheffield's XI v Australians 1884. Back row: J. Hide, W. G. Grace, A. Shaw. Seated: F. F. J. Greenfield, A. Shrewsbury, G. Ulyett, L. Hall, G. Harrison. In front: W. Flowers, H. Phillips (N. J. G. Sharp)

George Giffen and George Palmer had bowled unchanged throughout the match, which was completed inside two days. The local reporter was not dismayed and appears to have thoroughly enjoyed his visit to Sheffield Park:

That his Lordship's efforts in the cause of Sussex cricket and his desire to afford recreation and enjoyment to all classes, have been fully recognised and appreciated may be judged from the fact that on the opening day the park was visited by between 7,000 and 8,000 persons, and on Tuesday the attendance was still larger, more than 9,000 having entered the seven gates before half-past one, and the afternoon trains brought up the total to at least 12,000 persons of all rank and grades of society. The space appropriated to carriages was occupied by hundreds of vehicles from the lordly drag to the humble pony trap; and not only were the stands and the half-mile circle enclosing the cricket ground thronged and fringed with a wide circle of spectators, but the rising ground among the trees to the east was thickly dotted by groups intently interested in the progress of the play. The weather was again delightful, and the charming surroundings and accessories of the ground were viewed under the most advantageous circumstances. Probably there were many who scarcely saw a ball bowled, for during the whole day people were strolling about on the banks of the lakes and among the grounds, deriving pleasure from contemplating the beauties of nature in her most lovely garb and admiring the taste and skill which has been displayed in the construction of the cascades and the bridges by which they are spanned. Every body one met with at the close of the match were ready to acknowledge that, thanks to Lord Sheffield's kind liberality, a glorious holiday had been enjoyed.

The crowd was, we are glad to state, an exceedingly orderly one, and there was an entire absence of all attempts at rowdyism whilst so far as we saw, there was nothing done which in any way could cause the noble Lord to regret his very spirited and generous action. The arrangements for the match were, it is only just and fair to add, carried out in the most admirable and successful manner under the personal and active superintendence of his Lordship's respected home steward, Mr Nash.

Lord Sheffield's XI v Australians
13, 14, 15 May 1886

The Australians next toured England in 1886 and their opening fixture was again to be played at Sheffield Park against Lord Sheffield's XI over three days in May. The match was awaited with great anticipation and was announced as follows:

> The first match of the Australians in England this season will be against an eleven chosen by Lord Sheffield, and is to be played in his lordship's park on May 13, 14, 15 on which days arrangements have been made by the Brighton Railway to run special trains from both London and Brighton to the Sheffield Park station on the direct Croydon, East Grinstead and Brighton line, at convenient hours to the, no doubt, many visitors to this grand cricket match.

W. G. Grace was again asked to captain Lord Sheffield's team which was made up of leading north country professionals,

Australians v Lord Sheffield's XI 1886. Back row: G. Giffen, F. R. Spofforth, Major Wardill (Manager) F. H. Farrands (Umpire), J. Bates (Scorer), W. Bruce, J. McIlwraith, T. W. Garrett, E. Evans, J. W. Trumble, G. Salter (Scorer), R. Thoms (Umpire). Seated: G. J. Bonnor, J. McC. Blackham, H. J. H.Scott, S. P. Jones, G. E. Palmer. In front: A. H. Jarvis (N. J. G. Sharp)

Surrey's prolific batsman Walter Read and the Sussex wicket-keeper Harry Phillips.

The Australians were led by Henry Scott and although they had a strong bowling attack it was depleted because of Giffen's inability to bowl. The teams arrived at Sheffield Park on the eve of the match and the local reporter described the scene:

Most of the members of the two teams arrived at the park on Wednesday, and were received by his lordship. Quarters have been provided for them, during the match, at the village of Fletching and at farm-houses in the neighbourhood. On the afternoon of their arrival the Australians and several of the earl's team, including Dr Grace and Mr W.W.Read, engaged in practice in the park. During the night and early in the morning there was a very heavy fall of rain, and before nine o'clock more than one inch was registered in the park. After that hour rain ceased, but the weather was very threatening till noon. This no doubt interfered with the attendance, especially of ladies, but nevertheless the special and ordinary trains from Brighton and London were well filled, and upward of 6,000 were present in the park in the afternoon. Lord Sheffield and the opponent teams were present on the ground at an early hour of the forenoon, but it was found that owing to the heavy rains it was impossible to commence play at the usual time. About half-past twelve gleams of sunshine flitting across the ground gave promise of an improvement further on; and half an hour later, Dr Grace and Shaw went to inspect the wickets. Upon their report, it was decided not to commence the match till after the luncheon hour. In the meantime practice was indulged in outside the ropes, and the company present amused themselves by watching the batting of Messrs Grace, Read, Spofforth and others, or in strolling about the grounds, where the cascades were playing the whole day, or listening to the band.

The rain had stopped sufficiently for the Australians to meet a large party of Lord Sheffield's personal friends on the eastern lawn of the mansion. A sumptuous luncheon was then served in the eastern suite of apartments for a hundred guests while the Artillery Band performed on the lawn. On returning to the ground Scott won the toss, *Advance Australia* was the *mot d'ordre* and W. G. Grace led out his side at 3.10 p.m.

Lord Sheffield's bowlers made runs very difficult to come by on a damp pitch and they regularly took wickets. They were helped by William Newham of Sussex, who ran out the giant Bonnor from the boundary and then caught Palmer at long on, a capital catch which was much applauded. When the Australians were all out for 98 (Grace 4 for 50) at 5.55 p.m., play finished for the day.

Despite the short day's play the reporter from the *Sussex Agricultural Express* found much of interest to test his descriptive powers:

Sheffield Park has always been famous for its noble oaks, and a new plantation of these trees has been formed on the north-east side of the cricket ground, and south of the ladies' pavilion are planted groups of double scarlet thorn and double gorse. The interior of Lord Sheffield's pavilion, on the southern fringe of the ground, has been redecorated internally, and adorned with choice flowers and shrubs. On the north side a handsome tent, beautifully fitted was, as usual, erected for the Countess of Sheffield, and on the two other sides were stands, with seating accommodation for some 3,000 spectators. The flower borders round the two pavilions were bright with red and white tulips, and pansies, bordered with red and white daisies. The full band of the Royal Artillery, from Woolwich, occupied the covered stand near his lordship's pavilion, and at intervals throughout the day played choice selections of music in masterly style. Space was reserved at the south-eastern curve of the ground for carriages, of which there were a considerable number during the afternoon. The way to the plateau upon which stands the cricket ground, from the four entrances into the park thrown open to the public, was blazed with flags, and men, distinguished by a badge, were placed at intervals to keep order, prevent irregularities, and answer enquiries. In these duties they were assisted by a force of constabulary, under superintendents of the East Sussex division, but, so far as we heard, no occasion arose for their active interference. The whole of the general arrangements, comprising a mass of details of which only public entrepreneurs can form any conception, were entrusted by the noble earl to Mr W.T.Nash, the home steward at the park, who ably acquitted himself of the responsibility, and performed his arduous duties with much tact and courtesy.

On the second day
Australia's bowler Tom Garrett made batting very difficult for Lord Sheffield's XI when play resumed in unsettled weather and he was far more effective than 'The Demon' Spofforth. Garrett took six wickets for 22 after an opening stand of 31 between Grace (18) and Billy Scotton (30) and the innings closed just before two o'clock for 105, a lead of just seven runs.

The tourists began their second innings after lunch. Bonnor twice hit Grace over the ropes but wickets fell quickly and at five o'clock the Australians had collapsed to 70 all out. William Barnes's 23.3 overs had earned him seven wickets for just 26 runs and Lord Sheffield's XI were left to score 64 runs to win. By close of play they

Lord Sheffield's XI v Australians. 1886 Back row: F. H. Farrands (Umpire), J. Bates (Scorer), W. Flowers, W. Barnes, G. Ulyett, G. Salter (Scorer), R. Thoms (Umpire). Seated: A. Shaw, W. Newham, W. G. Grace, W. W. Read, A. Shrewsbury. In front: H. Phillips, W. Bates, W. Scotton (N. J. G. Sharp)

had reached 46 for two so on the last day were required to score a further 18 runs to win the match.

On the third day
Arthur Shrewsbury and William Bates quietly took Lord Sheffield's XI to an eight-wicket victory without further loss although Bates was dropped in the long field by Garrett off Evans.

Afterwards a scratch game was played between sides captained by W. G. Grace and H. J. H. Scott mixing up the players from both teams and introducing Rev. F. F. J. Greenfield (Sussex) and J. McIlwraith (Australians). Each team had eleven in the field but only seven batted for Mr Scott's side. The scratch game ended as a draw. Scott's XI scored 73 and Grace's XI replied with 57 without loss.

Lord Sheffield's XI had gained revenge for the defeat of 1884 and the match was considered to be another unqualified success:

Lord Sheffield may well be congratulated on the success of his endeavours to afford enjoyment to his neighbours and to further the interests of cricket in Sussex. During the three days, notwithstanding that the weather was by no means propitious, at least 25,000 persons visited the ground, more than half that number being present on the second day. On Friday and Saturday, the band of the 1st Sussex Artillery was present on the ground, and performed pleasing selections, under the conductorship of Mr Devin.

The whole of the arrangements were carried out without the slightest hitch, and great credit is due to Mr A.T.Nash, the home steward, who was chiefly instrumental in carrying out his Lordship's wishes and instructions; to Mr Fuller, who was deputed to watch over the comfort of the two teams, in the quarters provided for them; and to Mr Moore, the ground keeper. We understand that Lord Sheffield proposes to bring the Parsees down to Sheffield Park during their cricketing tour this season to meet an eleven selected by himself.

George Giffen, a famous Australian all-rounder, recalled an incident from this match. 'W. G.' caused the visitors some annoyance by calling for a gauge to test the width of bats used by Percy McDonnell and Alick Bannerman. McDonnell's bat was found to be a trifle too wide even though it was made in England and this was explained by the fact that many blades have a tendency to spread after severe usage. Giffen wrote: 'But annoyed though we were, a little fun was extracted out of the incident when somebody suggested that one of W. G.'s bats should be put through the gauge – and the very first one would not pass muster!'

Lord Sheffield's XI v Australians
8, 9, 10 May 1890

Sheffield Park was closed in 1888 for reasons that are explained later in chapter 11. The closure meant that the Australian cricketers who were touring England in that year were unable to play the opening match of their tour against Lord Sheffield's XI so did not experience the pleasures of Sheffield Park and a visit to the English countryside in springtime.

However, two years later when the Australians were again touring England, the *Sussex Express* made it clear that their opening fixture would be played at Sheffield Park:

CRICKET AT SHEFFIELD PARK
THE AUSTRALIAN MATCH

We beg to remind our cricket loving readers and those who take pleasure in delightful scenery that by the kindness of the Earl of Sheffield, his beautiful cricket ground and park will be OPEN TO THE PUBLIC on the occasion of the grand match commencing on Thursday next, May 8th, between the Australians and Lord Sheffield's eleven.

The cricket ground and its charming surroundings are in splendid order and are well worth a visit at any time, without the additional attractions of first-class cricket. Should the weather prove fine the boon conferred by the earl will doubtless be appreciated by thousands. There is a station at Sheffield Park, on the Croydon, Oxted, East Grinstead and Lewes railway and Lord Sheffield's domain is also easily reached by road from Uckfield, Haywards Heath and Lewes. Special facilities, we understand, will be afforded by the Brighton Railway company, in regard to service of trains.

The Australian team arrived at Sheffield Park the day before the match was due to commence and the arrangements for another keen contest were in evidence:

These arrangements were far advanced on Wednesday afternoon, when the Australian team arrived, and were received by his lordship at Sheffield Place. They left London about noon and, travelling via Croydon and East Grinstead reached Sheffield Park station at two o'clock. Carriages were in waiting to take them to the house, where they were entertained to luncheon before engaging in practice on the cricket ground. Those of us who have known and enjoyed the grand old park for many years were delighted to see that the flag of the head of the house of Sheffield again floats proudly over the mansion – the first time, we believe, for 40 years! And a grand piece of bunting it is. Upon a field of rich crimson silk, with a wide border of purple of the same material, are emblazoned the Sheffield Arms.

After practice on Wednesday afternoon the Australian team went to Brighton where they were staying at the Grand Hotel, a saloon carriage being placed at their disposal.

On the first day

The *Sussex Express* again takes up the story:

> The assemblage of spectators was extraordinarily large, and indeed in the early morning the keenest excitement was everywhere visible at the principal railway stations, this being particularly noticeable at Lewes. The scene outside the pretty little station at Sheffield Park was a very animated one. There were numerous vehicles to pick up passengers and carry them to the ground for a consideration, and they were largely patronised.
>
> The band of the Royal Artillery was present, and played selections of popular music throughout the day.
>
> At the commencement of the match there were between 4,000 and 5,000 persons present, and in many parts of the picturesque grounds they lined the ropes four or five deep. A splendid wicket had been prepared by Mr Moore, gardener and ground keeper, and the ground was in splendid condition, the showers of the few previous mornings having improved it rather than otherwise.
>
> The entrance to the park for foot people was through the gateway near the river bridge, and close to the railway station. The way to the cricket ground was 'blazed' with little flags of red, white and blue, and every opportunity was afforded to the spectators, on their way to the centre of attraction to view the grounds. The cricket ground itself presented a most inviting appearance. The wickets, it is scarcely necessary to say, were in perfect order. The Pavilions have been re-decorated, and surrounding Lord Sheffield's is an enclosure with a tent for ladies, lined with silk, a charming little al fresco boudoir. Just below is the bandstand, which has been placed on a new and more convenient site, and has also been re-decorated. At the steps leading up to the platform of this structure are medallions, with the Australian arms in gold, in honour of the visitors, and the border round this is very prettily planted. On the opposite side of the

carriage drive is a spacious marquee, with boarded floor, where Lord Sheffield, on the opening day, entertained the two teams and a large company of friends to luncheon. At intervals round the ground are placed stands for the spectators and to the south-west and north-east of the 'play' are large marquees in which Mr Welfare of the Sheffield Arms, and Mr John Diplock, of the Griffin, cater successfully for the wants of the British public when on holiday thoughts intent. The former well-known caterer also serves luncheon in the dining pavilion.

The rhododendrons are not yet in their full glory, but there are many bright patches of pink, white and crimson which, interspersing the clumps of rich golden gorse, make a picture very contenting to the eye. The lakes are connected with cascades which were playing throughout the match, and gave life, as it were, to the whole scene, producing an ensemble the like of which is rarely to be seen in the south of England.

The whole of the admirable arrangements were personally super-intended by the noble earl himself, who was assisted in carrying them out by his steward, Mr Colgate. Great credit is due to Mr Moore for the splendid condition of the ground, and indeed to all who have been engaged, including several Lewes and Brighton firms, in putting into execution his lordship's desires and directions.

After five years' absence W. L. Murdoch had returned to the Australian team as captain and there were four new players to England in Dr John Barrett, Charlton, Syd Gregory and Walters. Lord Sheffield's XI was a very strong one but as one newspaper put it:

We believe his lordship has intentionally omitted some of the best men of the present day from his side, whose services were available, in order that the colonists should not, in their first venture, have to contend against the best pick of the whole kingdom.

The two famous captains, W. G. Grace and W. L. Murdoch, were reunited in opposition and they were photographed together by Hawkins on the steps of Lord Sheffield's pavilion.

Two champions: Grace and Murdoch.

It was Murdoch who won the toss and at five minutes past twelve a loud cheer greeted the well-known form of Dr W. G. Grace as he emerged at the head of his team from the pavilion. The cheers were renewed on the appearance of the Australian batsmen Dr Barrett and Jack Lyons. After Lyons was dismissed at 20, Murdoch came in to bat and was greeted with a welcoming cheer. He quickly opened his shoulders to Briggs, despatching him to the off boundary for three and then was applauded for a brilliant cut for four, a lofted straight drive to the boundary and another late cut for four off Attewell.

The scoring after lunch was described as 'tediously slow' and the Australian captain survived a couple of chances to Lohmann and Peel. Humphreys, the Sussex lob bowler, came on at 110 but was later punished (although not reflected in his figures). He had famously performed the hat-trick for Sussex against the Australians in both 1880 and 1884. When stumps were drawn at six o'clock the Australians had lost some late wickets to finish at 190 for 8 and Murdoch was still there with 92. The day had finished with eight successive maiden overs.

Rain fell heavily on the second day of the match and play was abandoned without a ball being bowled. As one official commented: 'Although we are informed no less than two thousand persons were present, it was impossible to get in even half an hour's play, owing to the pitiless downpour.'

On the third day

The weather relented on Saturday morning and the day was bright throughout. The morning and afternoon trains to Sheffield Park were crowded with passengers, many of whom took an enjoyable walk in the lovely grounds, 'now approaching the height of their early summer beauty'.

The spectators were in for a shock when play commenced at 11.50 a.m. Murdoch and Charlton were both bowled by Lohmann for the addition of only a single and the Australians were all out for 191. The pitch on the first day was dry and true but now it was all in favour of the bowlers, Lord Sheffield's XI being dismissed by Turner and Ferris for just 27 runs. This was an ignominious performance and only W. G. Grace, who scored 20 of the total, gave the scorers something to do. 'The sun had already begun to take effect on the wicket and it was soon evident that the Australians were masters of the situation.' The visitors were only in the field for an hour and ten minutes and asked the stunned home team to follow on.

Stoddart and Shrewsbury opened the second innings with a stand of 31 – already in excess of the team's first innings effort – but the left-armed Ferris was not to be denied. This time he claimed seven wickets for 70 from 33 overs. After 'W. G.' had been well caught at point, Briggs and Peel added 45 in half an hour, their partnership producing some of the best cricket of the day. Briggs hit with great resolution but just as there seemed a remote chance of a draw he was run out attempting a third run. Lord Sheffield's XI were all out for 130 and lost by an innings and 34 runs.

The match was over just after 5 p.m. and twenty-two wickets had fallen for 158 runs. The local reporter felt that the colonials had all the luck because of the rain and added:

. . . Lord Sheffield may, on the whole, be congratulated upon the success of his opening cricket festival. He certainly afforded a most agreeable holiday on two of the three days appointed for the match to some fifteen or sixteen thousand persons. The event had another result of a curious nature from a financial point of view – it seems to have sent up the shares of the Brighton Railway Company. The traffic receipts of last week have to compare with those of the period of the Paris Exhibition last year and that there could possibly be an increase was wholly unexpected.

Lord Sheffield's XI v Australians
7, 8 July 1892

There was no official Australian tour to England in 1892 but there were sufficient leading Australian cricketers working or visiting for Lord Sheffield to contemplate a fixture at Sheffield Park in July. *Cricket* advised its readers:

> LORD SHEFFIELD is as a rule, and naturally, anxious when he arranges a match to provide for a display of first-class cricket. Nor is his fixture against the pick of the Australian cricketers now in England, at Sheffield Park on July 7 and 8, likely to furnish the exception. On the contrary, he has already got the backbone of a rather warm side. To Messrs W. G. Grace, H. Philipson, A.E.Stoddart, Briggs, Chatterton, J.T. Hearne, may be added Lohmann.

The cricket public was to be disappointed because the game clashed with an election in the area and was cancelled. In the following week's paper news was given of the cancellation of the match:

> The shadow of the poll has far reaching effects and outside the inner circle of the political arena. At all events it is responsible for the abandonment of the match between Lord Sheffield's team and the Australians in England fixed to be played at Sheffield Park on Thursday and Friday next. Polling is to take place in the district on the second day, and Lord Sheffield being, and rightly, of the opinion that his fixture might interfere to some extent with the progress of

Australians v Lord Sheffield's XI 1893 Back row: R. Carpenter (Umpire), V. Cohen (Manager), A. H. Jarvis, W. Giffen, W. Bruce, A. Bannerman, R. Thoms (Umpire). Seated: G. H. S. Trott, H. Trumble, G. Giffen, J. McC. Blackham (Captain), J. J. Lyons, R. McLeod, C. T. B. Turner. In front: H. Graham, A. Coningham, S. E. Gregory. (R. Packham)

the poll, has in the higher interests of politics very reluctantly made up his mind to cancel the arrangements he had made for the match.

Lord Sheffield's XI v Australians
8, 9, 10 May 1893

The enthusiasm for an Australian visit to Sheffield Park was even more intense in 1893 when Jack Blackham was the visitors' captain, Murdoch now having assumed that role for his adopted Sussex. The report in the *East Sussex News* sets the scene:

The match had aroused the evident possible interest in every quarter, and people came in their thousands, from far beyond the confines of Sussex to witness the game. The attendance on the opening day, as checked by Lord Sheffield's men at the various gates, was just under 8,000, of whom probably nearly 7,000 were present at one time in the afternoon.

The charming grounds of the park, though naturally, having regard to the dry and early season, not appearing at their best, were very beautiful. The yellow gorse was in full bloom and the rhodo-dendrons just breaking into flower, while trees were in glorious leaf, the only part burnt and brown being the turf, which gave every indication of the long and unusual drought. This by no means applies to the centre part of the cricket ground, which had been attended to by Mr Moore with the utmost care, and on Monday morning the pitch, as perfect as a billiard table, was surrounded by a large circle of perfectly green turf. Nearly all other arrangements were equally perfect and complete. Seating accommodation was provided for some 3,000 spectators, in addition to a large space reserved for coaches and carriages, occupied some half-dozen deep by conveyances of every description. Special pavilions had been provided for the ladies, for his lordship's private guests and for the representatives of the Press, though the provision for these gentlemen, owing possibly to an unexpectedly large attendance, was somewhat inadequate. A corner of their marquee was occupied by the telegraph department, under the care of Messrs Cox and Bennett, whose efforts to give satisfaction were as completely successful as they were untiring.

On the first day

Lord Sheffield's XI was a very strong one and 'except for the absence of Lohmann and Abel the eleven was as strong as it well could have been, and it is worthy of remark that seven were members of the team which accompanied Lord Sheffield to the Colonies in 1891.'

The Australians travelled from their headquarters at the Hotel Metropole, Brighton to Sheffield Park and soon found themselves in the field when Blackham lost the toss to W. G. Grace. 'W. G.' and Shrewsbury opened the batting against Giffen and Turner – all four being giants of the cricket field. 'W. G.' was in splendid form and after only 65 minutes Lord Sheffield's XI had reached 101 when Grace was first out for a chanceless 65. Shrewsbury was dismissed after lunch for 62 while William Gunn (56) and Herbert Hewett (30) also made useful contributions. After this only Lockwood and Briggs made any stand against Giffen and Coningham, who both took five wickets and the innings, 'which at one time promised to

W. G. Grace is pictured here during his opening stand of 101 with Arthur Shrewsbury in 1893. The Australian captain Jack Blackham is keeping wicket. Lord Sheffield's pavilion is in the centre. (*Cricket Field*)

produce three or four hundred, concluded with the total at 258.' This remains the highest score in matches between the teams at Sheffield Park.

The Australians had half an hour's batting in the evening and Harry Trott took three fours off the opening over from Attewell. The visitors finished the day at 40 for 1 but 'the interest in the day's play died out when the innings of the home eleven closed, and some thousands went away without waiting to see stumps drawn.'

On the second day

After the first day's play the match was evenly poised and with favourable weather conditions the scene was set for a record breaking crowd to watch the play on Tuesday:

On the second day there were very early evidences that the attendance would be a record one for any cricket match ever played in Sussex, or any event associated with Sheffield Park. By mid-day the ring of people around the ropes was more dense than at any period during

Monday, and while probably not less than 20,000 persons in all entered the Park during the day, there were at one time something like 15,000 watching the progress of the game. Nearly 10,000 arrived by rail. Many hundreds gave no thought to the cricket, but made of the visit a picnic, and among the shrubs or furze spread white cloths, laid out viands, uncorked bottles, and gave themselves over to social pleasure and the enjoyment of the glorious scene and delicious atmosphere. The weather, taken all round was perfect.

When the cricket resumed young Harry Graham showed that he had a good defence as well as 'plenty of hit if required' and he remained in good form for the Lord's Test match when he scored 107 on his debut. Graham apart, the Australians' batting was disappointing and Giffen, Turner, Trumble and Blackham all failed to score. From an overnight 40 for 1 the innings subsided to 138 all out, Attewell, Lockwood and Briggs sharing the wickets. 'The out-cricket of Lord Sheffield's team was up to the best standard and runs were very difficult to get throughout.' McGregor's wicket-keeping and Maurice Read's outfielding came in for special praise.

The follow-on was enforced and the Australians started more promisingly with a stand of 41 between Bruce and Lyons until Surrey's Bill Lockwood dismissed them both and went on to take five second innings wickets with his pace bowling. The visitors were all out for a second time just before the close of play for 173 and nineteen Australian wickets had fallen in the day for 271 runs, leaving Lord Sheffield's XI to score just 56 runs on the last day to win. The local reporter described 'a few wild hits by Coningham, who has a very rough, untutored style in his second innings 29 which included a hit for eight, four run out and four for an overthrow'.

The *Cricket Field* reporter enjoyed his day at the match:

The ground, probably the prettiest in the country was in splendid order and the spectators were most impartial, the Australians' hits being as heartily cheered as those of the Englishmen. Inside the charming pavilion, which was decorated with choice flowers, was a

2d.   2d.

Sheffield Park   **Cricket Ground**

MONDAY, TUESDAY & WEDNESDAY, May 8, 9, 10, 1893,

LORD SHEFFIELD'S XI. v. AUSTRALIANS.

LORD SHEFFIELD'S XI.	First Innings	Second Innings
1 Mr. W. G. Grace	c Trumble b Coningham 63	b Turner 18
2 Shrewsbury	c Trumble b Coningham 62	c Graham b Giffen......23
3 Gunn	c Graham b Giffen 56	not out 0
4 Mr. H. T. Hewett	c McLeod b Coningham 30	
5 Mr. A. E. Stoddart	c McLeod b Giffen 3	
6 M Read	c Coningham b Giffen ...2	not out......10
8 Peel	b Giffen 4	
7 Lockwood	not out......17	
9 Briggs	b Giffen 12	
10 Attewell	c Trott b Coningham 0	
11 Mr. G. McGregor	st Blackham b Giffen 2	

b.3 l.-b.3 w.I n.-b. Total...7   b.4 l.-b.1 w. n.-b Total...5
Total...258   Total...56

1-101 2-167 3-215 4-219 5-221 6-221 7-227 8-248 9-248 10-258
1-38   2-48   3-   4-   5-   6-   7-   8-   9-   10-

AUSTRALIANS	First Innings	Second Innings
4 Mr. H. Trott	b Lockwood 20	c Stoddart b Attewell ...14
1 Mr. W. Bruce	c Attewell b Lockwood ...8	c Briggs b Lockwood ...26
5 Mr. H. Graham	st McGregor b Attewell 32	c McGregor b Lockwood 12
2 Mr. J. J. Lyons	c Read b Briggs......21	b Lockwood 15
3 Mr. G Giffen	c and b Briggs......0	c McGregor b Lockwood 1
6 Mr. C. T. B. Turner	b Briggs......0	c McGregor b Lockwood 22
7 Mr. R. McLeod	c Grace b Briggs 25	b Briggs 24
9 Mr. S. Gregory	b Attewell......2	c Shrewsbury b Peel......15
8 Mr. A. Coningham	not out......26	c McGregor b Peel 29
10 Mr. H. Trumble	b Lockwood 0	not out 7
11 Mr. J. C. McBlackham	c Hewett b Lockwood......0	run out 8

b. l.-b.4 w. n.-b. Total...4   b. l.-b. w. n.-b. Total...
Total...138   Total...173

1-24 2-40 3-71 4-75 5-75 6-103 7-111 8-113 9-134 10-138
1-41 2-41 3-42 4-60 5-68 6-97   7-138 8-150 9-159 10-173

Umpires...Thoms and Carpenter.   Scorers...J. R. Bates and G. F. Salter.

Crowhurst, Printer to the S.C.C.C., 52 Market St., Brighton.

Scorecard for Lord Sheffield's XI v Australians 1893.
(N. J. G. Sharp)

small exhibition of some of his lordship's Egyptian trophies, including a 'Nile salmon' weighing about 250 lb. This was skinned by Alfred Shaw and set up on arriving in England. Photographs of the Nile and of Lord Sheffield's entourage, consisting of some thirty or forty natives, with about twenty camels, were objects of much attention, but that which caught the eye of cricketers was the bat with which W. G. Grace made his big score for Lord Sheffield's team in Australia. In the rear of the pavilion, a huge marquee had been erected, and in this some 300 guests were entertained to luncheon on Tuesday.

After the day's play the Australians were entertained at Sheffield Park when a large number of spectators stayed till late in the evening to watch a brilliant fireworks display.

At the end of the evening those visitors who left by train enjoyed a good service that merited a mention in the local press:

> The railway arrangements at Sheffield Park were most satisfactory, and we congratulate Mr Horn and those with him on their able management. On Tuesday the last train was got away at eleven o'clock, and would have started at least three-quarters of an hour earlier had not an engine run off the rails at Horsted Keynes and completely blocked the line.

On the third day

With a short day's play in prospect there were only about 600 people on the final day. They saw a steady opening partnership between Grace and Shrewsbury and although both were dismissed Lord Sheffield's XI easily obtained the 56 runs needed to win in 28.1 five-ball overs. The humiliating defeat of 1890 was avenged.

Lord Sheffield was congratulated for having made the 'most complete arrangements' for the visitors to Sheffield Park and for 'having furnished a spectacular display unrivalled for beauty and brilliancy'.

Lord Sheffield's XI v Australians
11, 12, 13 May 1896

The fifth and last visit of the Australians to Sheffield Park took place in May 1896. The game ended in a draw but in every other respect it outshone all the previous contests – spectacular though they undoubtedly were. On this occasion the crowd on the first day was estimated at 30,000 (although perhaps 25,000 is more realistic) and they came to see international cricket, Lord Sheffield's beautiful grounds and, in an age when royalty was revered, HRH the Prince of Wales.

Lord Sheffield's team had deliberately excluded all members of A. E. Stoddart's Ashes-winning team of 1894–95 because of a dispute

2d.   **2d.**

Sheffield   *Cricket*

Park   *Ground.*

MONDAY, TUESDAY and WEDNESDAY, May 11, 12, 13, 1896.

Lord Sheffield's XI. v. Australians.

AUSTRALIANS.	First Innings	Second Innings
Mr. H. Donnan	b Fry 32	c Hearne b Davidson 25
Mr. J. Darling	c Lilley b Mold 67	c Ranjitsinhji b Hearne 35
Mr. G. Giffen	c Lilley b Jackson....38	b Mold 18
Mr. F. A. Iredale	b Grace 14	c Lilley b Davidson....11
Mr. G. H. S. Trott (cap.)	c Ranjitsinhji b Hearne 43	not out 59
Mr. S. E. Gregory	b Grace 6	run out 0
Mr. C. Hill	c Lilley b Mold 32	b Davidson 23
Mr. C. J. Eady	c Hearne b Mold 2	c Lilley b Pougher 10
Mr. J. J. Kelly	not out 2	b Hearne 9
Mr. E. Jones	b Mold 9	c Ranjitsinhji b Pougher 0
Mr. T. R. McKibbin	st Lilley b Hearne 0	b Pougher 4
	b.10 l.-b.1 w.1 n.-b. Total 12	b. l.-b. w. n.-b Total
	Total- 257	Total - 194

1-92 2-110 3-145 4-175 5-192 6-242 7-243 8-245 9-256 10-257
1-52 2-68 3-87 4-89 5-126 6-168 7-168 8-186 9-186 10-194

LORD SHEFFIELD'S XI.	First Innings	Second Innings
1 Mr. W. G. Grace (capt.)	c Kelly b Jones 49	c Giffen b Jones....26
2 Mr. F. S. Jackson	c Hill b Jones 17	not out....25
6 Shrewsbury	c Donnan b Jones 1	
3 Gunn	c Giffen b Jones 5	c Hill b Eady 6
4 K. S. Ranjitsinhji	c Iredale b Jones 79	c Donnan b Jones 42
5 Mr. C. B. Fry	b Jones 0	b Trott 5
7 A. Hearne	c Kelly b Eady....4	
8 Lilley	c and b McKibbin 21	
10 Davidson	b Jones 4	
9 Pougher	not out 10	
11 Mold	run out 0	
	b.2 l-b.1 w.2 n-b. Total 5	b 4 l.-b.1 w. n.-b.1 Total 6
	Total — 195	Total—180

1-58 2-60 3-71 4-80 5-80 6-110 7-166 8-183 9-186 10-195
1-45 2-86 3-176 4-180 5- 6- 7- 8- 9- 10-

Umpires—R. Thoms & W. A. J. West   Scorers—Ferg. A. Lemon & E. J. Taylor

Crowhurst, Printer to the S.C.C.C., 50-1-2 Market St., Brighton.

Scorecard for Lord Sheffield's XI v Australians 1896.
(N. J. G. Sharp)

(see chapter 13) but it was certainly a strong one. The powerful batting line-up was W. G. Grace (captain), F. S. Jackson, A. Shrewsbury and W. Gunn, followed by the peerless Sussex pair of Prince Ranjitsinhji and C. B. Fry – all luminaries of a brilliant age. The local newspaper summarised the events of a glittering day of cricket:

The ground was delightful and flying over Lord Sheffield's pavilion was a flag with his coat of arms in rich silk, lovingly made by May

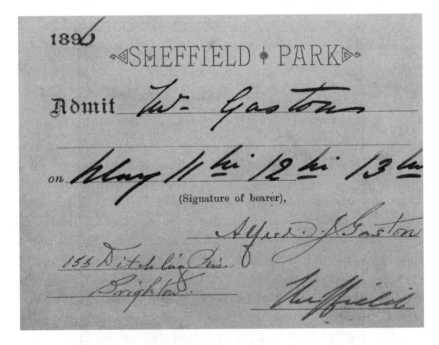

A. J. Gaston's Admission Card signed by Lord Sheffield for the 1896 match. (N. J. G. Sharp)

Attenborough. Just to the east of his lordship's pavilion was a very handsomely decorated marquee for the ladies and other friends because the Ladies' Pavilion had been given over to the Prince. The band stand next adjoined and then there was the carriage enclosure, Press and scoring tent and then the whole way round from west to south the ground was occupied by seats for the public.

The local report also acknowledged those involved with the arrangements:

The whole of the arrangements were admirably carried out by Mr Thos. Colgate (the well-known and courteous steward to Lord Sheffield), Mr W.T.Moore (who had the management of the ground), and Mr Alfred Shaw (who devoted his attention to the arrival and subsequent wants of the teams). On such an occasion there was, of course, a large number of police on duty, mounted constables from Brighton being present in addition to the East

Sussex Constabulary. We may add that the two extra marquees were provided by Messrs J.Parsons and Son, of Brighton, who also made the special white awning at the top of Lord Sheffield's pavilion. Messrs Berry and Bussey, of Lewes, did a considerable amount of work at the park in the building line. The public caterer, as usual, was Mr Richard Welfare, of the Sheffield Arms Hotel.

When the match got underway, the enormous crowd saw Harry Trott win the toss for the Australians who opened with two newcomers to English conditions in Harry Donnan and Joe Darling. Donnan played a stonewall game while Darling made many 'beautiful hits' and they batted beyond the lunch interval in a stand of 92. The left-hander Clem Hill had played attractively for his 30 not out when stumps were drawn at 241 for 5 – 'perhaps a little monotonous'.

On the second day there was another large crowd of 13,000 but at once there was a sudden change in the game when, in a few minutes, the Australians lost their last five wickets for 16 runs and were all out for 257. Their collapse was blamed on the pitch which was somewhat fiery after the recent drought and when Lord Sheffield's XI went in to bat Ernie Jones, the Australian express bowler, began by hitting 'W. G.' about the body with his first three balls but was then hit for two fours by the home captain off the last two balls of the over. This was the famous occasion when Jones was reputed to have bowled a ball through the great doctor's beard and the story is often recounted how 'W. G.' remonstrated with Trott about his wayward bowler. Trott responded with 'Steady, Jonah' to the tearaway who then replied to the shaken batsman, 'Sorry Doctor, she slipped.' The incident has become part of cricket's folklore.

Grace, who had enjoyed a prolific renaissance in his batting during the previous season, began to play some very attractive cricket shots and went on to score a 'perfect' 49 out of a disappointing lunch score of 80 for 5. All five wickets had fallen to Jones. 'Fortunately Ranjitsinhji was in no way incommoded by the eccentricities of the pitch nor by the pace and variety of the bowling and he began to make runs very quickly' before he too was dismissed by Jones for 79 – the highest score of the match. Lord Sheffield's XI were all out for

THE PRINCE OF WALES AT
SHEFFIELD PARK.

THE AUSTRALIAN MATCH.

THE RECEPTION OF HIS ROYAL
HIGHNESS.

BRILLIANT WEATHER.

ENTHUSIASTIC PROCEEDINGS.

Sussex Agricultural Express

195 (Jones 7 for 64) and conceded a lead of 62. When stumps were drawn the Australian second innings had reached 52-1, a lead of 114.

On the third morning Lord Sheffield's XI took quick wickets but they were held up by the Australians' captain Harry Trott, who 'showed all his old brilliancy in making 59 not out' and when the visitors were dismissed for 194 the home team required 257 to win. Although the pitch appeared to have become less lively there was insufficient time to get the runs 'but Jackson and Ranjitsinhji played beautiful cricket.' F. S. Jackson's 95 not out was the highest first-class score made at Sheffield Park and he took Lord Sheffield's team to an honourable draw at 180 for 4. The readers of the *Sussex Express* were left in no doubt about the success of the match:

The Earl of Sheffield, the noble patron of cricket at home and abroad, cannot fail to be gratified at the success of his efforts to render the inaugural match of the Australian Team of 1896 a notable event in the annals of the national summer pastime of English speaking people all the world over. The visit of the Prince of Wales, of course, gave great eclat to the opening day. The weather was brilliant throughout, and the beautiful cricket ground, the lakes below with its grand cascades, the parterres radiant with spring flowers, and the noble trees in the first flush of their spring garb of tender green, with the mansion at the distance above the water-system, made a picture, or rather a series of pictures, worth going miles to see, without taking count of the best cricket that the world can produce. The attendance was the largest ever seen at Sheffield Park on an opening day, and we should not be surprised to hear that the number of people present topped 30,000.

5

The Prince in the Park

The Prince of Wales paid a famous visit to Sheffield Park on 11 May 1896 for the first day of the cricket match between Lord Sheffield's XI and the Australians. Great crowds travelled to the ground to see the prince, as well as the Australians, the incomparable W. G. Grace and the beautiful gardens at Sheffield Park.

In 1896 the prince was 55 years old and awaiting his destiny to succeed to the throne. His mother Queen Victoria would in 1897 celebrate her Diamond Jubilee.

Although nearly 48, 'W. G.' was more popular than ever having completed a thousand runs in May of the previous year and finished the season with 2,346 runs.

The prince marked his visit by planting a tree at Sheffield Park on the north side of the cricket ground and the occasion was described by the local newspaper with great enthusiasm:

THE ARRIVAL OF THE PRINCE OF WALES

By an early hour in the morning thousands of spectators had made their way to the cricket ground. There was no tedious waiting, however, for what with the lovely scenery to admire and the constant influx of visitors from all parts by road and rail, the time passed away very pleasantly. The ground of play was cleared soon after 11 o'clock, and though most of the seats placed at the disposal of the public were soon occupied, and scores of carriages were taking up the more favourable positions under the welcome shade of the trees, the route to be taken by his Royal Highness the Prince of Wales was lined by crowds who were anxious to see the Heir Apparent, who was expected about noon. The special train by which his Royal Highness travelled arrived at Sheffield Park Station about half-past eleven, and

HRH Prince of Wales shakes hands with W. G. Grace 1896. (R. Mann)

the Prince was met at the station by the Earl of Sheffield, who, with Lord Harris and Sir Henry Fletcher, had previously given a hearty welcome to the Australians on their arrival by train from Brighton. The guard of honour at the station was furnished by the 1st Sussex Engineers and their band. With his Royal Highness were Lord Lathom and General Ellis (Equery). The Royal visitor cordially greeted his noble host on alighting from the train, and as they passed through the waiting-rooms the band played the National Anthem. Entering a state carriage drawn by four greys with postillions and out riders, the Earl and his guests proceeded to the park. The platform was decorated by flags, and outside as far as the entrance to the park there was a grand display of bunting suspended from Venetian masts in zigzag fashion. The approach of the Royal party to the cricket ground was heralded by the playing of 'God bless the Prince of Wales' by the band of the 1st Sussex Rifles stationed in the bandstand near the earl's private pavilion and the unfurling or 'breaking' of the flag on the mansion. As the Prince was driven up the strains of the band became mingled with the loud cheering of the assembled crowd. Those who took up places at the rear of the earl's private

HRH Prince of Wales leaves the Ladies' Pavilion 1896. (Mrs H. Rawlings)

pavilion – here were spaces roped off for the earl's tenants and the Fletching and Danehill school children – had a splendid view of the procession. At ten minutes to 12 the Prince reached the cricket ground, the carriage driving straight across the ground to the front of the special pavilion set apart for the Royal visitor's use. Another party of the 1st Sussex Engineers were here drawn up as a guard of honour, and the band with them played the National Anthem. The Australian cricketers were gathered near the pavilion when the Prince arrived and they gave him most hearty cheers as he passed. The cheering of the crowd was renewed again and again, being especially enthusiastic as the Prince stepped from the carriage and walked with the Earl to the pavilion. The volunteers, who were under the command of Captains Oakden and Gates, with whom were Lieuts. Martin R.Holman and Russell, then moved off. Major Savage and Captain Franklyn, R.E., of the Sussex Engineers, were also present. The cheers of the assembled multitude were quickly renewed as the Prince, accompanied by Earl Sheffield, walked across to the well-known pavilion on the south side of the ground. Here they met Dr W. G. Grace, the famous cricket 'centenarian' who was waiting

HRH Prince of Wales talks to Lord Sheffield 1896 (Mrs H.Rawlings)

for play to commence, and amidst the applause of those assembled
the Doctor was presented to the Prince. The Australians' captain (Mr
Trott) was also presented to His Royal Highness. Altogether the visit
of the Prince to the most charming cricket ground in the south of
England – if not in the whole kingdom – began under the most
auspicious circumstances, and the fact that the opening match of the
ninth Australian tour began under Royal patronage was clearly
heartily appreciated by all concerned.

SEVEN TRIUMPHAL ARCHES

The special preparations which Lord Sheffield had designed in honour
of the Prince's visit were of a character that may well mark the occasion
as historic. Neither labour nor expense was spared. His Lordship,
having regard to the time of year and the natural aspect of the park,
adopted a style of decoration which, while elaborately worked out, was
never out of harmony with the prevailing rural conditions. It was
decided that greenery should be used as much as possible, backed up
with wild and more costly flowers. In this latter department, his
lordship had the charming assistance of Miss Attenborough.

HRH Prince of Wales and Lord Sheffield 1896. (B. Gregory)

The first arch was at the station entrance to the park, this being composed of evergreen – bay, yew and box chiefly – studded with bunches of wild flowers, in which bluebells, primroses and cowslips predominated. It was flanked on either side with the Prince of Wales's feathers in the shape of shields and surmounted by the Royal Arms. Five other arches were similarly constructed as regards material, though each differed in design, some having smaller and what may be called Gothic-shaped arches at the side, while others had tastefully embellished bases, bearing the Prince of Wales's feathers, the Crown &c. The sixth arch erected at the bottom of what is known as the Oak and Ash Hill, was a particularly beautiful one. It was of large size and composed entirely of flowers.

The base was of dark blue – the Australian colours – and the pillars were of dark blue also, wreathed with flowers and interlaced with

Lord Sheffield's colours red, yellow and purple – in silk ribbon, while at the summit was the Australian arms, flanked by Lord Sheffield's flag and the flag of Australia. The whole length of the route – about a mile and a half – was marked out by lofty standards, connected with each other by chains of evergreens and wild flowers, with a flag or two just here and there. This work, as may be imagined, required a tremendous amount of material. A large number of women and children on the estate and in the neighbourhood were engaged, under the superintendence of Miss Attenborough in making the festoons and some twenty thousand bunches of wild flowers were used. The arrangements on the cricket ground were simply perfect as well as magnificent. On the east side a space was set apart for the Prince's pavilion and dining saloon. This was luxuriously upholstered by Mr Stead of Brighton. A splendid view of the game was afforded from it, and the entire front was hung with Japanese bead curtains.

Inside it was fitted up with Axminster carpets, with pannelled and decorated walls, hung with pictures, rare trophies and costly ornaments, brought home by Lord Sheffield from his travels in the East. The ceiling was fluted in salmon-coloured silk, relieved across the middle by darker silk embroidered fabrics; the two doorways and the side windows were in white enamel wood draped with russet satin; the cloak-room was tapestried with pink and brown silk and the furniture was in walnut and gold. In front of the luncheon tent was a verandah, having crimson plush supports all along, and a base of foliage and flowering plants, and over the verandah stretched a red and white striped sunblind. Outside in an enclosed space, edged in with yew, was a wonderfully pretty border of flowers, temporarily made up by Messrs Balchin of Brighton, The flowers included the beautiful variegated acer, liliums, hydrangeas, marguerites, genistas, geraniums, mignonette and stocks. The ordinary ladies' pavilion was, on this occasion, utilised as the Prince's retiring-room, and this again, was nothing less than a floral triumph, besides being luxuriously appointed in other respects. In the interior pink and yellow roses were lavishly used, relieved with the trailing greenery of smilax. The architectural features outside also received treatment, the blue and gold ironwork all round being festooned with the choicest flowers, intermingled with ever-green. In entering the pavilion his Royal Highness passed in turn under a bower of lilies of the valley and an arch of roses. Indeed, anything more lovely could not be conceived. Both this and Lord Sheffield's own private pavilion had been re-decorated in blue and gold by Mr Jesse Baker of Brighton, and from the summit of both floated the Royal Standard.

Charles Horn was stationmaster at Sheffield Park at this time and he must have proved highly efficient to handle the volatile Lord Sheffield and to take responsibilty for the royal visit. His son recalled life at the station in the mid 1890s:

We lived within a small community for, apart from the railway cottages, there were only seven cottages and a dairy anywhere near – all nice people. A great day for the locals was 11 May 1896, especially for the station staff, including my father as stationmaster. Lord Sheffield arrived at the station before 11 o'clock, and he was offered, and did accept, the privacy of our sitting room, which looked out on to the platform, until the royal train was due to arrive. At 11.30 the train steamed in bearing the Prince's emblem on the locomotive. Immediately on alighting, His Royal Highness went forward and heartily shook hands with Lord Sheffield, who stood, hat in hand, to welcome him. This unforgettable moment was witnessed by my mother, myself and my brother, from our sitting room windows, and I shall always remember it. Then after some introductions, the Prince and Lord Sheffield moved to the carriage, drawn by four fine grey horses. The bands played the National Anthem, while the Guard of Honour presented arms. The decorations, both inside and outside the station and along the roads, were also something to remember. Sheffield Park had never seen anything like it before.

A bedroom at Sheffield Park had been designated 'The Prince's Room' by a plaque on the door but the Prince of Wales left the Park about half past four to return to London. Nevertheless, as a newspaper reported,

The visit of his Royal Highness had a two-fold significance. The great Australian colonies cannot fail to appreciate the compliment paid to their representatives by the Heir Apparent to the Crown of the British Empire, and the people of Lord Sheffield's native county rejoice at the recognition which has thus been given to the noble earl's patriotic endeavours to strengthen the ties which bind the colonies to the Mother Country.

There is an amusing story, probably apocryphal, about the Australian fast bowler Ernie Jones being introduced to the Prince of Wales. When the Prince heard that Jones was from Adelaide he asked him if he had attended St Peter's College. The immediate reply was: 'Yes, sir, I take the dust-cart there regularly!'

6

Other Grand Matches at Sheffield Park

The celebrated visits of the Australian cricketers were by no means the only grand matches to be played at Sheffield Park during its heyday. We have already seen that, before the first visit of the Australians in 1884, Lord Sheffield's XI played a first-class fixture in 1881 against Alfred Shaw's XI and in 1883 against W. G. Grace's XI.

In 1880 Lord Sheffield invited Fourteen Gentlemen of West Africa to play at Sheffield Park. Later visitors included the Parsees, from India, in 1886 and the South Africans in 1894. Each of these three teams made cricket history as the first from their respective countries to play in England.

Lord Sheffield's Team v Fourteen Gentlemen Of West Africa
29 July 1880

Lord Sheffield's team included the Sussex county cricketers George Lynn and the young giant from Newick, Arthur Sclater, as well as some of his usual local friends such as Rev. Attenborough (Vicar of Fletching), Dr Treutler, Charles Greenfield (his gardener) and the ever reliable John Gilbert. The local press report of the match read as follows:

> An interesting match was played on Thursday on the beautiful grounds at Sheffield Park. Through the kindness of Lord Sheffield, the coloured gentlemen (who are studying for the learned professions) received an invitation to test their merits in the noble game on good wickets and with a moderate team to oppose them.

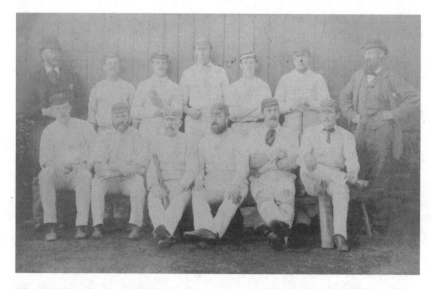

The initial first-class match at Sheffield Park was in 1881 when Alfred Shaw's team opposed that of Lord Sheffield. Shaw's team was: Back row: G. F. Salter (Scorer), T. Foster, W. Wright, W. Gunn, I. Grimshaw, W. Oscroft, C. Payne (Umpire). Seated: W. Bates, W. Clarke, J. Selby, A. Shaw, M. Sherwin, W. Scotton. (N. J. G. Sharp)

Rain had rendered the wickets wet but at 11.40 a brief glimpse of sunshine was taken advantage of to commence operations, the visitors going first to the wickets.

The visitors were dismissed for 133 before lunch and the reporter noted that 'a little latitude was allowed both in bowling and fielding, as the performers were scarcely up to county form.' Sheffield Park gained a first-innings lead of 20 when they were dismissed for 153 and at five o'clock the West Africans commenced their second innings which lasted for only 65 minutes. The home team, requiring 96 to win, completed the task at 7.05 p.m.

During the interval Mr F. D. Taylor gave some Shakespearian readings which were highly appreciated by the numerous assemblage. The attendance was the largest ever seen in Sheffield Park, though the storms of the morning kept many intending visitors away. At the close of the proceedings, Mr London, in a feeling and appropriate speech, thanked Lord Sheffield on behalf of himself and colleagues for his kind invitation to spend a day away from their studious labours amidst the fogs and smoke of the great city – in the clear and bracing air and amid the beautiful scenery of Sheffield Park to participate in a game of cricket and enjoy his Lordship's hospitality, a treat they should all remember with pleasurable pride; then, wishing health and long life to Lord Sheffield, Lady Sheffield and the Hon. Mr Holroyd, all joined in three hearty cheers. The Earl of SHEFFIELD responded, speaking of the great pleasure it gave him to find his invitation had proved so enjoyable, and ended by proposing three cheers for the visitors, which met with a hearty response, the cheers still ringing out as the waggonettes took their departure to the station with their occupants.

The scorecards of the game have survived.

WEST AFRICANS

First innings		Second innings	
Mr London b. Padgham	5	hit wkt b. Padgham	24
P.W.J. Stone b. Padgham	5	c. Lynn b. Gilbert	17
J.L. Stokes b. Padgham	26	c. Gilbert b. Padgham	0
J.Williams b. Greenfield	23	b. Martin	6
E.Williams c. Lynn b.Padgham	9	b. Gilbert	14
Rev. McLagen b. Martin	22	b. Padgham	29
G.G.M. Nicholl b. Dr Treutler	5	b. Padgham	0
Lake c. Martin b. Greenfield	12	not out	14
Hebron b. Treutler	1	b. Padgham	0
Rev. Willoughy c. Gilbert b.Treutler	9	c. and b. Gilbert	0
Pinnock run out	0	b. Padgham	12
Dr Kenner c. Gilbert b. Treutler	2	c. Lynn b. Gilbert	0
Lumpkin not out	7	b. Padgham	0
Extras	7	Extras	2
	133		**115**

SHEFFIELD PARK

First innings		Second innings	
Dr Treutler c. Williams b. Pinnock	4	b. Hebron	0
Rev. Attenborough run out	40	b. Lake	1
Rev. L.D. Kenyon-Stow b. Hebron	47	not out	47
A. Sclater lbw b. Pinnock	34	not out	41
G.H. Lynn run out	4		
J. Gilbert run out	3		
J. Martin b. Pinnock	0		
J. Fuller hit wkt b. Hebron	3		
Draper b. Hebron	1		
Padgham not out	0		
Greenfield run out	0		
Extras	17	Extras	8
	153		**97**

Lord Sheffield's XI v Alfred Shaw's XI
25–27 August 1881

Alfred Shaw, the famous Nottinghamshire and England cricketer, was employed by Lord Sheffield from 1883 but two years before, in August 1881, he led a team of northern professionals against the earl's XI in Sheffield Park.

Lord Sheffield's XI also included seven northern professionals and was completed by the current Sussex captain (Rev. F. F. J. Greenfield) and his immediate predecessor (Robert Ellis), Rev. Summers and John Gilbert. The last two of this quartet were regular cricketers at Sheffield Park but this was their only appearance in first-class cricket. Rev Summers, vicar of Danehill, was aged 48 and Gilbert was 50. Despite these ageing debutants, Lord Sheffield's side was a strong one but surprisingly no professionals from Sussex CCC were selected.

This was the inaugural first-class match at Sheffield Park and Alfred Shaw was destined to become a very important figure in Lord Sheffield's plans. At this time he was on the MCC ground staff at Lord's, was in dispute with his native Nottinghamshire CCC and was running the Belvoir Inn, Nottingham.

Seven of Shaw's team were involved in the Nottinghamshire v

Middlesex match that had finished at Trent Bridge the day before and were no doubt relieved that rain prevented any play on the first day of the match at Sheffield Park.

The local newspaper report indicates that the game was originally due to be played on the Thursday and Friday (25–26 August) but due to the washout the game was extended by Lord Sheffield to the Saturday – 'the result being that some brilliant cricket was witnessed'. In fact the cricket was not particularly brilliant. When play started on Friday it took Shaw's XI 84.1 overs to compile 106 all out between 11.05 a.m. and 1.35 p.m. when lunch was taken. An over consisted of four balls but even so a scoring rate of 1.2 runs per over was dull stuff only made bearable by an impressive over rate of 34 per hour.

When Lord Sheffield's XI replied, Rev. Greenfield was 'in grand hitting form' but the home team were all out for 117 in 76.1 overs to earn a first-innings lead of 11. By the close of play Shaw's XI were 20 for 4 in their second innings.

On Saturday 'the sun shone brightly, the wind had ceased and the cricket ground and its lovely surroundings appeared to the best advantage'. The pedestrian scoring rate continued, only relieved during one productive over from the Yorkshire slow left-arm bowler Edmund Peate:

> Peate, who bowled from the south end, had sent down six overs for two runs, when he was severely punished by Scotton, who drove the first ball of the over to the off for a couple, hit the next to square-leg for five in the direction of the lake, and (Bates in the meantime having made a single) got the last ball of the over to long leg for five, eliciting loud applause. Thirteen runs resulted from this over.

Scotton was a renowned stonewaller but he later hit Tom Emmett to long leg for a five and made the only fifty of the match before Shaw's team were dismissed on the stroke of lunch for 136 (off 82.1 overs) leaving Lord Sheffield's XI to score 126 runs to win. This was achieved at 5.00 p.m. from 88.1 overs for the loss of six wickets. The Yorkshire pair of Ephraim Lockwood (39) and Tom Emmett (27) top scored for Lord Sheffield's XI and the Danehill vicar had the satisfaction of scoring the winning run.

Lord Sheffield's XI v W. G. Grace's XI
5–7 July 1883
In 1883 Lord Sheffield began his association with the pre-eminent W. G. Grace by inviting him to bring a side to Sheffield Park to play against his team. The local newspaper report sets the scene:

THE GRAND CRICKET MATCH AT SHEFFIELD PARK
The noble patron of the Sussex County Cricket Club has displayed a liberality and munificence we would say without parallel not only in connection with Sussex, but with county cricket generally. His Lordship is evidently determined that every inducement shall be given to young men to come forward and interest themselves in cricketing matters, whilst he shows an equal desire to recognize talent, where it is shown by any Sussex player.

With a view to further increase the interest felt in the national pastime in Sussex, the noble Lord arranged for a grand match to be played on his magnificent ground this week, commencing on Thursday, the sides including many of the most prominent of English cricketers and Dr Grace captaining one, whilst Alfred Shaw acted in a similar capacity for Lord Sheffield's eleven. The match naturally excited much attention in cricketing circles, and there was a large and influential company present on the opening day. From the park entrance to the cricket ground, men were stationed to direct visitors, each of these men being employed on the estate, and having the badge 'S.P.' on his arm. Among the trees to the south of the ground, a platform had been erected for the use of the ladies, and near it a commodious marquee was placed, in which a public luncheon was served, that for the players &c, who were entertained by Lord Sheffield, being served, as usual in the Pavilion, now to a great extent covered with rose trees in full bloom. Opposite this was the scorers' and Press tent.

With regard to the players, some disappointment was felt at the absence of Mr W. W. Read, the well known Surrey gentleman, who was to have taken part in the match, but was unavoidably prevented from doing so.

The Earl of Sheffield was present throughout the day, and displayed the greatest interest in the play, his Lordship's splendid private pavilion being occupied by a numerous party, to whom invitations had been issued. The Countess of Sheffield was also present during part of the day.

W. G. Grace's XI included three Surrey professionals, two Nottinghamshire professionals and six well-known amateurs, including himself. Lord Sheffield's XI, according to modern cricket records, was captained by the Sussex amateur Rev. Greenfield but the above report gives that honour to Alfred Shaw. The team had four Sussex county players and the formidable Nottinghamshire and England quintet of Shaw, Shrewsbury, Scotton, Flowers and Barnes.

At mid-day exactly on Thursday, Dr W. G. Grace, the 'Leviathan,' left Lord Sheffield's pavilion amid loud applause and took his place at the south wicket. 'W. G.' (81) and his cousin Walter Gilbert (73) were the highest scorers in the visitors' 266 all out and when stumps were drawn at 6.45 p.m. Lord Sheffield's XI had lost Harry Phillips and were 9 for 1.

The match on Lord Sheffield's beautiful ground attracted, as was anticipated, very great interest in cricketing circles; indeed so large was the attendance on Friday, that it is estimated nearly 3,000 persons watched the match, many of the country gentry being present in their carriages.

The crowd witnessed an innings of 67 from Arthur Shrewsbury but Lord Sheffield's XI were dismissed for 231 – a deficit of 35 on first innings. In the evening 'W. G.' was again in good form taking his side to 99 for one at the close.

Play in the match was resumed on Saturday morning 'before a good sprinkling of spectators' but 'W. G.' was soon dismissed after completing his fifty. The innings declined to 167 all out (Shaw 6-43) and Lord Sheffield's XI needed 203 to win.

Resuming at 3.00 p.m. the home team had to bat positively to secure the victory and it was Alfred Shaw's score of 73 that ensured a comfortable win. 'W. G.' had bowled 49 overs in the match without taking a wicket.

Lord Sheffield's XI v Alfred Shaw's XI
21–23 May 1885

In 1885 the visitors to Sheffield Park for the annual grand match were Alfred Shaw's England team who had just returned from a successful tour of Australia under Shaw's management. He was also captain of the powerful Nottinghamshire team as well as being employed as a coach by Lord Sheffield and, although he did not play in the Test matches in Australia, he was the natural choice to lead the visitors at Sheffield Park.

Shaw's men had left Adelaide on board the SS *Potosi* on 6 April and reached Plymouth on 15 May, although half the party travelled overland from Naples and arrived home on the 12th. Shaw and four of his England players represented Nottinghamshire against Sussex at Trent Bridge on 14–16 May and then had a few days off before the start of the Sheffield Park match.

Maurice Read (Surrey) and John Briggs (Lancashire) were required to play for their counties and their places were taken by the stalwarts Shaw and James Lillywhite junior, both former England Test captains.

Lord Sheffield's XI, captained by W. G. Grace, included four Yorkshiremen (the players from that county missed the train from London and arrived just before lunch on the first day), three from Sussex (Hide, Newham and Phillips), the brothers Hearne from Kent and two from Gloucestershire (although because of a hand injury E. M. Grace was replaced by John Painter).

The match was awaited with great anticipation:

GRAND CRICKET MATCH AT SHEFFIELD PARK

We beg to remind our readers that the grand match of cricket given by the noble patron of the game in Sussex, the Earl of Sheffield, for the enjoyment of his friends and neighbours in all parts of the

South-Eastern counties, commences on Thursday next, on the beautiful grounds at Sheffield Park. The band of the Royal Artillery from Woolwich, is engaged and will play at intervals on the first day. Every arrangement has been carried out by his Lordship regardless of cost and all that is wanted to ensure success is fine weather.

Apropos of the match . . . it may be mentioned that Messrs E. Hawkins and Co., photographers, of 108, King's Road, Brighton, have received instructions from the Earl of Sheffield to photograph the two elevens. Messrs Hawkins and Co were selected last year to photograph several of the most famous elevens. A coach will be run from the Pavilion Hotel by Mr Harvie Jackson to Sheffield Park on Friday next, starting at nine o'clock. The fare is fixed at 10s.

The match was curtailed by rain but the local reporter was full of praise for the elaborate arrangements and the beauty of Sheffield Park:

With the history of Sussex cricket the name of the present Earl of Sheffield will be indelibly associated, not only for the support he has given for many years past to the advancement of young players to fit them to do battle for the county under the guidance of some of the best men of the day, but also for the grand expositions of game he has arranged, regardless of cost, for the amusement and enjoyment of the county, upon his splendid ground within the confines of his ancestral domain at Sheffield Park. Last year, it will be remembered, his Lordship brought the famous Australians into Sussex to play their first match of the season with a representative English team; this year the noble Earl invites the cricketing eleven under Shaw, who have recently returned from a most successful tour of the Antipodes to meet a well-selected team, captained by the champion of England, Mr Gilbert Grace. We have so often had the pleasure of enjoying cricket upon the Sheffield Park ground, and describing its charming surroundings, that to dwell upon the subject now would be superfluous. Suffice it, therefore, to say that nothing was omitted in the arrangements likely to give eclat to a most agreeable gathering, and that all that was wanted to ensure the attendance of a vast company, and render the event thoroughly successful, was fine weather, and this, unfortunately, so far, has been somewhat lacking, especially as regards the second day. The match commenced on Thursday, the wicket being in much better condition after a stormy night, than could possibly have been expected, the precaution having been taken of covering the ground in the centre of the play with tarpaulins. The greatest credit is due to those upon whom have devolved the duty of carrying out his Lordship's directions, which were as well devised as they were efficiently carried out. It need scarcely be said that the noble Earl entertained the players and a large number of friends during their stay at the park, nor that the attendance would have been much larger had only the weather been more genial, arrangements having been made for the receiving of special trains to the park station by the Brighton Company. As it was, nearly three thousand visitors availed themselves of the opportunity of witnessing the first day's play, and everything was done for their convenience that the practised skill in perfecting this part of the arrangements of Mr Nash, the home steward at the park, could carry out. Among those to whom a word of praise is due for the manner in which they assisted in the management are Mr J. Fuller, to whom was deputed the care and comfort of the two elevens; to Mrs Comber for the excellence of her catering, and to Mr Greenfield, the head gardener, for his floral decorations. The splendid band of the Royal Artillery played at intervals during the first day.

The noble Earl, having won the toss on behalf of his eleven, determined to act on the defensive, and play commenced shortly before noon.

Three days after the match had finished the same local newspaper expanded on the delights of Sheffield Park:

Although persistent ungenial and tempestuous weather marred the success of the grand match of cricket which the Earl of Sheffield had arranged for the enjoyment of the county in his beautiful park last week, between 5,000 and 6,000 persons availed themselves of the privilege of visiting one of the most charming places in the South of England. The chief attraction of Sheffield Park next to its splendid cricket ground is, of course, the noble expanse of ornamental water, with its pretty cascades and gently sloping banks, and the wealth of fine timber on every hand, and since we last had the pleasure of viewing the agreeable scene, much has been done to enhance its beauty, especially in the valley where are situated the new lakes extending, as seen from the cricket ground, almost from the foot of the eminences on which stands the mansion till they join the larger lake immediately below the plateau occupied by the cricket ground. On each side of the main cascade pools have been formed, surrounded by massive rocks, some of the pieces of stone weighing five to six tons, artistically planted with alpine shrubs and ferns, and a great variety of trailing plants, dotted here and there with specimen yuccas, among which we specially noticed the gloriosa and filmentosa species, and having beds of rhododendrons near at hand.

The noble Earl may fairly be congratulated upon the success of his landscape gardening on the banks of the lakes. The work has been carried out, we believe, under the Earl's personal superintendence, by Mr Moore, who has charge of the cricket ground and its beautiful accessories, whose own taste and skill have produced results of a most pleasing character.

The whole of the general arrangements were carried out under his Lordship's directions by Mr Nash, the home steward, with a regularity and smoothness which only long experience could possibly ensure. From the time when the two elevens arrived at Sheffield Park till they left on Saturday night, they were literally speaking, the guests of the noble Earl, and so were all the officials engaged in the match. Mr Fuller was deputed to attend to the wants and comforts of the party, and everyone had reason to be gratified at the sumptuous hospitality extended to them by his Lordship's commands. On Friday and Saturday the band engaged was that of the 1st Sussex Artillery, from Brighton, conducted by Mr Devin, whose performance was also much admired.

During their stay the visitors enjoyed some rook shooting, and those interested in agriculture inspected with evident pleasure, his Lordship's excellent herd of Sussex stock, in which Mr Nash is naturally so proud, after the successes achieved last Christmas. Some idea may be formed of the noble Earl's liberality when we state that the three days' festivities would not cost much less than £700!

For the record Lord Sheffield's XI were dismissed on the first day for 184 from 168 four-ball overs with the only substantial contributions coming from Frank Hearne (62) and Jesse Hide (40). Shaw's team lost Scotton's wicket to a brilliant one-handed catch taken by Irwin Grimshaw at mid-on to finish on 0 for 1.

Play was delayed on the second day when a fierce storm of hail and rain, accompanied by a gale and some thunder, burst over Sussex and almost deluged the ground. In a curtailed day's play, Shaw's XI moved from 0 for 1 to 80 for 3.

Shaw's team were dismissed on the last day for 200 – a lead of 16 – but it had taken them 205.3 overs ! George Ulyett (Yorkshire) top scored with 51 and Sussex's Jesse Hide took four wickets for 19. There was only time for Lord Sheffield's XI to reach 64 for 2 in their second innings (in 56 overs) but the crowd was rewarded when 'just at the finish some capital batting was shown by Messrs Grace and Newham'.

Parsees In The Park
Lord Sheffield's XI v Parsees
24–25 May 1886

In May 1886 Lord Sheffield hosted a match with the Australian tourists (see Chapter 4) but he was also keen to entertain another touring side – the Parsees from Bombay. There had been plans for the Parsees to tour England in 1878 and 1879 but they did not materialise and this match at Sheffield Park was the first to be played in England by a team from India. The local newspaper showed its customary enthusiasm:

ANOTHER GRAND MATCH AT SHEFFIELD PARK

We have much pleasure in stating that the Earl of Sheffield has made arrangements for the Parsee Cricketers, who have just arrived in England, to play their first match on his unrivalled cricket ground in Sheffield Park. His lordship has selected a team to meet the visitors from our great Indian Empire and the match will be played on Monday and Tuesday next. We understand that the park and grounds will be thrown open to the public on the same conditions as in the great match last week, that is to say, the usual customs and regulations of the park will be strictly enforced, and the right of refusing admission reserved. Thanks to the noble earl's liberality our friends in the south-eastern counties will again have an opportunity of witnessing some interesting cricket, and of enjoying the beauties of Sheffield Park.

The match was due to start nine days after the visit of the Australians but a wet spring day put paid to any cricket:

THE GREAT MATCH AT SHEFFIELD PARK LORD
SHEFFIELD'S ELEVEN v THE PARSEES

The match arranged . . . in which the Parsee cricketers were to have made their debut in England, against his lordship's eleven, was to have commenced yesterday morning upon the splendid ground in Sheffield Park, near Lewes, but rain fell heavily during the morning rendering play impossible up to three o'clock and it was not expected that the wickets could be pitched till today (Tuesday). The Indian gentlemen arrived at Fletching on Sunday evening and every arrangement for their entertainment had been made by his lordship's directions. The weather is now brightening and it is just possible that a full day's play may be witnessed today.

Flooding was in evidence on the road close to the lower entrance to the park, rendering that approach to the cricket ground almost impracticable. Play commenced a few minutes before half past eleven on the second day in the rain and the Parsees were given the option of batting or fielding. Choosing to field they must have been

The Parsee team at Sheffield Park 1886: Back row: A. B. Patell, S. Bezonjee. Standing: C. Payne (Umpire), M. P. Banajee, P. C. Major, S. N. Bhedwar, D. D. Khambatta, A. C. Major, J. D. Pochkhana Seated: A. R. Libuwalla, P. D. Dastur, Dr D. H. Patell, M. Framjee, B. P. Balla. In front: J. M. Morenas, B. B. Baria, S. H. Harvar (Sussex CCC).

satisfied to bowl out Lord Sheffield's side for 142 as the home team included seven Sussex cricketers with first-class experience plus the redoubtable Alfred Shaw. When it came to batting the Parsees fared less well and were dismissed for 46 (Arthur Huggett 5 for 12). They were asked to follow on and reached close of play at 53 for 4.

Despite the disappointing weather it had been a memorable visit and during the interval both teams were photographed by Hawkins and Co. of Brighton who 'had been honoured by the command of the Earl of Sheffield to photograph the Australian and also the Parsee cricketers at Sheffield Park'.

Lord Sheffield's XI v MCC
25–26 May 1891

It is surprising that the influential Marylebone Cricket Club visited Sheffield Park once only, playing a two-day first-class match in May 1891.

W. G. Grace captained the metropolitan club and his team was made up of William Attewell (Nottinghamshire) and ten amateurs

Sheffield Park Cricket Ground.

2d.   2d.

MONDAY and TUESDAY, May 25th and 26th, 1891,

Lord Sheffield's Eleven v. M.C.C. & Ground.

M.C.C. & GROUND	First Innings		Second Innings	
Mr. W. G. Grace (capt.)...	b Wright	19	c Barrett b Lohmann	2
Mr. A. J. Webbe..............	run out	0	b Wright	4
Mr. O'Brien	c Cantelupe b Lohmann	28	b Lohmann	21
Mr. J. G. Walker	st Phillips b Lohmann	8	b Wright	8
Mr. J. Cranston	b Wright	2	b Lohmann	3
Mr. R. J. Pope..............	b Lohmann	27	not out	11
Mr. G. F. Vernon	c Murdoch b Lohmann	3	b Wright	4
Mr. H. Philipson............	b Wright	1	l-b w b Wright	0
Mr. J. J. Ferris	c Phillips b Wright	15	st Phillips b Wright	5
Mr. J. S. Russell............	c Murdoch b Lohmann	0	b Wright	1
Attewell	not out	3	not out	3
	b.4 l-b. w. n.-b. Total. 4		b- lb.1 w. n.-b. Total.	1
	Total ...109		Total..	62

1-1   2-42   3-49   4-55   5-57   6-63   7-68   8-104   9-106   10-109
1-2   2-15   3-23   4-39   5-39   6-49   7-49   8-55   9-59   10-

LORD SHEFFIELD'S XI.	First Innings		Second Innings
Dr. Barrett....................	c Philipson b Grace	16	
Mr. W. Newham	c Vernon b Ferris	77	
Mr. W. L. Murdoch (capt.)	b Attewell	26	
Marlow	b Ferris	0	
Lohmann	l-b-w b Attewell	35	
Mr. A. F. Somerset	st Philipson b Ferris	1	
H. Phillips	b Attewell	0	
W. Wright	l-b-w b Ferris	7	
Mr. A. Harcourt	b Attewell	0	
Lord Cantelupe	b Attewell	1	
Lowe	not out	3	
	b.5 l-b, w. n.-b.1 Total. 6		b, l.-b. w. n.-b. Total...
	Total.. 172		Total...

1-47   2-107   3-108   4-133   5-148   6 155   7-166   8-166   9-168   10-172
1-   2-   3-   4-   5-   6-   7-   8-   9-   10-

Umpires... W. and T. Mycroft   Scorers...R. Taylor and G. F. Hearne

Crowhurst, Printer to the S.C.C.C., 52 Market Street, Brighton.

Scorecard for Lord Sheffield's XI v MCC 1891. (N. J. G. Sharp)

including the Australians Roly Pope and Jack Ferris. Lord Sheffield's XI also had two Australians: John Barrett and the famous Test match captain William Murdoch, as well as four players making their first-class debuts: Somerset, Harcourt, Cantelupe and Lowe. For Harcourt (Lord Sheffield's nephew) and Cantelupe (Gilbert Sackville, later Earl De La Warr who did much to promote cricket in Bexhill, attracting a visit from the 1896 Australians) this was to be their one and only first-class match.

There was no play before lunch on the first day because of rain and the local reporter described the scene:

In accordance with Lord Sheffield's custom, early in the season – a custom now of several years standing – a grand match of cricket was arranged to commence at noon yesterday at the noble earl's beautiful ground in Sheffield Park, between his lordship's eleven and the MCC. The former team was captained by Mr Murdoch, and the latter by Mr W. G. Grace. Everything was done on the part of Lord Sheffield that could possibly be conceived to afford enjoyment to lovers of cricket resident in the south-eastern counties. By arrangement with the London and Brighton Company, special trains were run to Sheffield Park from London, Brighton, Tunbridge Wells and intermediate places, and other traffic facilities were afforded to promote the convenience of the general public, and if the weather had only been fine the attendance would doubtless have been very large. Unfortunately, however, the elements were very unfavourable for out-door sports of all kinds. On the previous day (Sunday) the district was visited by smart showers, but the afternoon was fine, and the moon rose in an unclouded sky. Later on, however, heavy clouds came up from the westward, with occasional flashes of lightning, and the morning broke very unpromising, a north-west wind bringing continued rain. At 10 o'clock, however, prospects looked rather brighter, and rain ceased for a short time, but only to recommence as the trains arrived at the park station. The wickets were kept covered, and the rain was persistent rather than in volume, but it was impossible to commence play before luncheon.

The noble earl was himself early on the ground during the morning and received a large party of personal friends and the two teams at his pavilion. But although the rain was aggravating and disagreeable, it did not prevent many of the spectators from strolling round the lakes and grounds, which are now in lovely condition, notwithstanding that the severe winter and late frosts have sadly prevented the development of the bloom of the rhododendrons. The fine timber adorning the park has now assumed its spring garb, and the whole prospect is very contenting to the eye.

After luncheon, a few gleams of sunshine brightened the scene, and the view from the cricket ground looking over the lakes towards the mansion was very fine, bringing into relief bright patches of colour from the rhododendrons and the gorse on the banks of the water, and the noble marble fountain, newly erected on the lawn near the house. Advantage, too, was taken of the improved light to take photographs of the two teams.

The second day's play was well attended and proved to be very exciting. Lord Sheffield's XI gained a first-innings lead of 63 largely due to a faultless 77 by the Sussex CCC secretary Billy Newham. In a desperate struggle to stave off defeat against George Lohmann and Walter Wright – who bowled unchanged throughout the match – the MCC finished on 63 for 9. The match was drawn with the scores level and the last MCC pair at the wicket. An enthusiastic account appeared in the local press:

A MOST-ENJOYABLE AFTERNOON

We have much pleasure in recording that Lord Sheffield's generous efforts to afford enjoyment to the lovers of first-class cricket, and the public generally, were crowned with brilliant success on Tuesday. The morning play was slightly interfered with by local showers, but the afternoon was brilliantly fine, with continuous sunshine and crisp southerly airs. The attendance, too, was very numerous, some thousands being present. Not only was the wide circle round the cricket ground completely occupied, the spectators standing five deep in places, and the carriages on the east side being well filled, but large numbers availed themselves of the privilege of strolling round the lakes and through the charming grounds and park. Sheffield Park maintains its reputation as the most charming place of resort in the whole county.

Lord Sheffield's XI v South Africans
22–23 May 1894

The first ever appearance of South African cricketers in England was in a match played at Sheffield Park in 1894. Although not designated first-class, the game attracted much interest and the usual sizeable crowds. The event was announced in the local press by Lord Sheffield's steward, who stressed that his Lordship reserved the right to refuse admission or to eject unruly people.

The South Africans at Sheffield Park 1894: Back row: D. C. Davey, T. Routledge, C. O. H. Sewell, W. V. Simkins (Manager), G. Rowe, G. Glover, C. Mills. Seated: G. Kempis, G. Cripps, H. H. Castens (Captain), C. L. Johnson, A. W. Seccull. In front: F. Hearne, J. Middleton, E. A. Halliwell, D. C. Parkin. (Sussex CCC)

W. L. Murdoch, now captain of Sussex, led Lord Sheffield's XI and his team included eight Sussex county cricketers, the Brighton Member of Parliament Bruce Vernon-Wentworth, a local professional E. A. Bailey and the prolific Lancashire and England slow left-arm bowler Johnny Briggs. The match and the incomparable setting was recalled by the South African cricketer Arthur Seccull:

OUR MATCH AT SHEFFIELD PARK

Our first match was against Lord Sheffield's XI in which I had the honour of bowling the first ball in England. I failed to get a wicket but the honour of sending down the first ball in the first match of the first South African touring team remains mine for ever. The match, which we lost by ten wickets, was played in a drizzling rain, with a Scotch mist prevailing throughout at the seat of Lord Sheffield at

Sheffield Park, just outside Brighton. We all found Humphreys, the old Sussex lob bowler, very difficult to play, particularly so because of his habit of allowing his sleeve to hang down, which made it almost impossible to watch his fingers and to detect the spin.

Our initial defeat, however, was compensated for by the glorious conditions under which the game was played. Entering the magnificent wooded park along a lovely drive through an avenue of pines, we found on our arrival at the playing arena that the cricket field presented a truly superb view. The Castle stood high up in the distance, while a delightful streamlet wended its way snake-like through the slopes which led to the ground. Miniature waterfalls glistened at intervals all the way down through gorgeous gardens perfectly kept. Flowers of every description were growing in profusion, while the incomparable English birds were hailing the advent of spring with joyous song. The sight to most of us was almost in itself sufficient excuse for relaxing our vigilance in watching the bowler's arm. It was easily the most picturesque estate I had seen. In addition to all this elaborate arrangements had been made for our reception. The pavilion, though small, was unique and was replete with every conceivable convenience. An enormous marquee large enough to receive 300 guests was also provided, and a sumptuous repast filled our cup of contentment to the brim. Nothing was forgotten that could possibly have added to our enjoyment.

The reporter from the *Sussex Express* wrote enthusiastically about the South African visitors:

> The South African team were the guests of the noble earl at the Hotel Metropole, Brighton, and the entire party were conveyed to and fro each day in saloon carriages. A few words about the team may be interesting. They have come over, says a cricketing authority, with the reputation of good cricketers, but they have wisely refrained from arranging matches with the most powerful of the counties. The team contains men whose presence awakens old associations with the mother country. It is very difficult to regard as strangers a side which includes Frank Hearne, once a prominent member of the Kent eleven;

MEETINGS & ENTERTAINMENTS.

NOTICE.

SHEFFIELD PARK.

ON the occasion of the visit of the SOUTH AFRICAN CRICKETERS to SHEFFIELD PARK on the 22ND and 23RD of MAY, the Earl of Sheffield will OPEN THE PARK TO THE GENERAL PUBLIC. His Lordship reserves his right to refuse admission to the Park to any individual, and to eject any person at his pleasure.

Carriages may be placed in the space allotted to them at any time before seven p.m. on the day previous to the commencement of the match. All other arrangements as to horses and carriages must be made by the owners.

THOMAS COLGATE, Steward

Sheffield Park,
May 12th, 1894.

Sussex Agricultural Express

Charles Mills, who made a name in Surrey cricket; Mr H.H.Castens, a Rugby football 'blue' at Oxford; and Mr Halliwell, a son of the late Mr Halliwell-Bisset who stood up to the Middlesex fast bowlers on the old cattle market ground. Judging from his form on Tuesday, Mr Halliwell as a wicket-keeper seems quite capable of sustaining the fame gained by his father in this position. The Colonials played their three professionals – Frank Hearne, Middleton and Mills – and left out Messrs Kempis, Davey, Glover and Parkin. It is early yet to form a general judgment of the side. Their bowlers had to play on a pitch favourable to heavy scoring, but they kept a capital length, and at no time during the play did the batsmen obtain a complete mastery. The ground fielding, too, was clean and the returns were accurate.

On the first day Lord Sheffield's XI, after scoring 54 for the first wicket were restricted to 198 for 7, largely due to the slow left-arm bowler George Rowe who finished with 8 for 52 from 43 overs. On the second day they added a further 35 runs and were all out for 233. The South Africans were bowled out for 127 and 110 to give the home team a target of only five runs to win. The tourists found the classic slow left-arm bowling of Briggs and the underhand lobs of

Walter Humphreys rather too difficult although they may have been suffering from Lord Sheffield's well known hospitality. In a Test match at Cape Town in 1889 Briggs had taken fifteen wickets for only 28 runs and his bowling in English conditions was a severe test for the South Africans.

Despite the cold wind the local reporter was enthusiastic about the setting:

> During the last twelve months new vistas of great beauty have been opened up through the woods on each side of the two western lakes and beds of rhododendrons, choice conifers and fine foliage shrubs and parterres of flowers have been planted on the bank . . . The flower borders round the pavilions near the cricket ground are also planted with spring flowers. The arrangements for the comfort and enjoyment of the spectators were as complete as they could possibly be made.

7

Dining and Music
in the Park

High-class catering was considered by Lord Sheffield to be essential for the enjoyment of a day's cricket at Sheffield Park. For his invited guests, comprising the country gentry, senior naval and military figures, members of the clergy, members of parliament, personal friends and cricketers past and present, there was invariably a sumptuous lunch provided where no expense was spared. Mouth-watering details of the delights on offer can be gleaned from the printed menus, many of which have survived to become collectors' items.

Local newspaper reports of the day carried details of these splendid occasions and faithfully recorded the names of Lord Sheffield's guests who, when lunch was over, would enjoy mingling with the famous cricketers present, including W. G. Grace, W. L. Murdoch and Prince Ranjitsinhji. Some may have been tempted to ask the cricketers to autograph their beautifully printed invitation cards that Lord Sheffield always sent out.

In 1893 for the visit of the Australians the guests were particularly notable and included the Duke of Norfolk, Duke of Richmond, Earl and Countess De La Warr, Earl Winterton, Lord North, Viscount and Viscountess Cantelupe, Viscount Gage and General Lord Seymour. Also present were eminent Australians in the persons of the Agents General for New South Wales (Sir Saul Samuel), South Australia (Sir John Bray), Queensland (Sir J. Garrick), Tasmania (Sir E. N. C. Braddon) and Victoria (Hon. J. Munro) together with Sir Edwin Smith, the president of the South Australian Cricket Association. The colonial flavour of the occasion was completed with a cavalry contingent from New South Wales and a contingent of the Victoria

Horse Artillery. Even the captain of the *Orizaba*, the vessel in which the Australian cricketers travelled to England, was on the guestlist.

The cricket historian Alfred Gaston was a frequent guest and delighted in meeting a galaxy of famous cricketers, young and old. Edwin and William Napper (born in 1815 and 1816 respectively) were two famous old Sussex county cricketers regularly seen at Sheffield Park luncheons. Another old timer was Rev. J. Pycroft, author of one of cricket's best loved books, *The Cricket Field*, and he sat down to lunch in 1890 and 1893.

Members of the Sussex gentry who enjoyed Lord Sheffield's hospitality during one or more of the five matches against the Australians between 1884 and 1896 included Lord Leconfield (Petworth), Rev. Sir George Shiffner (Coombe Place, Offham), Major Sergison (Cuckfield Park), J. H. Sclater (Newick Park), Hon. C. Brand (Glynde), R. M. Curteis (Windmill Hill), Sir Anchitel Ashburnham (Ashburnham), W. H. Campion (Danny) and A. F. Somerset (Castle Goring). The civic side of Sussex life was represented on different occasions by the Mayors of Brighton, Chichester, Eastbourne, Hastings and Lewes.

By far the most memorable of these wonderful, colourful occasions took place on 11 May 1896 when the Prince of Wales attended the first day's play of the match between Lord Sheffield's XI and the Australians and members of the public turned up in huge numbers. On this occasion, Lord Sheffield's guest list was restricted to a select few and they were invited to a private luncheon which, not surprisingly, received some attention in the local press:

> Between one and two o'clock his Royal Highness was entertained to a very elegant luncheon by the noble earl. The luncheon party was a very select one, including only a few friends who had been invited to meet the Prince, and Lord Sheffield's private guests. The company included Lord and Lady Harris, Lord Lathom, Sir Spencer Ponsonby Fane, Lord and Lady De La Warr, Lord and Lady Evelyn Somerset, Lord Zouche and Sir H. Fletcher, M.P. and Lady Fletcher.

The second day's play saw a return to the lavish luncheons on a large scale when a party of 500 was catered for by Messrs Booth 'in a handsome and spacious marquee erected on the lawn in rear of the private stand'. On the top table Lord Sheffield was accompanied by his adopted daughter, Miss Attenborough, and another famous prince – Ranjitsinhji.

The preparation for each grand occasion at Sheffield Park included the siting and construction of one or more marquees at different parts of the cricket ground. There was a permanent dining/refreshment pavilion on the west side of the ground and this was used in 1881 with a marquee opposite. The dining pavilion was surmounted with a clock and was sometimes referred to as 'the clock pavilion'. It may also have had dressing rooms for the players as there are references to the 'players' pavilion'.

For the first visit of the Australians in 1884 a luncheon was served at the great house for the players and about 150 personal friends of Lord Sheffield. On the first day of the 1886 match with the Australians 'a large party of the noble earl's personal friends invited to meet the Australians repaired to the eastern lawn of the mansion where they were received by Lord Sheffield. A sumptuous luncheon was served in the eastern suite of apartments.' While this was taking place the professionals and officials were enjoying a 'capital repast' in the dining pavilion, presided over by Lord Sheffield's steward, Mr Nash. On the second and third days the teams, officials and a circle of Lord Sheffield's friends enjoyed luncheon in the refreshment pavilion. Elsewhere on the ground John Diplock's marquee for luncheons and refreshments was 'largely patronised'.

For the Parsees match in 1886 the dining pavilion was used on both days for players and friends while local caterers provided luncheons for the public in large marquees on other parts of the ground.

On the first day of the Australian match in 1890, luncheon was served for the players and 200 guests in a large marquee 'to the right of the players pavilion' but the dining pavilion (perhaps the same as the 'players pavilion') was used for the third day.

For the MCC match in 1891 'Mr Booth's elegant refection was served in a marquee erected in the enclosure to the south of the earl's pavilion while luncheon was served by Mr Welfare in the refreshment pavilion on the second day.'

A large marquee was sited behind Lord Sheffield's private pavilion for the grand matches of 1893, 1894 and 1896 where the teams and friends were entertained. For the visit of the Prince of Wales in 1896 the permanent Ladies' Pavilion was utilised as the Prince's retiring room and redecorated for the occasion. Adjoining it was an ornate marquee for the royal visitor's dining saloon and the frontage was hung with Japanese bead curtains. These luxurious buildings were photographed with the future Edward VII and Lord Sheffield standing outside. Elsewhere there was a separate tent for the ladies to take tea.

Lord Sheffield's menus for the guests at several of the important cricket matches were expensively produced and, along with the printed invitations, are now much sought after by collectors. The edges of the menus are thick and gilded and do not fold flat because they were designed to stand on the decorated tables. The menu for the 1894 South African match 'included a View of Sheffield Park House, the lakes, cascades and grounds with the arms of South Africa and the noble earl emblazoned in gold on each outside page'. They were, in their own right, works of art, produced locally by Mr John Beal and Son of Brighton.

An example of the superb cuisine on offer is taken from the menu for the 1890 match with the Australians when Edwin Booth was the caterer:

Salmon   Daubed Capons

Ox Tongues   York Hams

Pigeon Pies   Lobster Salads

Lobster Mayonnaise

Roast Fowls   Plovers' Eggs

Pate de Foie Gras

Ribs of Lamb   Roast Beef

Croustades of Quails

Croustades Chickens and Peas

Jellies – Macedoine, Dantzic, Belgrave, Wine
Maraschino, Noyeau
Creams – Strawberry, Italian, Vanilla, Peach,
Charlotte Russe
Boudin, Venetian   Peaches and Cream

Pine Apple   Grapes   Strawberries

Amontillado   Rudesheimer
Bollinger, vintage 1884
Giesler, vintage 1884
Chateau Margaux   Brandy Whisky

Lord Sheffield had great faith in the licensees from two local public houses to perform the challenging task of catering at the great events at Sheffield Park.

At the Sheffield Arms, Mrs Comber (1881–5), her successors (1886) and then Richard Welfare (to 1896) attended the cricket matches while, from the Griffin at Fletching, John Diplock's name appears throughout the 1880s and in 1890. Their terrific efforts were augmented by the celebrated cuisine of Messrs Booth of Brighton. The latter was under the direction of Councillor Edwin Booth, a member of the Sussex CCC committee, who had a restaurant in East Street, Brighton where Lord Sheffield's cricketing friend Alfred Gaston was entertained to a testimonial in 1895 for his services to cricket. It was usually Booth who attended to Lord Sheffield's personal guests at the matches, including the players, and presented them with sumptuous lunches.

Lord Sheffield always took care to ensure that his guests' luncheon rooms were elegantly appointed and the following report from 1885 sets a typical scene:

The tables were tastefully decorated with beautiful flowers and epergnes of luscious fruit, including some magnificent pineapples, grapes and strawberries from the extensive gardens and houses near the mansion, of which Mr Greenfield, the head gardener, is the presiding genius. This part of the arrangements reflected much credit on him.

These caterers made a real contribution to the success of many events in Sheffield Park over 20 years and in doing so undertook some enormous tasks. The vast quantities of food and drink for the massive crowds had to be brought to a remote ground, presumably by horse-drawn vehicles, in the days before refrigeration and pre-packed food. Perhaps there were reinforcements at intervals from the Sheffield Arms and the Griffin and it may be that many spectators brought their own food or went hungry. The newspapers do not refer to any toilet arrangements but it would be surprising if this were overlooked. There were toilets in Lord Sheffield's pavilion and the Ladies' Pavilion for invited guests. There may also have been a facility in the dining pavilion.

The only criticism of the catering arrangements was made during the visit of the Australians in 1893 when it was reported that:

> Refreshments and luncheons were served from the permanent pavilion and two large marquees, but the staff engaged was utterly inadequate to supply the needs of hungry and thirsty thousands, and so small was the serving space that quite half an hour's struggling was the general experience before wants were satisfied.

Music in the Park
Lord Sheffield was fond of music and believed firmly that an enjoyable day's cricket would be further enriched by a programme of music and he employed several different bands who played from one or more of the permanent bandstands around the cricket ground.

William Moore's diary for 1896 records that the Chailey Industrial School Band was usually in attendance for a fee of £3 at the frequent club matches and occasionally a local band from Newick was employed.

For the important matches, though, more established bands were engaged and for Lord Sheffield's XI v Alfred Shaw's XI in 1885 the

Luncheon menu for Lord Sheffield's XI v South Africans 1894. (N. J. G. Sharp)

band of the Royal Artillery from Woolwich played choice selections beside the pavilion during luncheon. For the Australian match of 1886 the same band performed on the lawn by Sheffield Park House while the players and guests took lunch.

In 1890, while Lord Sheffield's XI, the Australians and guests enjoyed their lunch in the dining pavilion on the ground, 'the fine band of the 14th Hussars (the King's), under the talented conductorship of Mr H. Hemsley the bandmaster, performed a pleasing programme of choice music and they continued at intervals during the play'. The 1893 Australians were treated to an excellent programme of music by the full band of the 6th (Inniskilling) Dragoons from Brighton 'which was stationed outside the marquee while lunch was in progress'.

On the first day of the MCC match in 1891 the players and guests were also treated during the day to music 'by the fine band of the Inniskilling Dragoons which occupied the bandstand on the east side of Lord Sheffield's pavilion. On the second day it was Mr Devin's famous band from Brighton that performed a choice selection of music during luncheon, occupying an enclosure in front of the pavilion.'

For the Parsees in 1886 the fine band of the First Sussex Artillery from Brighton performed selections on both days commencing with the National Anthem in honour of the Queen's birthday. It is not recorded what the visitors from India thought about the programme for the second day, which included the march *Cornelius* by Mendelssohn, the overture *L'Intrepide* by Bousquet, a polka entitled *Garden Party*, a selection from Gilbert and Sullivan's *Mikado* and, topically, 'Life's A Bumper' by Wainwright.

Lord Sheffield employed the band of the 1st Sussex Regiment of Volunteers for the grand matches against the 1894 South Africans and the 1896 Australians. It was described as 'a fine military band' and performed on a bandstand near Lord Sheffield's pavilion. The players were relieved at intervals by the boys from Chailey Industrial School.

For the Grand Reviews of volunteer soldiers at Sheffield Park the volunteer bands were much in evidence and it was the Brighton Volunteer Brigade of Artillery Band that greeted the Maori rugby footballers on their arrival at the cricket ground in 1888. The band, under Mr Devin's leadership, 'had already taken up its position on the bandstand near his lordship's pavilion and was performing popular selections of music in pleasing style. While the players were entertained to lunch the Artillery Band played on the lawn.'

Lord Sheffield was keen to record events at the grand matches played on his ground and the Brighton photographers E. Hawkins & Co. took photographs of practically every team that played there including some of the less well known ones. During the luncheon interval the teams were carefully arranged in front of Lord Sheffield's pavilion and photographs were taken. As soon as prints were available they were sold commercially. They are now sought after by collectors as they provide a splendid record of those who played between 1881 and 1896, including great cricketers like W. G. Grace, W. L. Murdoch and Ranjitsinhji, as well as the teams from Australia,

The licensees of the Sheffield Arms, pictured here, were regular caterers at Lord Sheffield's grand matches (R. Packham)

South Africa and Bombay. Messrs Hawkins also photographed the Middlesex and Maori rugby teams in 1888 and the Sussex Martlets football team that played Nottingham Forest in 1894.

Lord Sheffield's hospitality always extended to the army of workers employed to stage the cricket matches. In 1883 'the workmen also had lunch supplied them in Mr Diplock's marquee by his lordship's instructions' while at the Parsees' match in 1886 there was a large marquee 'where the special park men, the police and other officials enjoyed the noble earl's hospitality. Even the cabmen were not forgotten and it is needless to say that his lordship's kindness was much appreciated.' In 1894 the cabmen were banned from the park for an unspecified reason, dealt with later in this work, but 'those engaged in duties connected with the match were entertained to luncheon by Lord Sheffield in the refreshment pavilion'.

The Maori rugby team that played at Sheffield Park in 1888 was treated to one of Edwin Booth's delicious luncheons before the match. The players sat down to turkey, roast beef, ox tongues, york hams, lobsters, roast fowls, pigeon pie, quails, chicken, pheasants, partridges and grouse. This was followed by conserve of apricots, jellies, strawberry cream, ice pudding, champagne and other liquors.

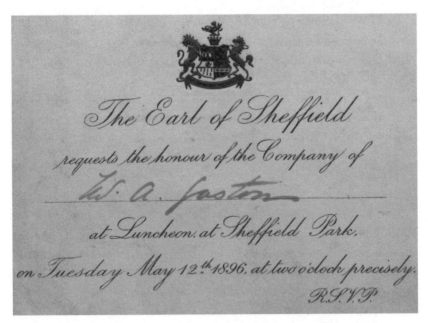

The Earl of Sheffield requests the honour of the Company of
W. A. Gaston
at Luncheon at Sheffield Park.
on Tuesday May 12th 1896, at two o'clock precisely.
R.S.V.P.

Alfred Gaston's invitation to luncheon at Sheffield Park 1896. (N. J. G. Sharp)

Many of the team were inclined to lie down and sleep rather than to play against a strong Middlesex team and when the pre-match photographs were being arranged two of the Maoris were found to be missing. Officials went in search and soon found the errant boys peacefully napping in the bracken. They had the grace to look rather shamefaced when escorted to the dressing room by their irate captain.

The famous Nottingham Forest team and the Sussex Martlets were entertained at the Sheffield Arms after their match at Sheffield Park in 1894 when 'Host Welfare provided an excellent repast'.

Richard Welfare of the Sheffield Arms was entrusted with the catering arrangements for the Grand Reviews for the volunteer soldiers, described in chapter 17. In 1889 he served luncheon to the crew of the *Heloise*, Lord Sheffield's yacht, in the pavilion and later served refreshments to the soldiers on the eastern side of the cricket ground while Lord Sheffield, the officers and a numerous party of friends partook of a sumptuous 'tea' served by Booths of Brighton in a marquee on the cricket ground.

In 1890 Welfare catered for the non-commissioned officers, the rank and file and the general public. There were regimental canteens on the north-east side of the cricket ground in a spacious marquee while the public was catered for at the luncheon pavilion on the cricket ground. For Lord Sheffield's personal guests 'a large and handsome marquee had been erected south of his lordship's private pavilion and Mr Booth and his staff were preparing to serve elegant refection'.

That year the public was admitted for a march past and the pavilions and refreshment tents plied a roaring trade. Mr Welfare supplied the men with excellent bread and cheese and beer or lemonade. In one corner of the cricket ground was an officers' field mess where, even today, old champagne bottles are occasionally ploughed up. There was a vast indoor picnic for the troops and bullocks were roasted by the lake.

In 1895:

> the modestly described tea proved to be on a par with the noble Earl's munificence in all other respects. In fact the menu was of such a nature as to more readily suggest a banquet and the inclusion of bright, sparkling champagne affords considerable corroboration to a description of that sort. It was one of those recherche affairs for which Messrs Booth are famous and, favoured with a carte blanche order from his lordship, they once more added to the renown of the firm. The decorations were particularly pleasing and the bouquets laid for each visitor were a charming memento of the occasion. Guests to the number of 250 were laid for and the military uniforms and ladies toilettes combined to make a strikingly pretty scene. The Earl of Sheffield presided at the principal table, Colonel Tolson and Miss Attenborough being his immediate supporters. A band played outside during the time the guests were at table.

John Diplock was the energetic landlord of the Griffin at Fletching for the duration of Lord Sheffield's grand matches and he was responsible for much of the catering on the cricket ground at the Park. The public house prospers still and visitors can enjoy some

The Griffin, Fletching High Street. (B. Gregory)

interesting cricket memorabilia. In addition to his catering at the matches, Mr Diplock hosted dinners for famous cricketers on occasions, starting with the initial first-class match in 1881. On this occasion the players dined on successive evenings at Lord Sheffield's expense 'when the catering of Host Diplock was highly appreciated'. Alfred Shaw proposed a toast to the health of the Earl of Sheffield and speeches or toasts were made by Tom Emmett, Charles Payne, Frederick Greenfield and Robert Ellis. In Lord Sheffield's absence his steward Mr Nash remarked that Lord Sheffield had been much pleased with the brilliant cricket displayed by both sides during the day.

For the match between Lord Sheffield's XI and Alfred Shaw's Australian team in 1885 the players and officials dined at the Griffin on each evening: 'Mr Colgate presided on the first evening and Mr W. G. Grace on the second. Need it be said that the health of Lord Sheffield was drunk with all the honours or that a most pleasant evening was spent?'

8

On Tour in Australia
1891–92

Lord Sheffield had entertained Australian cricketers at Sheffield Park in 1884, 1886 and 1890 in some style, and so it is not surprising that in an era before central authorities organised cricket tours he should undertake the arrangements and finance of an England tour to Australia in 1891–92. He accompanied a team who played their matches wearing Lord Sheffield's colours of purple, crimson and gold with an armorial 'S' on their caps.

Lord Sheffield wrote a letter to the Melbourne *Leader* to explain his initiative:

> I have long waited to see your country and your cricket and as I was compelled by my failing health to decide upon taking a long sea voyage and spending a winter away from England, it occurred to me that if it was convenient to you in Australia to see us I could combine a voyage for health with a visit of English cricketers . . . I was very much afraid you might find that a visit of English cricketers would do much to dislocate local cricket but the Australian clubs have most generously waived all objections, for which I am deeply grateful and which I warmly appreciate.

A letter was sent to Arthur Shrewsbury by Lord Sheffield seeking his advice about the trip and Harry Boyle, who managed the Australian team to England in 1890, was also sounded out. To ensure the tour's success it was felt essential to enlist the services of England's most famous cricketer, Dr W. G. Grace, who was now 43 years old and had not been to Australia for 18 years.

W. G. Grace's cap for the England tour to Australia in 1891–92. Note
Lord Sheffield's emblem. (MCC)

'W. G.' was no stranger to Lord Sheffield, having played several
times at Sheffield Park but he declined the invitation to tour feeling
that he would be tired after a long English season and that he had his
medical practice to consider. Perhaps, more importantly, he felt that
his fee would be too costly for Lord Sheffield.

It is quite possible that 'W. G.' was playing hard to get because he
was duly summoned to Sheffield Park and a deal was struck. It was
an extremely lucrative one for the champion amateur cricketer: a fee
of £3,000, first-class tour expenses, invitations for his wife and two
children, and a locum to run the medical practice. The authors of
W.G. Down Under (1994) wrote: 'Taking inflation into account, no
other cricketer has received anything approaching this for a single
summer's work.'

The tour plans were being made when the following cable
message appeared in the Australian press on 10 February 1891:

A scheme has been put forward under the auspices of the Earl of
Sheffield to take a team of English cricketers to Australia in the
autumn.

On 21 March 1891 the news was released in Australia about 'W. G.' being included in the England team and the incredulous Victorian Cricket Association cabled Lord Sheffield to confirm whether he really was involved. An emphatic reply was sent confirming not only 'W. G.'s' availability to tour but also that of Lord Sheffield.

In August an advertisement appeared in many of the Australian newspapers:

> Lord Sheffield's eleven will arrive in Australia about the beginning of November, and as they will have a few vacancies for country matches, secretaries of country clubs are requested to write to Mr F. Illingworth, care of Scott and Boyle, stating terms etc.

The touring party consisted of eight professionals and five amateurs (including 'W. G.') and the former were offered £300 plus all travelling and hotel expenses 'exclusive of wine and cigars'. Some professionals, notably Shrewsbury and Gunn, declined invitations to tour but nevertheless the team was reckoned to be the strongest ever to leave England. Lord Sheffield announced that he would distribute any tour profits to the professionals and the itinerary showed that there would be eight first-class matches (including three Tests) and 19 minor matches. The team was announced as:

W. G. Grace (Gloucestershire) (Captain)

R. Abel (Surrey)	R. Peel (Yorkshire)
W. Attewell (Nottinghamshire)	H. Philipson (Oxford University)
G. Bean (Sussex)	O. G. Radcliffe (Gloucestershire)
J. Briggs (Lancashire)	J. M. Read (Surrey)
G. Lohmann (Surrey)	J. W. Sharpe (Surrey)
G. MacGregor (Cambridge University)	A. E. Stoddart (Middlesex)

The manager was Lord Sheffield's trusted employee Alfred Shaw who had great experience of touring Australia.

The anticipation of the team's visit and the return of 'The Champion' provoked much excitement and Tom Horan ('Felix'), recalling Lord Sheffield's hospitality to Australian cricketers, wrote:

When it first became known that an England cricket team would probably visit us, some opposition arose; but as soon as our cricket authorities ascertained beyond doubt that the Earl of Sheffield was identified with the team, and that he himself intended to come out, all manifestation of opposition disappeared and the cricket associations of Australia unanimously decided to accord the team the heartiest support.

Departure

The team was given an enthusiastic farewell when it left Liverpool Street Station on 2 October. There was 'a very large assemblage' including a considerable number of well-known cricketers who accompanied the team to the Albert Docks to board the P & 0 Company's RMS *Arcadia*, 'the finest of all steamers'. The farewell party included W. L. Murdoch, C. Aubrey Smith, Hon. Ivo Bligh, W. W. Read, C. W. Alcock, W. Mycroft and Walter Humphreys.

Lord Sheffield in particular received a hearty reception from the spectators as the engines of the *Arcadia* began to set the huge vessel in motion just before one o'clock . . . Lord Sheffield is accompanied by his nephew, Mr Harcourt, and Major Warren.

The Journey

The usual rough weather was met in the Bay of Biscay and even the captain was obliged to miss out on some meals. A cricket net was organised on board and Alfred Shaw's bowling was still reckoned to be formidable. Lord Sheffield turned out to be a good sailor: 'His berth is not exactly sybaritic, being near the ever throbbing engines, while an adjacent baby cries most of the night.' The ship docked at Malta and a match was played on the Naval Ground on a pitch of asphalt covered by coconut matting against a team of eighteen soldiers and sailors.

After being entertained at the garrison the players returned to the Arcadia and the next stop was at Brindisi where the team was joined by Hylton Philipson who had preferred to travel overland. A fellow traveller on the ship was H. M. Stanley, the famous explorer.

The next stop was at Colombo when another match against a

local eighteen was played and the party arrived at Albany, Western Australia on 6 November travelling on to Adelaide shortly afterwards for the first match at the Adelaide Oval.

The Matches

England started the tour with an innings victory over South Australia and then travelled to Melbourne where 'W. G.' carried his bat for 159 not out in another innings victory. Grace though had found himself doing far more public speaking at the receptions than he had bargained for partly because Lord Sheffield had arrived in Melbourne two days after the team. Both were reluctant public speakers and 'W. G.' is said to have commented that had he known he would be called on for so many speeches he would probably have stayed at home.

However, Lord Sheffield was on the ground shortly after lunch on the first day and he was greeted with a hearty reception. Amidst applause the band played 'A Fine Old English Gentleman'. He had arrived in Port Phillip Bay, Melbourne on the mail steamer *Ballarat* and was met by a special steam launch containing dignitaries from the Victorian Cricketers' Association. Lord Sheffield transferred to the launch and caught the train to the cricket ground where a great reception awaited him: 'Cheer after cheer rent the air as the Earl walked out to inspect the wicket.' Australian cricket writer David Scott reported:

> I was delighted to see the grand reception that was given to Lord Sheffield from 20,000 people and I know that his Lordship thoroughly appreciated the kindly feeling towards him. I have had two or three chats with him, but there has been so many wishing to speak to him that we did not get much time together. However, when he returns from Sydney later on he will be longer in Melbourne and then we can have a chat about the game he loves and supports so well.

The team moved to Sydney where they beat New South Wales and were entertained to a sumptuous banquet: 'The toast eulogised the great and unostentatious work the Earl of Sheffield had done in the interest of cricket. The Earl in replying said if he deserved any praise

Lord Sheffield wears a dark blue shooting coat with a
newspaper parcel in a pocket at Melbourne in 1891

at all it was for introducing the champion, W. G. Grace, once more
to Australian cricket fields. He most warmly spoke of the cordial and
hearty welcomes he and his team had received from the moment
they landed at Adelaide.'

After winning the opening three matches against strong sides
Lord Sheffield's team played six minor matches in country districts
before the First Test at Melbourne on New Year's Day. Despite
achieving a first-innings lead England lost the match but Lord
Sheffield could console himself with an attendance of 60,000 and a
profit of £2,600.

There were six further minor matches before the Second Test and
Lord Sheffield was reported as being present at a town hall lunch at
Malvern near Melbourne.

The Second Test was at Sydney where there was further disappointment for the tourists. On this occasion a first-innings lead of
162 could not prevent a defeat by 72 runs. Lord Sheffield was
reported as watching every ball very closely accompanied by Lord
Jersey, Governor of New South Wales. During the match 'W. G.'
refused a substitute for the injured Harry Moses but 'Earl Sheffield

Lord Sheffield is depicted as financially exploiting
Australian cricket, but in fact he lost a considerable sum
of money

once more showed what a true sportsman he is by urging Dr Grace
to let a man field and W. G. gave way.' Surrey's Bobby Abel had
batted throughout England's first innings for 132 not out and he
was rewarded with a cheque for £50 from Lord Sheffield. When Jack
Lyons scored 134 in Australia's second innings it was again Lord
Sheffield who made a presentation to him of a silver matchbox
donated by a group of Sydney ladies.

The defeat surrendered the Ashes to Australia and Lord Sheffield
was in poor health, 'the climate and Australia generally not agreeing
with him'. This was resolved when he decided to stay on in Tasmania
after the team moved on to play Victoria in Melbourne and the final
Test Match in Adelaide. From Hobart he retained a keen interest in
the team and when he learned that Victoria was unlikely to field its
strongest team he sent a telegram to Melbourne threatening to cancel

This photograph of the Sydney Test Match was presented to Lord Sheffield by the trustees of the Sydney Cricket Ground in appreciation of his efforts to revive Australian cricket. It is the earliest known photograph of a Test Match in Australia and has been returned to Sydney by the late Sussex CCC librarian H. A. Osborne (pictured).

the match. Major Wardill, the energetic secretary of Melbourne Cricket Club, was deputed to visit a local bank manager for the release of Trumble and McLeod and Bruce also agreed to play. 'All these concessions were of course gained because of Earl Sheffield's generosity and because of the fillip he had given to cricket by spending so much money in bringing out the team.'

Lord Sheffield's team won the third and final Test Match by an innings but it was something of a consolation victory. Australian cricket had been revived and Lord Sheffield's assistance was acknowledged in the following letter:

To Lord Sheffield
March 28, 1892
Tasmania

Dear Sir,
The representatives of the New South Wales, Victoria and South Australian Cricket Associations in conference to-day desired me, as their Chairman, to convey to you their warmest appreciation of the

interest you have shown in Australian cricket by bringing into competition with it, in the Colonies, the greatest champion of England. It is gratifying that the international contests have been characterised by the kindest social amenities which it is hoped may have an enduring influence for good. So far as Australia is concerned it will not stop upon the steps of the pavilion nor fade away at the gates of the cricket grounds.

I remain yours very faithfully,
H.Y SPARKS
Chairman
Australasian Cricket Conference

Tasmania suited Lord Sheffield and he planned to return with another team of English cricketers. Readers of *Cricket* were informed:

Lord Sheffield who, by the way, left Australia in the *Arcadia* some little time after the team would appear to have had a very pleasant experience on his first visit to the Colonies. The climate of Tasmania seems to have impressed him very favourably and it is already announced positively that he will spend next winter in Australia. According to a special cablegram from the Melbourne correspondent of the *Times*, under date of March 29, he proposes to collect the strongest possible team of English cricketers, including Shrewsbury and Gunn, to visit Australia next winter. The idea is to play three test matches against the pick of Australian cricketers, the first at Adelaide in December, the others at Melbourne and Sydney. Though Lord Sheffield is reported to have said that W. G. will not make the trip again all is mere rumour as yet. The new Australian Cricket Council according to the same message is to keep the matter of another English visit open till May.

The proposals for Lord Sheffield's team to return in 1892–93 and later years failed to materialise but there was no doubting Lord Sheffield's popularity on his sole tour. One of the team in an interview said: 'Lord Sheffield's popularity was universal, it was unbounded; he was, in fact, quite the most popular sportsman who has ever visited Australia.'

Australian Views of Lord Sheffield

The Australians were fascinated by the cricket-loving English earl and he was described in the *Bulletin* for 12 December in some detail:

> A little fat, stumpy man, for all the world like an English farmer of the old standard type. Hair long and straggly, lips and face roughly shaven, and a little fringe of a beard left under the chin, eyes small and cute, thick-necked, heavy jowled, obstinate, good natured and shrewd, his lordship is just the sort of man that would make a fine landlord for a bush pub.

This amounted to high praise and another description of Lord Sheffield appeared in the *Australasian* at the time of his walking out to inspect the pitch at Melbourne Cricket Ground:

> His lordship is genial, jovial, hearty and a thorough sportsman, cricket being his especial hobby. He cares little for vanity of wearing apparel, but dresses himself for comfort and in a style all of his own. He wore an Alpine hat with the colours of his eleven (yellow, red and dark violet) as a band, dark blue shooting coat, and roomy, nankeen trousers. A newspaper parcel was in one pocket and a warm-tinted handkerchief in the other. He chatted heartily with all and sundry who were presented to him, and when he made a tour of the ground, the crowd cheered him, recognising a true sportsman and a fine old English gentleman into the bargain, who had always been the first to welcome 'our boys' on English soil.

Financial

The tour had succeeded in Lord Sheffield's stated aim of fostering Australian cricket and he showed little disappointment in losing the Test series. The estimated cost of the tour had risen from £11,000 to £16,000 and this left a deficit of £2,700, seemingly of little concern to Lord Sheffield. One unforeseen item of expenditure, according to historian Chris Harte, was a payment of £90 made by Lord Sheffield to settle a writ in Sydney served on one of his team for assault and a dispute over a barmaid! Major Wardill, the secretary of Melbourne

Cricket Club, had worked hard on behalf of the team and Lord Sheffield later expressed his gratitude by forwarding him five silver dessert service pieces of the choicest design and workmanship.

Welcome Home
Lord Sheffield received a 'right loyal and hearty welcome home' at a splendid day at Sheffield Park on 4 June. He was early on the ground where a cricket match was to be played between the tenants of the estate and the residents of Fletching. 'He appeared in excellent health and spirits after his sojourn at the Antipodes and subsequent long sea voyage' and received many old friends, neighbours and deputations from 19 local cricket clubs, including those from Brighton.

Luncheon for a very large party was served in the luncheon pavilion where the walls were hung with photographs of Australian scenery and cricket grounds 'including a splendid picture of the Sydney ground with the players in the second test match between Lord Sheffield's Eleven and United Australia'.

Two addresses were then made to Lord Sheffield representing the good wishes of the tenants, parishioners, friends, neighbours and cricket clubs, the second of which containing nearly 300 names. The accompanying gift was presented by former Sussex county cricketer R. M. Curteis:

> It consisted of a silver-mounted field glass, and gold-mounted umbrella and walking stick, enclosed in a case of polished oak, having on the lid an earl's coronet and the letter S in silver. Mr Curteis said, 'I need only assure your lordship of our gratification at seeing you here again safe and sound and in good health and spirits.'

Lord Sheffield was overwhelmed and after thanking everyone he spoke of his pleasure at being home and the reception that he and the team had received in Australia:

> Well, gentlemen, all these congratulations, these gifts, these addresses, have a priceless value in my mind because they seem to show me that whatever may be my own shortcomings I have at any

rate a little corner in your affections (loud cheer) as I can assure you gentlemen you have a very large one in mine (renewed applause). If it is a gratifying thing, as it always must be, to come home from abroad to mix again with one's old friends, to see the old familiar faces and those to whom one is so much attached, I can scarcely describe to you how the pleasure is enhanced and heightened when, after a long expedition, full of risks and anxieties, after a long travel by sea of something like 30,000 miles, one comes back to find one's arrival is the signal for a spontaneous display of cordiality and good feeling such as I have this day experienced . . .

Gentlemen, continued his lordship, it is no exaggeration to say that the reception given to myself and to the English team, for its splendour, for its extent, for its variety and for its continuity (for it began when we landed in Adelaide in November and only ceased when the team in March set foot aboard the *Valetta*) was unparalleled in the history of cricket in Australia, and I am quite sure I may also say it is without parallel in the history of cricket in England (great cheering). I hope therefore when the Australians come to England next year – as they are coming – and when they visit this park – as they intend to do (cheers) – that the people of Sussex will assemble on this ground in their thousands and give them such a ringing welcome as Sussex throats know how to give, and as will show them that you have recognised and appreciated the magnificence of the welcome that they gave your fellow country men last winter in far away Australia (prolonged cheering).

Lord Sheffield's plea for future Australian teams to be lavishly received at Sheffield Park resulted in the tourists of 1893 and 1896 being entertained in the most spectacular style imaginable.

9

The Sheffield Shield

Lord Sheffield's most enduring legacy to cricket, and to Australian cricket in particular, must be the Sheffield Shield.

It is a magnificent trophy and was bought for £150 donated by his lordship during the tour of Australia in 1891–92. His purpose in donating the shield was to stimulate competitive cricket between the Australian states.

He certainly succeeded. Over the years the Sheffield Shield has come to be regarded as the strongest first-class cricket competition in the world, excluding Test matches, and has largely contributed to the seemingly endless supply of great Australian players.

In 1999 the need for sponsorship of the Australian domestic competition signalled the demise of the shield after 107 years. It was replaced by the Pura Milk Cup sponsored by National Foods, and the change brought benefits valued at $A22 million per year to Australian cricket. Lord Sheffield's shield was consigned to a museum, albeit as an Australian sporting icon.

Happily for the 2008–09 season Australia's domestic competition again became known as the Sheffield Shield. The trophy itself was in very poor condition and 200 hours of craftsmanship went into its restoration. In a breakfast handover in July 2008 at Melbourne Cricket Ground the new sponsors Weet-Bix presented the restored shield to the chief executive of Cricket Australia and, to everybody's great pleasure, announced that the sponsor's brand name would not be added to the name of the trophy or to the domestic competition.

So, very appropriately in the one hundredth year since the death of Lord Sheffield, the shield has been restored to the Australian sporting arena.

It is hoped that the Sheffield Shield will be on display at Sheffield

The Sheffield Shield

Park at the end of June 2009 when the restoration of Lord Sheffield's cricket ground will be celebrated. The trophy was last in the area in 1990 when it was on show at Fletching, where an Old England XI played an Old Australian XI to mark Lord Sheffield's contribution to cricket in both those countries.

At an early stage of Lord Sheffield's tour to Australia in 1891–92, arrangements to create the shield were entrusted to the Melbourne CC secretary, Major Ben Wardill. On November 20 the Major wrote to his opposite number at the New South Wales Cricket Association, John Portus, and brought up the matter of a trophy:

> Lord Sheffield has asked me if the Associations would accept a Trophy of the value of £150 or thereabouts for competition by the three colonies in any way agreed upon by them. I said I would ask the Associations if any regulations could be drawn up and agreed to, so that the Trophy might be won, say, by two consecutive wins by any Colony. Will you bring the matter before your Association and offer any suggestions you think fit?

The centenary of the Sheffield Shield was commemorated by the issue of this philatelic item. (R. Packham)

Major Wardill obtained Lord Sheffield's permission to suggest an equal division of the £150 between the three colonies and this, together with the above letter, was discussed in Sydney on 14 December. In early January 1892 Wardill again wrote to Portus:

> Lord Sheffield spoke about the Trophy business this afternoon and he made a suggestion that the trophy (if only one agreed to) should go to the Colony holding it against the other two Colonies for two seasons – I pointed out that we played S.A. only once each season and NSW twice – here comes the difficulty.
>
> He wishes to give gold medals to each member of the winning team etc. Until I hear from the other Associations about their ideas, I don't see what can be done. Lord S has got the needle about Creswell and he says he is going to write to the SACA to ask them to appoint someone *pro tem* with whom he can correspond.
>
> I think myself the difficulties attending a triangular match so great that we shall have to fall back upon a Trophy for each Colony to do what they like with.

Major Wardill had doubts about the cricket associations of Victoria, New South Wales and South Australia being able to come up with a suitable proposal and he confided to Lord Sheffield: 'I fancy that they will find it so difficult to arrange that they will fall back on your idea of giving a trophy to each Colony.'

Long after Lord Sheffield's return to England the matter had still not been resolved but at a meeting of the newly formed Australasian Cricket Council at Sydney on 13 September 1892 the terms and conditions of the Sheffield Shield were decided. After a proposal from the Victorians to divide Lord Sheffield's money, an amendment was put forward by Augustus Robinson, a South Australian delegate. Robinson's proposal was that 'the money be devoted to the purchase of a premiership shield, to be held by the premier colony for the year and that a sub-committee be appointed to draft the necessary rules'.

After discussion the vote was taken and Robinson's proposal was approved by just one vote. The rules for the Sheffield Shield were drawn up by the sub-committee that evening and ratified by the Council.

So the Sheffield Shield was inaugurated in the 1892–93 season, but at the end of the season there was no trophy to present to the successful Victorian team and it took until 3 July 1893 for Lord Sheffield's £150 to be released by Major Wardill.

With funds available the following advertisement appeared in the Sydney, Adelaide and Melbourne newspapers on 29 July:

To Silversmiths and Others
Tenders for the manufacture and supply in silver of 'The Sheffield Shield' will be received by the undersigned up to 31 August 1893. Each tender must be accompanied with the design of the Shield suitably engraved. The value of the Shield to be £150 sterling and it must be delivered as directed. The lowest or any tender not necessarily accepted. For further particulars, apply to John Portus, Hon. Sec. Australasian Cricket Council, Box 32, GPO, Sydney.

The advertisement failed to produce a satisfactory tender and Portus was obliged to place a further advertisement in October:

THE SHEFFIELD SHIELD

Tenders accompanied with the design of a suitably engraved cricket Shield will be received by the undersigned up to 30 November. The approximate weight of the Shield, which shall be of the full value of £150 sterling, must be supplied with full particulars by each tenderer. The members of the Australasian Cricket Council will decide on the tenders and designs in Melbourne on 28 December 1893.

John Portus, Hon. Sec.
Australasian Cricket Council
Harbours and Rivers Office,
Phillip St., Sydney, NSW.

There were 21 tenders tabled at the annual general meeting of the Australasian Cricket Council at the Vienna Cafe, Melbourne on 28 December 1893. After consideration the successful design was that of Philip Blashki, a jeweller of Bourke Street, Melbourne whose company still trades today.

Mr Blashki was a Polish Jew born in 1836 in the village of Blaszki. His real name was Uri Wanczewski and he emigrated to Manchester in 1854. Newly married, he arrived in Melbourne in 1858 where he worked as a hawker and gold trader. He went bankrupt, but managed to start a jewellery business in Melbourne in 1875. In 1893 he retired from the prosperous family business and handed over to a son. His design of the Sheffield Shield is likely to have been one of his last transactions, though he was only 57, and the manufacture of the Shield is thought to have been the work of his son Henry. The design was described in the *Australasian*:

> The shield is of silver, the centre-plate representing the Sheffield Park cricket ground where so many Australian teams have played. On either hand is a bowler and a batsman in action. In the centre-piece the men are shown in the field and the wickets, bat and ball will be of gold, as well as some sixteen little tablets which are to bear the names of the winning teams. The Australian arms and the Sheffield arms will be correctly enamelled in colours and rest on shoulders of the shield. The shield, which is to be crowned with a bust of the donor, will measure 40 inches by 30 inches.

Instructions were later given to Mr Blashki to replace the bust of Lord Sheffield with a statuette of the goddess 'Victory' but it is not known what the reasons were behind the alteration. Otherwise the Shield remains faithful to the original design and it contained 200 ounces of silver, several ounces of gold and the following inscription on the bottom:

Presented by Lord Sheffield for competition between the Cricket Associations of Victoria, South Australia and New South Wales, commencing season 1892–93

The second Sheffield Shield season was that of 1893–94 when South Australia proved victorious but the trophy was still not ready for presentation until the close season. The first official handover was made on 14 July 1894 at the Adelaide Oval during an Australian Rules football match between Norwood and Port Adelaide. The chairman of the South Australia Cricket Association, Mostyn Evans, presented the Sheffield Shield for safe keeping to the Association's president Sir Edwin Smith, who had been at Sheffield Park in 1893 for the visit of the Australians.

It has been calculated that, from the time Lord Sheffield first suggested giving a shield to the date of the first presentation, 964 days had passed!

The competition has gradually been expanded to include Queensland, Western Australia and Tasmania and, despite Lord Sheffield's threat in 1897 to take back his trophy, (see chapter 13) the Sheffield Shield has become a much-loved part of Australian sporting tradition.

In 2009 the Sheffield Shield, now beautifully restored by Messrs Hardy, returned to public prominence in Australia. It would be fitting if the shield were to make an appearance at Sheffield Park during the summer festivities.

10

Parties in the Park

Lord Sheffield's name will be remembered for his cricketing activities with Sussex County Cricket Club, with the grand matches at Sheffield Park and his tour with an England team to Australia in 1891–92. But there is no doubt that he was fond of other sports and had a genuine desire to provide entertainment for people of all classes. Some of the other sporting and recreational activities held at Sheffield Park are described here.

Children in the Park

Lord Sheffield's ideal of providing sport and entertainment for the general public extended to organising treats specifically for children. He particularly sought to look after the poorer classes and even invited children from deprived parts of London. The following reports are typical of many such occasions:

GREAT SCHOOL TREAT AT SHEFFIELD PARK 1892
His Lordship generously entertained 2,000 Sunday School children. The weather was delightfully fine and the faces of hundreds of little children, accompanied by their teachers, as they filed into the Park were radiant with happiness. The children hailed from Newhaven, Danehill, Fletching, Chailey and Newick. The Newhaven town band travelled with the contingent from that town.

The Earl had provided a most thorough and complete programme for the delectation of the children, the first item being an aquatic tournament in one of the lakes by members of the Brighton Swimming Club, at the conclusion of which was a display of daytime fireworks. Tea was a most gigantic affair as the 2,000 were appeasing

Children are in evidence in a prizegiving ceremony in front of Lord Sheffield's pavilion c.1890. The lady in a white dress on the steps is believed to be Mabel Attenborough. (N. J. G. Sharp)

their sharpened appetites, and seated in the lovely grounds, and, encircled with beautiful flowers, two bands played enchanting music.

The fact of over a mile of tables and seating being required, gives some idea of the dimensions of the party. When the time came to start for home, the bugles collected the children into various groups around the cricket ground, the line of assembly marked by bunting which went round the entire length of the ground. When all were ready the combined bands of Newhaven and Chailey stationed in the centre of the cricket ground, struck up 'Onward Christian Soldiers' and the final procession – not less than a mile in length – started with flags and banners held high and the children singing. The procession moved along before Lord Sheffield's private pavilion on the balcony of which His Lordship was standing surrounded by his friends. The children cheered as they passed and Lord Sheffield raised his hat and smiled his acknowledgements of their hearty greeting.

East End children at Sheffield Park 1895

A DELIGHTFUL AFTERNOON

This was one of the frequent generous acts on the part of Lord Sheffield. The Park on Saturday was thrown open to over a thousand children from London who were accompanied by about 100 adults. These youngsters were poor 'companions' of The Children's Order of Chivalry – an order formed in connection with Lord Winchilsea's agricultural newspaper *The Cable*.

700 children from the East End and 700 from Old Ford visited Sheffield Park travelling in two separate trains (girls/boys). Ever thoughtful, the Earl had made arrangements for the youngsters to be conveyed from the station to the park and had chartered from Mr Golding of Haywards Heath three brakes, three 'buses and 15 landaus to and from the station. (Refreshments on arrival: then dispersed). The one great object of every child was of course to thoroughly enjoy himself and herself and there seemed to be not a single failure if the many happy faces to be seen all around can be accepted as proof of this statement. Messrs Brock of firework fame, gave a long display of daylight fireworks and the many curious things which developed in the air after a couple of explosions created surprise, wonder and delight to the youngsters who eagerly strove for possession of the large paper cows, horses, men &c which floated some distance off, or scrambled for the small india-rubber balls which came in a shower from out of the air. About four o'clock, tea took place and the welcome meal was served at a pleasant spot in the rear of his lordship's private pavilion – exactly the same spot that the great gathering of children at tea took place in 1892. The tables arranged in two rows were just about 400 yards long and the ground they occupied was encircled with Venetian masts on which were about 80 large flags with about twice that number of bannerets used at various points, festoons of evergreens hanging from mast to mast. His lordship mixed amongst the children the whole of the time they were present and took a keen interest in their doings. It was a capital tea that Mr R. Welfare of the Sheffield Arms provided.

The complex earl had a genuine affinity for children and there is a report that on May Day 1900 he allowed children to clamber about the interior and roof of his private cricket pavilion.

Coursing in the Park

One of the sporting activities taking place at Sheffield Park when Henry's father was the Earl of Sheffield was hare coursing. In February, 1871 the following appeared in the *Sussex Express*:

SHEFFIELD PARK COURSING

We understand that the Earl of Sheffield, with that kindness which always distinguishes him, has again placed his domain and hares at the service of the coursing men of Sussex and that a meeting will shortly take place. Early application should be made for nominations in the two great events of the day – the Sheffield Cup and the Pevensey Cup – to Robert Loder Esq, the High Beeches, Crawley, Honorary Secretary.

In 1888 the local newspaper recalled the encouragement given to coursing by Henry's father: 'The late earl, for instance, for many years placed his game and his land at the disposal of the coursing men of Sussex and Surrey and many an enjoyable day in the early months of the year has been spent in the glades and on the uplands which surround the cricket ground. Soon after the accession of the present earl to the estate he gave most of the shooting to his tenantry and ceased to preserve game. The natural consequence was that the coursing meetings were discontinued.'

Cricket on the Ice

Winter sporting activities at Sheffield Park were organised on several memorable occasions, notably in the harsh winter of 1890–91. On 17 January 1891, a particularly cold day when the lakes were iced to a depth of between 12 and 16 inches, cricket was played on Upper Woman's Way Pond (nearest the cricket ground). Lord Sheffield had arranged for the photographer to be present and on the same day curling took place on Middle Lake and football on Ten Foot Pond.

Cricket on the Ice, Upper Woman's Way Pond, 17 January 1891. Sheffield Park House can be seen in the distance. (N. J. G. Sharp)

The cricket on ice was recalled by E. V. Lucas and a report in the *West Sussex Times* (27 August 1898) provided Lucas's description:

A. Payne then joined Charlwood and they collared the bowling entirely and gave their opponents plenty of healthy exercise. One man in particular was made busy. There was a dogged perverseness about him that seemed to encourage the batsmen. While others of his colleagues were thankful if they could stop and return the ball on their feet, he seemed to be saddened if he kept upright. He was faithful to the notion that the best fielding is done on the back of the head. Perhaps he once saw Mr Royle field that way. Anyhow, he put his principles into practice and must have done a mile at least on the back of his head during the game. In whatever part of the lake you might be you would be sure to hear a dull thud every few minutes, followed by a peal of laughter. It was his head. Other fieldsmen were not much less unlucky. Once a very tempting catch was sent to mid-on. He forgot all about his skates and leaped high in the air to grab the ball, with his right hand high up. He failed to reach it and then began to come down again. He came down flat. When Charlwood had made 30 and Payne 33, they retired. Osborne, who followed, did not stay very long; and then Watson and the captain were together. Now when Harry Phillips was on his feet, he batted excellently, showing, in fact, some of the form that so electrified the Australians in 1884; but – the pity of it – he was hardly on his feet at all. It is no exaggeration to say that of the 30 minutes he was in he spent five on his stomach, five on his back and three on his knees. Harry was one of the few players who wore skates, and though he could skuttle as well as anyone there, he could not pirouette. Cricket on the ice demands pirouetting. Watson was only a little better. Yet, in spite of their falls and flounderings, Butt could not put down their wickets. One exciting series of overthrows ended in a tableau that everybody present must regret was not photographed. Phillips, on his hands and knees, two yards from the wickets, was tearing away at the yielding surface of the ice with his nails, trying in vain to get some purchase, he had flung his bat away long before. Butt, two yards behind the wickets, spread out as though he had been rolled, was also wriggling. Harry Phillips got in first. The match, though cut short, progressed sufficiently far to enable the observer to note the following points of difference between the winter and the summer game:- In summer, the fieldsmen pick up the ball as it rolls; in winter, they wait till the ball stops, which may be a matter of minutes, then describe an arc round it and pick it up at the finish of the curve. In summer they throw it in as they run; in winter they sit down first. In summer, the bowlers take a run before making their attack; in winter they stand as still as possible, press their knees together and thank Heaven if they can get rid of the ball without falling. In summer, the batsmen, in running, just touch the popping crease with the tip of -their bats and hurry back again; in winter they shoot a dozen yards past the bowling crease, beat the ice with their feet, wave their arms round their heads, plunge their bodies backwards and forwards, and then start for the other wicket. It will be seen that cricket on the ice is more exciting than cricket on the turf.

Cricket on the Ice, 17 January 1891. (N. J. G. Sharp)

Four years later cricket was again played on the ice but Lord Sheffield, who had missed the 1891 ice match through illness, was again absent owing to an accident. The laws of cricket were followed except that no extras counted and batsmen were compelled to retire after making 20 runs. The ordinary allowance for a boundary hit to the edge of the lake was 3. 'Needless to say the match was productive of considerable fun.' Score:

MR BLACKMAN'S XI – A. Blackman retired 20, G. Bean retired 20, F. Worger b. Tate 0, W. Marlow retired 20, A. Bramwell b. Butcher 3, W. Mitchell retired 20, J. Meaden lbw b. Butcher 0, F. Geake c. Lever b. Midgley 15, F. Swan b. Butcher 9, R. W. Kellow not out 6, W. Hague b. Butcher 0. TOTAL 113

MR MIDGLEY'S XI – A. Midgley run out 12, C. F. Butcher retired 20, H. Budgen retired 20, F. Tate retired 20, Markwick b. Worger 10, W. Meaden b. A. Bramwell 13, F. Bramwell run out 3, P. Crowhurst b. Worger 5, W. Moore b. Worger 3, G. Goord run out 10, C. Leaver not out 3. TOTAL 119

The above teams include seven Sussex first-class cricketers as well as William Moore, Lord Sheffield's hard working groundsman.

Curling in the Park

In January 1891, the same day that cricket was played on the ice of the long pond, the sport of curling was also in evidence at Sheffield Park:

A novel game – curling – which aroused a good deal of interest, and which had probably never been played in the south of England before, was played throughout the day on the middle lake. The game is a popular one on the ice in Scotland, and is played with heavy granite stones, shaped like a flat Dutch cheese, with a handle on top, which is propelled along the ice with the object of causing the stone to remain in a ring marked in the ice some thirty yards away, whilst the players are equipped with besoms, with which they vigorously sweep the ice in front of the stone should its speed of progress indicate that it would not reach the goal. The players, in throwing or pushing the stone, stand on cocoa-nut matting, and in turn send the curling stones in the direction of the ring, in the centre of which is placed a marble ball. Two matches were played, which resulted as follows:

1st Game

A. Harcourt (captain)	R. Surtees (captain)
J. Webber	Capt. R. Sharp
H. Wool	A. J. Lewis
E. Hobbs	T. Colgate

Mr Harcourt's team won by six points to four

2nd Game

H.Wool (captain)	A. J. Lewis (captain)
W. Gates	J. Sheppard
J. Webber	Capt. Sharp
W. Humphrey	F. Wood

Mr Wool's team won by 10 points to six

Cyclists in the Park

Lord Sheffield showed considerable interest in the town of Newhaven and many of its sporting activities. In 1891 the cyclists of Newhaven were invited to Sheffield Park:

FORTHCOMING CYCLISTS' TEA

by kind permission of the Earl of Sheffield, Mr Gray will be enabled to entertain the Newhaven Cyclist Club members at tea in the pavilion on the cricket ground in Sheffield Park. The date fixed for the outing is July 8th.

Four years later the Brighton cyclists also had cause to be grateful to Lord Sheffield and expressed it in a handsome manner:

PRESENTATION TO THE EARL OF SHEFFIELD

Lord Sheffield has been presented by the members of the Quadrant Cycling Club with a handsome badge as a mark of their esteem on consenting to stand as President of the club. The badge is composed of silver and is in the form of a shield surmounted by a cycle wheel. The whole is encircled by a laurel wreath and capped by a coronet. The monogram 'QCC' in gold plated letters appears in the centre of the shield. The badge is enclosed in a morocco case, lined with blue velvet upon the outside of which appears the following inscription:-

Presented to
The Right Honourable
THE EARL OF SHEFFIELD
By the officers and members of the Quadrant Cycling Club
January 1895

Fireworks in the Park

In his desire to entertain on a grand scale Lord Sheffield sometimes included fireworks as part of a day's activities, as seen with the display for the East End children in 1895. The most spectacular display at Sheffield Park however, was without doubt during the cricket match between Lord Sheffield's XI and the 1893 Australians, photographed by Messrs Hawkins and puting to the test the superlatives of the *East Sussex News* reporter:

There were probably many hundreds among those who went to the Park on Tuesday who did so solely to witness the illuminations arranged for that evening in honour of the colonial visitors. Indeed this was proved by the fact that whole train loads of passengers arrived from Brighton and elsewhere long after stumps had been drawn for the day. Quite an army of operators had been for two days engaged in hanging coloured lamps and lanterns and building up set firework pieces at every conceivable point where beauty of effect was obtainable, and even before the sun had fairly set men had commenced the enormous task of lighting the former. As darkness fell, it was seen by the thousands who had assembled on the northern slope of the cricket ground that the lake plateaus between that spot and the noble mansion, with all the undulating woodland upon their banks, were crossed and re-crossed, festooned and bedecked with lights of every describable hue, in some spots, particularly over the waterfalls and bridges, so thick as to present the appearance of continuous narrow lines of variegated fire. The gaunt trunks of firs and the stems of the more massive oaks were entwined with lamps, fancy lanterns hung in graceful festoons from bough to bough, high spreading branches had pendants of brilliant lights reaching to the ground; every walk was bordered and every group of shrubs encircled with tiny flashing fires; bright stars shone upon the water's edge and even among the dancing spray of the cascades. As darkness came on and the distant house faded from view, the scene grew more and more brilliant, and as far as the eye could reach, till seemingly lost on a dim and distant horizon, there was a veritable fairyland of extreme beauty and variety. Those who know the open-air café chantants of the Champs de Elysees can imagine some thousand of them grouped upon a sloping plain, and even then they would scarce picture the true brilliancy and beauty of the picture which night disclosed to view in Sheffield Park. At a given signal the woods on every side were formed

Fireworks and illuminations for the visit of the Australians in 1893. (Sussex CCC)

into a background of magnificent green, changing to purple, again to blue, then to a delicate pink, and, indeed, colours of all tints, the most distant foliage being brought more clearly into vision than ever day made possible. Then began the discharge of rockets – such combinations of colours, such myriads of shooting stars, such wonderful fiery meteors, such groupings of beauty as pen cannot possibly describe. They flashed to the sky above, they darted and hissed on the waters below and in such numbers that one was bewildered and knew not which way to glance, fearing to miss some new sight, whilst awed in contemplation of another. Then came the set pieces. Great revolving circles within circles, squares and triangles of enormous size, moving elephants, dancing sailors, performing acrobats, cascades of sparks that no words can picture. Presently a great cheer arose as clear and distinct on the margin of the lower lake appeared the words, in orange coloured fire, "Welcome Australians. Good wishes and hearty thanks for your reception of our team in Australia." Then came a repetition of much of that which we have already endeavoured to describe, and so the mysterious and lovely sight continued for quite an hour. Reluctantly the great crowd turned from the charming spectacle, and it is not too much to say that the recollections of that

night will never fade from the memories of those who had the good
fortune to witness the spectacle, which was verily a triumph of the
illuminator's art. Before the crowd separated, cheers were given again
and again for the noble Earl.

Flowers in the Park

An annual Flower Show organised by Miss Attenborough was held
during the 1890s with prizes from Lord Sheffield. In 1896 entries
were confined to inhabitants of Fletching parish, Lord Sheffield's
tenants outside the parish and cottagers on any part of his estate. The
prizes totalled £60 – £70. The show for 1898 was cancelled because
of the death of Rev. Attenborough.

Football in the Park

Lord Sheffield had excelled at the Eton versions of football in his
schooldays and interested himself in the development of association
football and the advent of professionalism.

In 1894, with his customary desire to promote sport and provide
entertainment for large numbers of people, he invited the renowned
Nottingham Forest Football Club to Sheffield Park to compete
against a representative amateur Sussex team, the Sussex Martlets.

Before the big day Lord Sheffield invited the Sussex County F.A.
to play a trial match at Sheffield Park on 3 October, the sides being
captained by E. H. Polehampton ('Whites') and G. H. Arlington
('Colours'). Arlington had made his Sussex cricket debut during the
summer and his team won by three goals to one. 'Mr Alfred Shaw
had made admirable arrangements on behalf of his lordship and
Mr W. Moore, the well-known ground man had evidently been to
considerable trouble in preparing the turf which was in splendid
condition.'

After the trial match the teams were entertained by Lord
Sheffield at the Sheffield Arms where George Cole, in the chair,
proposed the health of Lord Sheffield with 'Success to Football at
Sheffield Park'. He said it was scarcely necessary for him to tell
those present of the enthusiasm with which his lordship upheld
all manly sports. The Australians and South Africans had been

delighted to open their tours at Sheffield Park, and the Sussex Association felt it to be an honour to inaugurate their present season on the same ground. He hoped the trial in that afternoon would be the forerunner of many happy football gatherings at Sheffield Park.

Exactly a week later, on Wednesday 10 October the famous professional team, Nottingham Forest, overwhelmed the amateur Sussex XI that included the athletic C. B. Fry and fellow Sussex cricketer Frank Guttridge, a sometime Notts County footballer.

The local newspaper enthused:

A very interesting and attractive match of football took place on the famous cricket ground, which has been the scene of many notable events both in cricket, volunteer manoeuvres and football during the last eighteen years. That the general public appreciate and do not abuse the noble earl's kindness was shown by the fact that on this occasion the gates of the park and the grounds were thrown open to all comers, and a large number of spectators, estimated at from 1500 to 2000 availed themselves of the privilege afforded them. It need hardly be said that Lord Sheffield with his usual generosity, defrayed all the expenses of the match, nor that under his directions the arrangements were as complete as they could possibly be. The eastern portion of the cricket ground was appropriated to the match, the goals being placed in front of Lord Sheffield's private pavilion, looking north. No doubt the visitors from the Midlands, who only on Saturday defeated the renowned Aston Villa team, had a great initial advantage from the fact that they have long been accustomed to play together. Both teams arrived early, and were photographed in groups in front of his lordship's pavilion.

A Mummy in the Park

Lord Sheffield had a considerable interest in history and brought back many historic objects from his travels overseas. He was also a vice-president of the Sussex Archaeological Society. In 1893 one of the treasures he had brought back from a recent visit to Egypt was to be spectacularly unveiled on the cricket ground at Sheffield Park in front of some guests and the reporter from the *East Sussex News*.

A Remarkable Scene At Sheffield Park, Unrolling A Mummy

At Sheffield Park on Saturday in the presence of some 40 or 50 of Lord Sheffield's friends and neighbours, Professor Budge of the British Museum, unrolled a mummy brought by Lord Sheffield from Egypt in the early part of this year. On a number of tables placed together in front of his Lordship's private pavilion in the cricket ground lay a strange object in human form and from this the experienced fingers of the Professor were seen unwinding yard upon yard of brownish linen, brittle with age, until at length the shapely face and head and small but well moulded form of a priestess of twenty centuries ago was unveiled. A hieroglyphic inscription was thus described by Dr Budge: 'Look, O Osiris, the President of the Underworld, the Great God, the Lord of Abydys, and do thou protect the deceased Sheret-Meht, daughter of Nes-Heru.'

At the close of the investigation, which was followed with the deepest interest by all present, the remains of the priestess were returned to the sarcophagus where they had rested for so many centuries.

Rugby in the Park

The first rugby tourists to England were the Maori team of 1888–89 and they played a staggering 74 matches on the British Isles leg of the tour. Lord Sheffield arranged for the Maoris to play Middlesex at Sheffield Park at a time when the park had been closed to the public because of the poison pen letters. The local newspaper enthused:

LORD SHEFFIELD AND THE MAORI FOOTBALL TEAM
We understand that the Earl of Sheffield has arranged a football match at Sheffield Park between the New Zealanders and an English Fifteen chosen by Mr Rowland Hill. The match will be played on the beautiful cricket ground above the lakes and the day fixed is Monday, October 22nd. This will be a particularly interesting occasion for many reasons besides the interest attaching to the game. It is, we believe, the wish of the noble earl, as an individual Englishman to give the New Zealanders as cordial a reception as he gave the Australians – a reception which has never been forgotten in Australia. The park will

Sussex Martlets football team opposed to Nottingham Forest at Sheffield Park in 1894: Back row: F. J. Lawrence (Linesman), E. G. Wilson, F. Guttridge, W. P. Meates, F. J. Wall (Referee), E. W. Everest (Hon. Sec. Sussex County F.A.). Seated: F. Street, C. B. Fry, E. H. Polehampton (Captain), H. C. Stewart, Rev. C. H. Bond. In front: T. Orphin, E. C. Cooper, H. E. Landon. (N. J. G. Sharp)

only be open to those who are specially invited, on account of the annoyance to which his lordship, we regret to hear, continues to be exposed on the part of local people. So long as this continues, the general public will not be admitted to the park on these occasions.

A fortnight later the same newspaper recorded a historic match between Middlesex, with six internationals, and the tourists. Middlesex won by nine points to nil:

The weather on Monday morning was foggy but towards noon the atmosphere cleared and the remainder of the day was fine. Autumn has as yet laid a very light hand on the foliage at Sheffield Park. The fine old oaks are still verdant, and although the chestnuts, maples, and many other trees display the mellowing influences of October frosts, a wealth of colour – gold, ambers and browns – is produced, richer, if not perhaps so pleasing to contemplate than the tender green of spring. The cascades played throughout the day and the scene looking westward from the cricket ground over the lakes towards the mansion was very grand. Both teams arrived at the Park station before noon and vehicles were in waiting to convey them to the cricket ground, where the band of the Brighton Volunteer Brigade of Artillery, under the leadership of Mr Devin had already taken up its position on the band stand, near his lordship's pavilion, and was performing popular selections of music in pleasing style. Shortly before one o'clock the two teams wended their way to the mansion, where, with a few of Lord Sheffield's personal friends, they were entertained to an elegant and recherche luncheon, served in the best style of Mr Councillor Booth, the famous caterer, of East-street, Brighton. Lord SHEFFIELD himself presided, having on his right hand the Middlesex team and on his left the New Zealanders. Among those also present at luncheon and on the ground were Lord Monk Bretton, Sir G. C. Shiffner, Sir William Grantham, Sir George Pocock, General Hepburn, Colonel Holden Rose, Colonel Dudley Sampson, Mr Blencowe, Major Campion, Colonel Tamplin, Mr Sclater, Mr R. M. Curteis, Dr Blakey, Mr Chatterton, Captain Hemming, Mr Cooke, Dr Jones and several gentlemen well known in the football world, including Messrs A. Bond, (president of the Rugby Union), F. I. Currey, S. E. Sleigh, F. W. Burnand, C. W. Alcock, W. Newham, H. L. Ashmore, J. A. Murdoch and H. Furniss (Lord's), &c. The teams were:

NEW ZEALANDERS - D. Gage (Poneke, Wellington) (back), W. Wynyard (North Shore), E. M'Causland (Gordon, Auckland) (captain) and C. Madigan (Grafton) (three-quarter backs), J. Keogh (Dunedin), F. Warbrick (Tauranga) and W. Elliott (Grafton, Auckland) (half-backs), T. Ellison (Poneke, Wellington), Art Warbrick (Malata), W. Karauria (Hawke's Bay), G. Williams (Poneke, Wellington), W. Anderson (Thames), H. Lee (Riverton), A. Webster (Hokianga) and R. Taiaroa (Dunedin) (forwards).

MIDDLESEX - A. S. Johnston (Blackheath) (back), W. E. Maclagan (London Scottish) (captain), A. J. Gould (Richmond) and G. C. Lindsay (London Scottish) (three-quarter backs), J. H. Roberts (Richmond) and D. G. Anderson (London Scottish) (half backs), F. C. Cousins (Richmond), G. L. Jeffery (Blackheath), R. E. Inglis (Blackheath), J. H. Hedderwick (London Scottish), T. W. Lockwood (Middlesex Wanderers), J. Hammond (Blackheath), J. G. Patterson (London Scottish), A. A. Surtees (Harlequins) and E. S. M'Euen (Old Cheltonians) (forwards). Umpires: Messrs J. Warbrick (New Zealand) and J. I. Ward (Middlesex County). Referee: Mr G. Rowland Hill (hon. sec. Rugby Football Union).

During the repast the Artillery band performed on the lawn. Following the precedent set by his lordship some years ago – and a very good one it is on such occasions – there were no speeches and therefore, shortly after two o'clock the whole party returned to the cricket ground where, before play commenced, the teams were photographed in groups, in front of Lord Sheffield's pavilion, by Messrs Hawkins of Brighton.

The goals were placed north and south in front of the refreshment pavilion and play commenced at five minutes past three.

Skating in the Park

In February 1895 Lord Sheffield engaged two champion skaters to race and to give an exhibition of skating in Sheffield Park. The contestants were Lindahl of Norway and Smart and the event happened a fortnight after the Great Cricket Match on Ice between Mr Blackman's XI and Mr A. Midgley's XI. The skating contest brought forth the following from the *Sussex Express*: 'Lord Sheffield has given many and varied treats to Sussex folk and his action on Saturday has only added another to the long list of debts which we owe his lordship but have unfortunately no expectation of ever being able to pay.'

Stoolball in the Park

Stoolball has many similarities to cricket and perhaps enjoys an even longer history. It was revived in Sussex in 1917 by Sir

The champion skaters Lindahl of Norway and Smart display their skills at Sheffield Park in 1895. (N. J. G. Sharp)

William Grantham, KC and flourishes to this day especially in Sussex and Kent where ladies and mixed teams compete. Lord Sheffield's adopted daughter, Mabel Attenborough, played stoolball and encouraged local girls of all classes to follow her example. In 1900 her all-female XI played against Lieut. F. Attenborough's XI, made up of gentlemen, at Sheffield Park: 'The two elevens with friends were kindly entertained to luncheon by Miss Attenborough, and also photographed in the ground during the interval.' The following is a typical account from the *Sussex Daily News* of 2 June 1905:

STOOLBALL AT SHEFFIELD PARK

A stoolball match was played on Wednesday at Sheffield Park between Miss Attenborough's XI and the Ringmer Stoolball Club, resulting in a draw. The play of the visitors was very slow and as many as nine of the home team were given a trial with the ball in the hope of getting them out. Miss L.Hyder took the three wickets that did fall for 14 runs in sixteen overs, of which seven were maidens. During the interval between the innings both teams were entertained to tea by Miss Attenborough.

Swimming in the Park

An aquatic tournament in one of the lakes involving members of the Brighton Swimming Club took place in 1892 for the entertainment of 2,000 Sunday School children.

11

Scandal in the Park
1886–1889

For Lord Sheffield, 1886 had been a busy year. In May he had entertained both the Australians and the Parsees from Bombay in grand cricket matches in his famously lavish style. In his capacity as president of Sussex CCC he had helped to acquire the freehold of the County Ground at Hove and had also assisted the cricketers of Eastbourne by sending his team to play in the inaugural match that marked the opening of the Saffrons cricket ground.

Lord Sheffield's name was revered amongst cricket lovers for his generous staging of important matches at his splendid ground to which the public were always admitted free of charge. His popularity can also be inferred from the guest lists at these matches. They show that his efforts were supported by a good section of the nobility and gentry of the county as well as by eminent people from the cricket world including the great W. G. Grace.

In the autumn of 1886, then, Lord Sheffield should have been satisfied that his considerable efforts in the cause of cricket were successful and widely appreciated. However, all was not well at home. According to a report in December:

> Lord Sheffield has been most annoyed over the past autumn by a series of anonymous accusations regarding his estate and has closed his cricket ground until the culprits are discovered and punished.

These anonymous accusations were in the form of poison pen letters, and they continued throughout the autumn and winter of 1886–87. In March 1887 it was reported that:

Lord Sheffield is becoming increasingly concerned regarding anonymous letters being sent to him, one referring to adultery and whoremongery in Sheffield Park. Another says everybody is laughing at the Lord and that he should get out and about to see how his cottages and farms have fallen down.

Lord Sheffield was distraught and in the same month he resigned his presidency of Sussex CCC and closed Sheffield Park for cricket for the forthcoming season of 1887. There was an immediate reaction to this regrettable state of affairs:

The decision of Lord Sheffield to have no more cricket matches at Sheffield Park this season has naturally excited a good deal of regret among the lovers of the game at Brighton. A petition is now going the round of the town asking that his lordship may reconsider his decision, and show, by his continued encouragement of the game, that he cannot be influenced by the anonymous rumours which are supposed to have caused him so much annoyance.

Happily Lord Sheffield was persuaded to withdraw his resignation of the presidency of Sussex CCC and the club's secretary issued the following press release:

Sir, I am sure the public will hear with great pleasure that I am authorised to say the Earl of Sheffield has, yielding to the earnest appeals addressed to him by lovers of cricket throughout the country, consented to at once withdraw the resignation of the presidency of the Sussex County Cricket Club, which he had felt compelled by annoying circumstances to tender to the committee as previously announced.

Yours &c
GEORGE GOLDSMITH
11 Prince Albert St.
March 31, 1887
Brighton

At a committee meeting of Sussex CCC on 21 April relief was expressed that Lord Sheffield had withdrawn his resignation and it was felt that the chairman, W. H. Campion, should write to convey the club's sympathy:

> The Committee of the Sussex County Cricket Club have requested me to express to you their very great regret at the serious annoyance which you have recently experienced and their sincere sympathy with you under these painful circumstances – and that they have heard with great satisfaction that you will not allow them to interrupt the relations which have so long existed between you and our Club.

Lord Sheffield's reply is preserved in the Sussex CCC minute book:

> Sheffield Park
> April 22, 1887
> Dear Campion,
> I am extremely obliged for the Resolution you have forwarded to me and passed by the Committee of the Sussex County C. Club.
> It is very gratifying to me to receive it and I cordially reciprocate the kindly feeling expressed in it.
>
> > Believe me
> > Sincerely yours
> > Sheffield

In May, 1887 Lord Sheffield sent his cricket team to play a match against Brighton Brunswick on the occasion of the formal opening of the cricket ground at Preston Park near Brighton, although he did not attend. In the after-dinner proceedings at the match, however, he received a vote of support from the Mayor and Corporation of Brighton and the town generally when references were made to events of an 'annoying and irritating character' to Lord Sheffield.

Public meeting at Fletching
In May Fletching was preparing to celebrate Queen Victoria's golden jubilee but Lord Sheffield reluctantly withdrew his patronage

Clapwater, Fletching. (B. Gregory)

'for causes with which everyone is acquainted' and it appears that the letters were continuing.

By September he was so aggrieved that he announced his intention to move from Sheffield Park. This news created a stir and a public meeting was called at the National School in Fletching 'to express outrage at the reprehensible letters and to beg the Earl to stay at Sheffield Park'. The meeting was advertised in the *Sussex Agricultural Express* where it was urgently requested 'that all persons of every class in the entire neighbourhood should make an earnest effort to attend'. Lord Sheffield's provision of employment for labourers was a major economic factor and the absence of cricket would reduce many local incomes.

However, before the date of the meeting Lord Sheffield sent a telegram to Rev. Attenborough demanding action not words and scorning any suggestion that he should spend his money amongst those who failed to assist him when he had appealed to them. He 'would be so bitter and outspoken that matters would be ten times worse afterwards than before'.

The meeting was then condemned by Lord Sheffield as a 'mischievous farce' and faced with such implacable hostility there was no alternative but to cancel it.

The Rose & Crown, Fletching. (B. Gregory)

Mr Churchwarden Gibbons

One local man, Gibbons, was not going to attend any meeting in support of Lord Sheffield and he wrote an indignant letter claiming that he had been insulted by the earl:

To: The Right Honourable the Earl of Sheffield

Mr Churchwarden Gibbons would wish the Earl of Sheffield to know he had nothing whatever to do with the meeting called, and if he thinks he would attend a meeting to express sympathy with such a farce, he is vastly mistaken. If the Earl of Sheffield has anything to say of or to Mr Churchwarden Gibbons, his address is Clapwater, Fletching, Sussex, but at the same time he would caution him how he uses his names in public, or to his private friends, as his pen and words may have the effect of causing him, the Earl of Sheffield, further trouble. Mr Gibbons has been over 50 years in Fletching, and never insulted in such a cowardly manner before. Had any farm labourer conducted the correspondence for the Earl of Sheffield, it would have been done in a more dignified style and more noble spirit.

Clapwater

Sept. 12th, 1887

It seems that Mr Gibbons was suspected of being behind the anonymous letters because on receipt of the above letter Lord Sheffield forwarded it to the newspapers together with some withering comments of his own, including:

> I do not of course suppose that the Churchwarden had anything to do with the 'anonymous letters', but if anyone read the 'anonymous letters' and then compared them with the Churchwarden's letter, he would not be at a loss to understand why the Churchwarden's sympathies would naturally be with those whose style and taste, and possibly opinions, are like his own.

There is no record of a further exchange with Mr Gibbons or of any further letters during early 1888 but at a Sussex CCC committee meeting on 5 April, Grover Ashby (treasurer) reported Lord Sheffield's intention to withdraw his subscription for the future 'under certain circumstances'. This suggests that all was not well and there was every likelihood that the Australian cricketers would not be entertained as usual at Sheffield Park in May.

In the autumn Lord Sheffield fulfilled his wish to host the touring Maori rugby footballers. The match took place on 22 October but the park was closed to the general public 'on account of the annoyance to which his lordship, we regret to hear, continues to be exposed on the part of local people'. The report went on: 'So long as this continues, the general public will not be admitted to the park on these occasions.' A report of the match stated that:

> Sheffield Park was guarded against other than privileged visitors with the care which would be exercised in the event of an Imperial visit within the dominions of the Tsar and this exercise provoked further abuse in the pages of a London sporting paper.

Jack the Ripper 1888

If the public felt that the rugby match was an indication that normality was slowly returning to Sheffield Park they were in for a shock. At the end of October, while the Whitechapel-murders in London were at their height another letter arrived with the intention of making the maximum impact. The letter was so menacing that Lord Sheffield offered a reward of £250 for information leading to the writer's arrest. He also had a facsimile copy on display and released it to the press:

England
October 27th 1888
Dear Lord Sheffield,
I am sorry, but feeling it my duty to let you know, as I do not think you do, or you would not have the heart to turn out an old tenant like poor Mrs Grover out of her home after such a hard struggle to maintain and bring up her family. Not only that, but allowing anyone to get an honest living there in the butchering line, or that have done for a great number of years. But it seems to me as though you and your faithful steward want it all, and if you had my wish you would get more than you wanted.

Remember, this is a warning to you, but at the same time I should be much obliged to you if you can arrange it for your steward to sleep under the same roof as yourself on Monday night, October 29th, or else I shall have to bring an assistant. My knife is nice and sharp. Oh for a gentleman this time instead of a lady. I am sorry for troubling you, but don't forget the 29th.

I remain
Yours truly,
JACK THE RIPPER

It was not difficult to deduce that the letter came from a local butcher taking up a grievance of Mrs Grover, an elderly tenant of Lord Sheffield. The letter writer had to be Edward Grover, formerly a butcher using a slaughter house on the smallholding of his unfortunate mother but now a labourer on the Belaggio estate near Lingfield. The letter was particularly hurtful to Lord Sheffield because he had wanted Mrs Grover to stay in her own house for as long as possible. Only when the Fletching surgeon, Mr R. Gravely, realised that the old lady was incapable of looking after herself was she advised to move in with another son, Alfred.

Edward Grover

Grover claimed on two separate occasions that he had written the letter. Walking down Fletching High Street near the Rose & Crown on 3 November he met Henry Fuller (the local Prudential insurance agent) and Thomas Venus (a Piltdown plumber) and admitted that he wrote the letter. Later that afternoon inside the Rose & Crown, Grover was with Thomas Bourne (a tenant farmer on the Sheffield Park estate), Mark Newnham and Robert Welfare. When Bourne read out the letter from the newspaper, Grover admitted it again and added:

> Lord Sheffield ought to be shot; if I had a gun I would shoot him. I will on Monday. The —- ought to be shot. He's no good in this place. I will give anybody a sovereign to shoot him. If no-one will shoot him I will myself.

Bourne stepped outside, wrote down Grover's speech and persuaded the others to sign it. He then handed his notebook to Mr Butcher, the Brighton detective who was engaged by Lord Sheffield to investigate the letter.

Although the evidence was taken very seriously it took nearly three weeks for the police to call at Grover's lodgings in East Grinstead. On being arrested Grover exclaimed:

> I never threatened to murder Lord Sheffield; if I did I must have been drunk at the time.

Grover then gave the police the slip by climbing from an upstairs window and he later admitted walking the 12 miles back to Fletching without shoes.

The next day PC Barnard visited Grover's house opposite Fletching church but he again escaped after his wife denied that he was at home. Supt. Diplock and Sergt. Tom Huggett from Uckfield made enquiries locally and the sergeant heard that Grover was being harboured at Splayne's Green by the family of Henry Packham, who, like Grover, lived at Fletching, lodged at East Grinstead and worked at Belaggio. Det. Sgt Goldsack was summoned specially from Eastbourne and two constables accompanied Sgt. Huggett.

Despite the Packhams protesting Grover's absence, Huggett found him in a locked attic and conveyed him into custody at Uckfield. The following afternoon, Monday 26 November, Grover appeared at the Magistrates' Court in the packed public hall at Uckfield where he was described as 'an intelligent looking man in the prime of life, apparently of the better class of labourers'. The charge he faced was that on 5 November

> he did wickedly and unlawfully solicit, encourage, persuade or endeavour and propose to divers persons (Bourne, Newnham, Venus, Fuller, Greening and Welfare) to murder the Right Hon. Henry North, Earl of Sheffield against the peace of our Sovereign Lady the Queen, her Crown, and dignity.

Grover's application for bail was refused because of his liability to a sentence of penal servitude if convicted and his record of absconding.

His case was heard the next day. Lord Sheffield had H. J. Verrall (of Messrs Verrall & Borlase of Brighton) prosecuting with Marshall Hall ('The Great Defender' 1857–1927) acting on their behalf in court. For the defence another celebrated lawyer, J. K. Nye, acknowledged the distress the letters had caused Lord Sheffield but portrayed Grover as overwrought rather than malicious.

After being remanded Grover was sent for trial at Lewes Assizes on 18 December for incitement to murder. The charge of sending the anonymous letter about his mother was dropped after Nye objected to Marshall Hall asking Henry Fuller if he suspected Grover. There was also a likelihood that Lord Sheffield's affairs concerning his tenants could be debated.

At Lewes Lord Sheffield's stance had softened because Grover had uttered the offending words in a public house making it hard to prove serious intent. Grover pleaded that his bragging was that of a half-drunken man and expressed deep regret. The judge trusted that Lord Sheffield would not be annoyed any more by him and that he would be severely punished if brought up again with similar charges. After a verdict of not guilty Edward Grover was discharged and although the letters persisted they faded from prominence.

Tiresome Ruffians & Cowardly Brutes

While the poison pen letters were being received, Lord Sheffield made persistent attempts to resign the presidency of Sussex CCC. It was only by gentle diplomacy that he remained in office but his generous annual contributions appear to have ceased at this time.

A few months after Grover's trial at Lewes Assizes Lord Sheffield was still in a state of high indignation and he wrote a letter to the new Sussex CCC secretary, William Newham, who read it at the club's annual meeting at the Town Hall, Brighton on 18 April 1889. It appeared that letters threatening assassination were still being received:

Dear Mr Newham

As the County Cricket Club is, I think, entitled to ask and to know the reason why I, though President of the Club, have withdrawn my subscription, I beg to state that it is because Sussex people for the last two years and a half have been amusing themselves by pestering me with anonymous letters, and lately with letters containing serious threats of assassination. These tiresome ruffians live in the parish of Fletching or Maresfield. I have done my utmost to bring them to book in order to put an end to a state of things, not only injurious to cricket but to other local interests. But, owing to the Fletching people giving me not the slightest practical assistance, and not only that, but in some cases to their doing what they could to prevent information being brought to me, and, in other cases to their trying even to injure those who brought it, and otherwise tried to help me, to such a degree that those who brought it came to me in downright fear and trembling; the task of bringing the offenders to light has been very difficult, and has been thwarted by Sussex people as much as possible, especially by those who ought to have aided me. It is under these circumstances, and feeling deeply the manner in which I have been treated by these Sussex people, so deeply that, perhaps the action I am taking is more natural and excusable than strictly logical, I have decided to withdraw all subscriptions from all Sussex public objects until these cowardly brutes are discovered and punished. I may add that as soon as these ruffians, who live in Fletching, have been punished, I shall gladly continue to subscribe to your funds, and so glad shall I be to do so under the altered circumstances that I will increase the amount to £300 annually. I am sorry to have had to refer to my personal and individual concerns at all, but it would have been impossible to have given the full and proper explanation to the meeting, which I think they have a right to expect, without doing so.

Believe me,
Very truly yours etc
London, April 16
SHEFFIELD

The Sussex members resolved to forward a letter to Lord Sheffield expressing the sympathy of the meeting and acknowledging the great support that he had given for many years to Sussex cricket.

Return of the Australians

It had been suggested that the anonymous letters began to appear when Lord Sheffield's ten-year programme of winter work on his estate had been completed. The local workforce undoubtedly found it difficult to make ends meet in the winter and some labourers may have been resentful.

At last the letters ceased and Lord Sheffield was able to invite the Australian cricketers of 1890 to Sheffield Park, a treat not extended to their immediate predecessors. In May the grounds were open to the public once again but with a few exceptions:

We are authorised to state that the park will on those days be open to the general public, and indeed to all comers with only a few local exceptions. Of course Lord Sheffield, as on former occasions, reserves the right of refusing admission to any one whose presence, in his opinion, is not desirable.

Lord Sheffield's 'Partner'

It is difficult to assess Lord Sheffield's position in these difficult years for him. Certainly he was quick to write to the newspapers in high dudgeon but he also showed a certain amount of restraint and compassion in the Grover affair. He believed that certain newspapers were more favourable towards him than others partly based on political considerations.

The newspaper *Cricket: A Weekly Record of The Game* recorded some of the incidents involving the anonymous letters because of Lord Sheffield's position as Sussex CCC president. It is though a little surprising to find a later report in its issue dated 21 April 1892 that can only be described as rumour mongering. Lord Sheffield was returning from his tour of Australia and *Cricket*'s readers were informed:

> LORD SHEFFIELD followed in the P & O Steamer, the *Arcadia*, returning without the partner anyone who did not know him would have been led to expect from the cablegrams which reached here from Australia. Rumour has been true to her proverbial character of untruthfulness once more, for Lord Sheffield is coming back to England single as he left it.

The identity of the 'partner' remained a mystery but in the language of the day it can be inferred that the partner was female and because of his stated intention to return to Tasmania in a year's time, it may be assumed that Lord Sheffield had met and befriended a Tasmanian lady. This and the heat on mainland Australia would explain his reluctance to travel around the country with his team.

The story probably stemmed from journalistic licence exercised by some reporters but nearer to home in 1895, an official announcement was made concerning Lord Sheffield that caused a major stir among local residents and gave rise to a great deal of speculation.

12

The Vicar's Daughter

Elements of Lord Sheffield's private life have been discussed briefly earlier in this story. Much of it can be summarised as without foundation but one established fact that had the tongues wagging in Sheffield Park and beyond is that in 1895 Lord Sheffield, aged 63, adopted as his daughter Miss Mabel Strey Attenborough, aged 24, the eldest daughter of the Vicar of Fletching. Miss Attenborough left the family home to live at Sheffield Park and it was announced that a suitable chaperone had been engaged. She was to remain there as companion and hostess until Lord Sheffield's death in 1909.

The convenience of staying at Sheffield Park was obvious and it may be that for the sake of Victorian propriety and Lord Sheffield's sensitivities the course of adoption was agreed. It is not recorded what the views were of Miss Attenborough's family but it does appear at this distance of time to be an unusual arrangement.

Before the death of the earl's mother in 1889, Mabel (always known as May) Attenborough was often asked to present prizes and gifts to the villagers and tenants at the various functions at Sheffield Park. She appears to have been a charming, accomplished young woman.

Her parents were the Rev. William Frederick Attenborough and his wife, Sarah, who came to Fletching in 1863 from the curacy of Runcorn, where they had met and married. William had been educated at St John's College, Cambridge (BA 1849, MA 1852) and was ordained deacon in 1854 and priest in 1855. After nine years at Runcorn the couple arrived at the Vicarage, Fletching when he was 36 and in a short space of time their five children were born: Henry (1867), Mabel (1870), Ethel (1871), Hilda (1873) and Frederick (1875). The family was complete with Rev. Attenborough's unmarried sister, Amelia.

Miss Mabel Attenborough (1870–1954)
(Mrs H. Rawlings)

William's duties included being domestic chaplain to the Earl of Sheffield (father and son), although there is evidence of a dispute in 1889. He 'displayed more than ordinary interest in everything appertaining to the parish church and promoted in every possible way the well being of the national schools'. From 1866 to 1871 he was Diocesan Inspector of Schools for the Chailey Deanery and he partly rebuilt the parish school at Fletching. When he died in 1898 his widow was presented with the following address:

We, the parishioners of Fletching, desire to express our deep sorrow and sympathy with you and your family in the sad bereavement you have sustained by the lamented death of our long-respected vicar, the Rev. W. F. Attenborough, who has ministered in this parish for over 35 years, and who, by his universal kindness, has won the love and esteem of all who knew him, and whose memory we shall ever cherish with deepest respect. That strength will be given you to bear your greatest trial is the earnest prayer of . . .
[a long list of signatures followed.]

A sorrowing Sarah Attenborough was comforted by her family and graciously replied:

> My dear friends and his friends, I feel I must personally thank you although it is so hard to do so. We shall never forget the beauty of the offering you all sent as a last token of affection to one we all loved so well. He took up the cross so bravely, whatever it might be. I think it was the heaviest when he had to sit powerless and could not teach or work for you any more. He loved his people and his beautiful church more than any earthly possession and sought nothing beyond them in this world, and when he thought of things done and left undone he simply said, 'I have always tried to do my best.' He chose his own resting place to be as near as possible to his church and to the path he had traversed so often. There his body 'Rests in Peace' and every soul that continues in well-doing or turns from any known sin from his teaching will add one more jewel to his everlasting crown. Your heartfelt sympathy touched us all greatly. We are bound together by a common sorrow and we as a family shall always remain your grateful friends.
>
> SARAH ATTENBOROUGH
Fletching Vicarage

There is a record of Rev. Attenborough playing cricket for Sheffield Park as early as 1869 and he appeared for the team for many years. He was a Nottingham man by birth and it is easy to picture him discussing cricket with Alfred Shaw, Rev. Walter Summers (vicar of nearby Danehill), and, of course, Lord Sheffield. There is a delightful photograph of Rev. Attenborough and his son Harry when they appeared for John Gilbert's team against Rev. Summers' team in 1886. When William Attenborough died, Lord Sheffield provided a large house, 'White Lodge', in Fletching for his widow, son and two youngest daughters.

However, his eldest daughter, May, was firmly established at Sheffield Park. She had proved to be a capable organiser long before her adoption by Lord Sheffield and emulated her father's encouragement of the local children. In 1893 she started a cricket club known as 'Miss May Attenborough's Fletching Junior CC'. This was taken seriously and results and averages appeared in local newspapers. In 1894 the results (6 wins, 3 losses) were identical to the initial season and the club provided competitive cricket for many local boys – Welfare, Diplock, Fuller, Moore – whose fathers were all well known to Lord Sheffield. The opposition included junior teams from Newick, Nutley, Maresfield, Horsted Keynes and Danehill. Only one home match was played at Sheffield Park but the Park was used more frequently in later seasons. As late as 1907 there is a report of a junior match at Sheffield Park, by kind permission of Lord Sheffield, when the Fletching and Danehill boys were entertained to tea.

May Attenborough also organised stoolball matches for the ladies and from 1900 (at least) there are stoolball reports involving her XI against local rivals such as Cowfold, Danehill and Glynde. In 1900 Miss Attenborough's XI (ladies) competed against her brother's XI (Lieutenant Frederick Attenborough) at Sheffield Park when 'the two elevens with friends were kindly entertained to luncheon by Miss Attenborough and also photographed on the ground during the interval'.

Concern for local children occupied much of Miss Attenborough's time, which was something she shared with her father and Lord Sheffield. In 1896 there was a school treat for 230 children at Sheffield Park and William Moore's diary for July 29 records: 'Had tea on the Lawn round Fountain. Miss Attenborough took Photos of them all before tea. After children had tea they went to the Cricket Ground where Swings, rounders, stoolball, cricket, bowls and French and English was played until 8 o'clock when Buns were served out to all of them before returning home.'

The following winter was notable for a different style of entertainment when the pantomime *Aladdin* was performed at the riding school at Sheffield Park. The school had been transformed into a theatre with curtains, stage, footlights and comfortable seating: 'These entertainments are given annually by Lord Sheffield and Miss Attenborough to the villagers of Fletching, the schoolchildren and his lordship's tenants and servants.' The pantomime was produced and stage-managed by the talented May Attenborough who also took the

Mrs Sarah Attenborough (1824–1907)
(Mrs H. Rawlings)

part of Aladdin. Her brother Frederick, home on leave from the navy, was Widow Twankey and sister Hilda impersonated the Vizier 'complete with moustache, pig-tail and enormous spectacles'. The press report continues: 'The children's ballet was one of the prettiest sights ever seen in private theatricals . . . a crowd of little girls all differently dressed in muslin, chiffon and silk dancing in constantly changing lights.' The little boys had to be content with parts in a chorus of mandarins but the three evening performances and a matinee proved a great spectacle for the children.

Life at Sheffield Park was considerably enhanced by Miss Attenborough's presence. In 1897 a report of the Sheffield Park Flower Show noted that 'Miss Attenborough, who had the entire management of the show is deserving of the highest praise.' The following year the flower show, 'usually organised by Miss Attenborough', was cancelled because of the death of her father. In 1896 she presided over a jumble sale at Fletching School having acted in a similar capacity with Mrs W. L. Murdoch at Lord Sheffield's stall at the Sussex CCC bazaar in 1894.

In 1896 William Moore's diary records May Attenborough on shooting parties at Sheffield Park with Alfred Shaw, Captain Donovan, Mr Verrall, Major Broomfield and Thomas Colgate when the quarry comprised wild ducks, birds and rabbits. In the same year she took much interest in the new pheasantry. Moore's diary also noted: '12 Oct Started planting roses in Miss May's oval bed in the grounds; 30 Nov Labelled Miss May's roses and oak tree on lawn' The diary also records a momentous occasion on 23 October: 'Planted on the Lawn 1 Oak to commemorate the visit of HRH The Prince of Wales to Sheffield Park on May 11, 1896. Lord Sheffield, Miss Attenborough, self and Reed and Mitchell planted it 4pm.'

The historic visit of the Prince had involved Miss Attenborough in organising the extensive floral decorations and arches at Sheffield Park and under her supervision a large number of women and children had been employed in making festoons involving twenty thousand bunches of wild flowers. When the future King was entertained to lunch in a marquee on the cricket ground May Attenborough was on the top table and her father, Aunt Amelia and sister Hilda were also present.

William Moore's diary hints at a very busy year for Lord Sheffield's charming young companion and he also briefly mentions short visits to Belgium, Ryde, London and Brighton.

During her years at Sheffield Park (1895–1909) May Attenborough's energies and abilities were much in evidence. During this time her busy life was saddened by the deaths of her father (1898), Aunt Amelia (1900) and mother (1907). Lord Sheffield too, as he became older began to suffer from heart problems, and often spent his winters abroad as a consequence. When he died in 1909 Miss Attenborough left Sheffield Park but her generous guardian had arranged for her to move to 'Clinton Lodge' in Fletching High Street.

She continued to work for the people of Fletching, especially the schoolchildren, and among other good deeds she helped institute a parish nurse for Fletching and arranged a splendid tea for the village to celebrate the 1911 coronation: 'In anything for the good of Fletching Miss Attenborough was the first to give her valuable assistance and her energy, ability and enthusiasm had on many occasions been used for the happiness of the parishioners.'

In 1912, three years after the death of Lord Sheffield, May Attenborough, now 42 years old, prompted 'joyous scenes at Fletching' by her marriage to G. Roy Fitzpatrick, an officer of the 3rd Battalion Welsh Regiment, whose parents lived in Highgate, London. It is not known how or where they met but it is clear that Miss Attenborough had fallen in love with a handsome soldier. When told that the local people felt that her fiancé was very nice, she replied that she thought that he was 'extraordinarily nice'.

Two days before the July wedding all roads led to Fletching School when the parishioners' handsome wedding gift was presented by Rev. Hood, Vicar of Fletching:

> The large gathering, representative of practically every family in the village, showed how strong is the bond of affection existing between the parishioners and the bride, and the presence of so many children brought to mind the many happy occasions on which Miss May Attenborough has ministered to their enjoyment and well being. No wedding presentation was ever taken up with greater eagerness and the fact that the names of 288 subscribers appeared on one address and 124 school children on the other bore testimony to the great appreciation of Miss Attenborough's efforts for the welfare of Fletching and to the wide spread desire for her future happiness.

The two addresses read as follows, the second one being illuminated by Hilda Attenborough:

> We, the parishioners of Fletching, beg to offer to Miss M. S. Attenborough our hearty good wishes and congratulations on the occasion of her marriage, July 3rd, 1912 and ask her acceptance of this address, together with a silver kettle, as a token of our warm appreciation of the keen interest she has always shown in the welfare and happiness of the parishioners.
>
> We, the children of Fletching National Schools, desire to take this opportunity of acknowledging the many kindnesses we have received

G. R. Fitzpatrick (Mrs H. Rawlings)

from Miss Attenborough and to offer her our best wishes and congratulations on the occasion of her marriage, July 3rd, 1912.

At eight o'clock on her wedding morning the bride attended a choral service at Fletching Church with several of her relatives and friends who were staying at 'Clinton Lodge'. The wedding though was held at Herons Ghyll, some miles distant, in the Catholic church because Roy Fitzpatrick belonged to that communion. The bridal party and guests made the journey in motor cars, and never before had Fletching seen so many of those vehicles.

Early in the morning the inhabitants were busily engaged in hanging out flags and emblems of good luck and from one end of the street to the other the scene was quite enchanting. After the service at Herons Ghyll the Fletching church bells rang merrily and a warm welcome awaited the happy couple. The car slowed down as it reached the village and Mr and Mrs Fitzpatrick acknowledged in the happiest manner the kindly greetings they received on all sides: 'the school boys cheered them in hearty fashion and a charming scene

The White House, Fletching can be seen behind the Attenborough graves in the churchyard. (Mrs H. Rawlings)

was enacted when they reached Clinton Lodge. About fifty school girls dressed in white lined the footpath and strewed roses in the way of the bride and bridegroom.'

The newlyweds later motored to Haywards Heath en route for London and North Wales for the honeymoon.

Lieutenant and Mrs Roy Fitzpatrick remained at 'Clinton Lodge' after their marriage pursuing their interests in the Welsh Regiment and village life respectively.

After only two years of marriage Great Britain was at war with Germany and Lieutenant Fitzpatrick (3rd Battalion Welsh Regiment) left England with the Expeditionary Force on 12 August 1914 and was attached to the 2nd Battalion Welsh Regiment. Six weeks later he was killed in action at an unspecified location, presumably France, and the newspaper cursorily reported that 'A well known Fletching lady is bereaved by the death of her husband, Lieutenant Fitzpatrick.' A further report added that 'the death had aroused much local sympathy for the widow, who is well known and highly esteemed in the district.' The body had been returned to England and the grieving widow and her sisters attended a requiem Mass at the Uckfield Catholic church on 23 September.

On the day that the Sussex cricketer and Indian maharaja, Ranjitsinhji, offered a thousand men to the Allies, the *Sussex Express* reported a second Mass on 1 October for poor Fitzpatrick at Herons Ghyll – the scene of his joyous wedding in 1912. At the east end of the nave a catafalque had been erected and this was covered with the Union Jack on which rested the helmet, sash and sword belt of the deceased. Over the altar were grouped the flags of England, France and Belgium and above them was a laurel wreath surmounted with palm. On the church tower the flag of the Fitzpatricks floated at half mast.

It was later reported that, a fortnight before he was killed, Lieutenant Fitzpatrick had obtained his promotion to the rank of Captain.

The death of Captain Fitzpatrick and the great sadness of the loss of other young men from Fletching brings the curtain down on this part of the eventful life of the Vicar's daughter. Universally loved, she employed her many talents for the benefit of those less fortunate. She had dined with the future King Edward VII, been the mistress of a great estate and found love – but it had all been taken from her.

Her later life is difficult to unravel but after nursing wounded soldiers she married Major Willoughby Tottenham towards the end of the Great War and they later moved to Fiji where she died in 1954, aged 84.

Some of the momentous events in May Attenborough's life were recorded in her scrapbook, largely in the form of press cuttings. Some events at Sheffield Park are also recorded. The precious scrapbook is now kept locally and there is a copy in the East Sussex Record Office.

The Attenborough graves can still be seen close to Fletching Church by the path to the entrance so well trodden by Rev. William Attenborough for 35 years. Here one can pay tribute to May's father, mother and Aunt Amelia and May's siblings Hilda (died 1943), Frederick (died 1951) and Ethel (died 1952).

13

Disputes in the Park

The remarkable generosity of Lord Sheffield contrasted unfavourably with a capacity to demand his own way. If he failed to achieve this he was quick to take offence and reacted immediately by writing strongly worded letters or telegrams.

In his role as president of Sussex CCC he was involved in a dispute with Henry Perkins, Secretary of the Marylebone Cricket Club, and arranged for the correspondence to be published. He threatened to resign from Sussex CCC if John Raven remained on the committee after a selection blunder and he managed to quarrel with the local Brighton cricket clubs after increasing subscriptions to help pay for the freehold of the present County Ground at Hove.

Nearer to home there was some bitter rivalry with the Maryon-Wilsons, fellow landowners in Fletching, and there is a report in 1889 that a letter of complaint from Lord Sheffield caused uproar in the Fletching vestry. The letter concerned a robbery at Fletching Church three years previously when Lord Sheffield had criticised a churchwarden for refusing to assist in the investigations. The vicar of Fletching, William Attenborough, regarded the earl's letter as an attack on his chairmanship.

The amiable England cricket captain Andrew Stoddart was also the subject of a bitter dispute that led to the exclusion of all the members of the England team from Sheffield Park.

To a disinterested onlooker most of the disputes that raised Lord Sheffield's blood pressure would seem trivial. To his Lordship they gave reasons aplenty to man the barricades.

The 'battle' of Shefield Park 1894

In the reports of the grand matches at Sheffield Park there are references to Lord Sheffield's generous treatment of the horse-drawn cab drivers who took spectators from the station to the cricket ground – 'even cabmen ferrying visitors to the games were fed at his expense'. In 1894, however, that privilege appears to have been withdrawn and the cab drivers were angry.

The occasion was the first ever match played by a South African team in England. Lord Sheffield's XI had entertained the tourists in a two-day match but when the South African team were leaving Sheffield Park at the end of the match there was an ugly confrontation with the cab drivers. Arthur Seccull, a member of the team, recalled the incident:

> We were billeted at the Hotel Metropole in Brighton as the guests of Lord Sheffield and our host had arranged for special conveyances to take the team to the station after each day's play. His Lordship had forbidden any ordinary carriages for hire to enter the estate. This evidently caused great annoyance to the cabbies who were plying for hire and who had lost innumerable fares in consequence. To our astonishment, on leaving the estate on the last day we found the cabbies had obstructed the pathway, presumably with the object of forcing us to miss the train to Brighton and to use their conveyances afterwards for this purpose. They had completely blockaded the fairway with their vehicles and we found ourselves held up by a number of cabbies ready with picks and shovels. Some dirty work looked imminent. Fearing that damage might be done and finding it quite impossible to pass, we determined on battle and declared war. Boy Johnson and myself led the attack, followed by other members of the team. On jumping from our carriages we were greeted with all kinds of missiles and various weapons were used against us. After a desperate fight we managed to push the enemy back and to clear their cabs away. Breaking through their lines amidst ringing cheers, we just succeeded in catching our train after a record drive.

Dispute with A. E. Stoddart 1895

Stoddart was a famous Middlesex and England batsman and he had been a member of Lord Sheffield's team in Australia on the 1891–92 tour. Three years later he captained the England team on their next visit there and won the fifth Test match to take the series 3-2. After his team had played its final match in Melbourne and were about to start for Adelaide on the way home, Lord Sheffield cabled Stoddart to invite his team to play a match at Sheffield Park against the next XI of England.

Stoddart replied to Lord Sheffield stating that he was unable to accept the invitation. His reason was that F. G. J. Ford had arranged to return home via Japan, Leslie Gay intended to stay in Ceylon and A. C. MacLaren intended to remain in Australia, but Stoddart had omitted mentioning these matters in his reply because of pressure of business and illness. Back in England the victorious captain decided to visit Lord Sheffield to explain why he had declined the invitation but, before he could do so, Lord Sheffield, who was strongly incensed by Stoddart's refusal, ended all friendly contact between the two. It was said that the sympathies of the leading English cricketers were entirely with Stoddart who, they pointed out, was the last person wilfully to give offence.

However when Lord Sheffield selected his team for the famous visit of the 1896 Australians, not one member of Stoddart's team was included.

A dispute with Walter Quaife 1891

Walter Quaife (1864–1943) was a successful young Sussex professional from Newhaven who would later be overshadowed by his younger brother William. Walter first appeared in the Sheffield Park trial matches in 1884 and made his county debut the same year. In 1887 he became the first ever Sussex player to score 1,000 runs in a season and he represented the Players against the Gentlemen at Lord's in 1890 when Albert Craig ('The Surrey Poet') published the following:

Walter Quaife (1864–1943) (N. J. G. Sharp)

QUAIFE
The Popular Sussex Batsman's Success
at LORD'S, JULY 7th 1890, in the
Gentlemen v Players Match

Gallant Quaife ! 'Tis right to cheer you
When we view your past career
Friendly foes have cause to fear you
When you at your post appear.
In each sharp decisive struggle,
In each stiff, unflinching fray,
Doubtings vanish like a bubble,
Vain misgivings melt away . . .

Walter Quaife was also described as a fair medium-paced change bowler and in 1888, bowling with Walter Humphreys, he helped Heron's Ghyll dismiss Nutley for 4 and 6!

In 1891 the 27-year-old Quaife was in his prime, but halfway through the season he was dismissed from the Sussex team when the club's committee summoned him to answer rumours that he was qualifying for Warwickshire. Quaife refused to answer but later claimed that when the Sussex CCC secretary William Newham had asked him the same question at Tonbridge, Newham had threatened to knock him down with a bat. Quaife justified his approach to Warwickshire on the grounds that his application to the Sussex CCC committee for winter employment two years previously had, because of an incapacity, been unsuccessful. For five successive winters he had lived entirely on his summer earnings.

It is at this point in the sorry affair that Lord Sheffield becomes involved. Quaife wrote a letter to the *Sportsman* to justify his actions and concluded thus:

> I wish to thank the right honourable the Earl of Sheffield for the benefits which, in common with the other members of the county team, I have received from the practice from Mr Shaw, and for which his lordship has been generous enough to pay. This is, however, the full extent of my indebtedness. I have never received any special practice at his lordship's expense. His lordship has, however, taken consistent action in the matter by cutting off my younger brother from the benefit of that practice in consequence of my leaving Sussex, and he has informed the chairman of the cricket committee of my native town that, unless I resign membership of the club to which I have belonged since its formation, he will withdraw any support which he may have felt inclined to give.
>
> I am yours &c
9 South-road
W.QUAIFE
Newhaven
July 21

Lord Sheffield was outraged by Quaife's conduct and as president of Newhaven Cricket Club he demanded Quaife's resignation from his local club in the following two letters:

Sheffield Park
July 25th

DEAR SIR – in consequence of one of the members of the
Newhaven Cricket Club, a professional, W. Quaife, having received
various payments of money from me on the understanding that he
was willing to continue (if asked) to play for the county of Sussex,
and having, as I understand, for a long time been endeavouring to
complete arrangements for playing for another county, I regret to say
that I cannot any longer remain president of the Club if this man
continues to be a member of it.

Yours faithfully
SHEFFIELD

Sheffield Park
July 28th

DEAR SIR – Since sending to you my first letter, Quaife has
addressed a letter to the public journals in which he very needlessly
introduces my name, and he does so in a manner which at once
relieves me of any reluctance I might otherwise have felt to give you
the fullest account of the conduct of this young professional towards
me. He seems, or pretends, not to know or understand the real
reasons why I decline to remain in the same Club with him as a
member. As I informed you in my first letter, they are not cricketing
reasons at all. Quaife only did what was entirely within his undoubted
rights to do, however dishonourable we may think his whole conduct,
and I should not have been justified in withdrawing from your
presidency and club simply because Quaife had pursued a course
which, however regrettable, it was within his undoubted right to
pursue. My reasons were of a more personal and entirely a grave
character. I found, I am sorry to say, that Quaife had been in the habit
of receiving payments of money from Shaw during the last two years
which would never have been paid or authorised by me if Quaife had
not concealed from me the fact that he was at that very time
attempting to qualify for other counties. It was under this *suppressio*

veri, which in this case was a distinct *suggestio falsi*, that I paid this man's expenses on the occasion of his 'special practice' with Shaw – this very special practice which he has now the absurd effrontery to try to repudiate. He knew perfectly well that if he had told me that he was negotiating with other counties I should not have paid one farthing of his expenses. He concealed the fact and took my money.

On these grounds I decline to remain the President or member of a Club which numbers such a professional amongst its members.

Yours faithfully
SHEFFIELD

The Newhaven CC committee, faced with Lord Sheffield's ultimatum, were forced to ask Walter Quaife to resign his membership but the young professional responded to Lord Sheffield by writing to the *Birmingham Daily Mail*:

Alfred Shaw is engaged to coach all those players who are fortunate enough to have their names placed upon Lord Sheffield's 'special practice list.' For this 'special practice' I received the sum of 5s 6d per day when not engaged in county matches - 2s 6d of which I paid for rail fare, and usually about another 2s for refreshments. I generally travelled by the eleven o'clock train from Newhaven, and returned at seven in the evening, so that for the eight hours I was away from home I had a bonus of one shilling. I will correct yet another error which the public might possibly be led to believe – viz. that I have been receiving these aforesaid payments for the past two years while qualifying for another county. As a matter of fact my qualification for Warwickshire only began in April last. My terrible offence, as far as I can judge, is this – since I began my qualification for Warwickshire I have had eight practices from Shaw, for which I have received the ordinary sum of 5s 6d per day. I do not intend now, or at any other time, to write more concerning this petty affair. I leave the matter in the hands of an impartial public.

And so the affair ended. Walter Quaife appears to have been a strong minded character quite capable of championing the cause of the

J. E. Raven (1851–1940) played for Sussex in
1874 but his committee work incurred the wrath
of Lord Sheffield. (*Cricket*)

professional cricketer. Sympathy must also be with Lord Sheffield in
an era when there were strict qualification rules for county cricketers.

Undoubtedly it was Sussex CCC who were hardest hit because, as
well as losing Walter Quaife to Warwickshire (not yet a first-class
county) they also lost his younger brother William who became a
famously prolific batsman during 35 years at Edgbaston.

The Raven Affair 1880
The Sussex v Hampshire match at Hove in 1880 marked the 'debut'
of the Harrovian George Grundy in the home side. There is a story
that Grundy, not quite 21 years old, was introduced to the Sussex
captain, Robert Ellis, on the morning of the match prior to Sussex
taking the field. After one over, one of the Hampshire batsmen
noticed that there were 12 fielders! Billy Tester left the field but at
69 for 2 he returned to replace Grundy.

The selection of the Sussex team was in the hands of the general committee and it is not surprising that mistakes occurred. The committee member who had invited Grundy to play was John E. Raven, an old Lancing schoolboy who had played once for the county in 1874 and who played in a Sussex trial match at Sheffield Park just before the Hampshire match. Mr Raven wrote to the newspapers alleging that there was a fiasco in the match and justified his own action in inviting Grundy to play. He also denied the committee's assertion that he had misunderstood what had passed at the meeting. The affair angered Lord Sheffield and he wrote in response to Raven's letter:

SUSSEX COUNTY CLUB

Sheffield Park
Fletching
July 10th

To The Editor

Sir, Allow me to state, in answer to Mr Raven's letter, that the minute he refers to does not represent quite clearly what took place. Mr Raven's statement that he was empowered to finally engage Mr Grundy and Mr Trevor is entirely at variance with the facts of the case. The minute should most clearly have stated that he was only instructed to ascertain in what match the above-named gentlemen would play, that selection to be referred back to the committee for final decision. No doubt you will receive further communications on the subject; meanwhile, I beg to state that I have decided to withdraw, not only from the committee, but from the County Club altogether, so long as Mr Raven is allowed to remain on the committee.

I am, yours faithfully,
SHEFFIELD

PS – I send this in haste in order to give without a moment's delay a most emphatic denial to Mr Raven's assertions, to assure the cricketing public of Sussex that Mr Raven was never empowered to finally engage Mr Grundy, and to remind them that the question is not what the minute says, but what really and actually took place before the committee, whatever the minute may have recorded, are unanimous. On another occasion I shall have to ask you to open your columns in the best interests of county cricket to a correspondence which has taken place between Mr Raven and myself, as a member of the committee, a correspondence which, I believe, will place that gentleman's conduct in a worse light even than, in my opinion, it appears in at present.

The situation had developed into a crisis with Lord Sheffield's threatened resignation and at a committee meeting on 13 July Mr Raven, in the interests of peace, tendered his resignation. On the same day Lord Sheffield wrote another letter to the *Sussex Express*:

Brighton
July 13, 1880

TO THE EDITOR
Sir, Mr Raven's appeal to the judgment of cricketers generally, as between him and me, will probably be answered in the same spirit as the committee of the Sussex County Club have answered his attack on them, in his letter to you in your issue of Saturday last. However strong and perhaps violent my letter of Monday may have been, it will not be seen by Sussex cricketers that the committee of the County Club – composed of Sussex gentlemen – who are in full possession of all the facts of the case (and, possibly of some facts which are not publicly known), and who have also had the advantage of hearing Mr Raven's explanation, take precisely the same view of the matter as I, individually have done and have expressed a very strong and significant censure upon him in the resolution which is published in your columns this morning, and which was unanimously agreed to at a very full meeting of the committee of the County Club yesterday afternoon.

I am, sir, yours faithfully
SHEFFIELD

One has to feel sympathy for Raven but Lord Sheffield was not to be denied. Later the same year his position as Sussex CCC president was seen to much better advantage when he allowed the Sussex match against the Australians to be postponed thus enabling the very first home Test match to take place.

Lord Sheffield and the Press

Lord Sheffield was sometimes quick to air his disputes in the local and national newspapers and he used the advertising columns to publicise his cricket matches at Sheffield Park. He does seem to have been sensitive about any references to him and towards the end of his life he confided to A. J. Gaston, the Sussex cricket historian:

'I generally find any flattering references to me much better reported in the Liberal papers than in the Conservative: I was much struck by the way the *Sussex Daily News* cut out what you said about me. I must thank you all the same for what you did say which I need not tell you, gave me much pleasure – as a proof that the support I have given to Sussex cricket was not forgotten by you at any rate.'

There is much to be found about Lord Sheffield in the *Sussex Agricultural Express*, published in Lewes, and it is consistently favourable to him in its reporting. In July 1891 Lord Sheffield wrote to that paper to state his displeasure with the London press for ignoring his volunteer reviews:

Sheffield Park
July 27, 1891

THE SHEFFIELD PARK REVIEW
Sir – Allow me to call the attention of the volunteers of Sussex and the public also to the extraordinary conduct of the London Press in ignoring and boycotting all accounts of the two gatherings of Sussex volunteers in this park. Last year not a line in any London paper – morning, evening or weekly – appeared, in reference to the field day held here by 3,000 volunteers in the presence of 6,000 or 7,000 spectators. This year last Saturday's gathering of 2,500 volunteers

was treated with the same contemptuous and intentional silence. I say 'intentional' because I myself sent notices of the intended review to the *Times*, *Daily Telegraph* and *Standard*.

Surely this is an ignoble specimen of the manner in which the volunteers of this county are slighted by those whose duty it ought to be to support and encourage all efforts of the volunteers to increase their efficiency and enlarge their experience of military duties.

I am yours etc
SHEFFIELD

The Australian press found Lord Sheffield eccentric but they generally approved of him on his visit of 1891–92. Some years later, in July 1896, Lord Sheffield took offence to an article in the *Australasian* and hurriedly sent a telegram to Major Wardill, Exchange Buildings, Melbourne:

> Version in Australasian most one sided. Unfair, very cowardly to insert such partisan version without reference to me. Will you or my friends protest for me against this cowardly action on part of Australian papers.

Major Wardill was secretary of Melbourne Cricket Club and acted as an unofficial agent for Lord Sheffield. Seven months later he received another telegram from the English earl:

> I hear Australian papers grossly insult me. If true will not tolerate further Australian insults. Will take action – probably withdraw Challenge Shield. Will write. Deep regrets.

It is not clear what had raised Lord Sheffield's indignation but Wardill's reply advised him that he had been misinformed and that the Australian press was entirely loyal.

Perhaps Lord Sheffield was too sensitive or perhaps he felt that he was not always accorded the respect that his position and support of cricket merited.

He may have been influenced by another incident with the Australian press 10 years earlier. In July, 1886 readers of *Cricket* were informed:

Some time since a disgraceful attack on the Earl of Sheffield and Mr W. G. Grace appeared in one of the most influential Melbourne papers. The subject was the opening match of the Australian tour of 1884, and the remarks made were so unwarrantable as well as so untrue that an expression of regret appeared. Lord Sheffield though has been subjected to considerable annoyance by a repetition of the attack, this time in the *Melbourne Punch* and concerning the visit to Sheffield Park of the 1886 Australians:

> Luncheon then took place and no more cricket was played on the opening day. To be entertained and rub shoulders with a real live earl at a banquet must certainly be very nice but our boys went to play cricket and to play cricket with sharpers too at that – and therefore should not have allowed themselves to be got at. I use the word sharpers advisedly. There were men playing in Lord Sheffield's eleven who would use any means fair or unfair to defeat the Australians. If an Australian's defence of his wicket was impregnable, then his body was aimed at by an infuriated giant, who nearly stumbled every ball he delivered, till the batsman was maimed and had to retire.

The *Melbourne Punch* article then referred to the incident in 1886 when 'W. G.' challenged the width of the bats of the Australians which would 'catch the Australians on the hop and by inciting the passions of the English mob against them, and by having them hooted and jeered at as they left the ground to get their bats planed down, to completely unnerve them for the contest'. The editor of *Cricket*, Charles Alcock, felt sure that 'no one will be more thoroughly annoyed at such a gross attack on one of the most munificent patrons cricket has ever had than Major Wardill' and he attacked the *Melbourne Punch* for inserting 'such a combination of ignorance and malice'.

Major Wardill, manager of the 1886 Australians, replied on behalf of the team:

> I entirely repudiate the statements and sentiments contained in the article. Nothing could have been more hospitable than Lord Sheffield's treatment of myself and team and many Australian friends on the

occasion referred to, and no match could have been played with a more friendly feeling between the rival teams. I am positively certain that no previous Australian team visiting Lord Sheffield's Park were ever treated otherwise than in the most hospitable and cricket-like manner, and all those who know the great interest and love which Lord Sheffield entertains for the game, and the pleasure it gives him to see good cricket, would never dream of attributing to him any of the vile charges made in the issue of the *Melbourne Punch*. My team have not found in any of the games that they have played that they have met any of the 'Sharpers' alluded to. We have been met by all classes of cricketers in the most straightforward, honourable and pleasant manner. I trust that English cricketers will disassociate Australian cricketers of trying to impute the most sinister motives to Lord Sheffield, Dr W. G. Grace and others, who have always been sincere friends of the Australians whenever they have appeared on English cricket fields.

Dispute with Brighton Cricket Clubs 1885

In November 1884 Lord Sheffield headed a sub-committee of Sussex CCC in an attempt to carry out the purchase of the County Ground at Hove from the representatives of the freeholder Mr Benett-Stanford. A ground purchase fund was set up and Lord Sheffield agreed to defray the expense of a list of donations being published. As part of the purchase scheme the charges to local clubs and schools using the ground for practising and playing matches was doubled from 10s to £1 and privileges withdrawn for free entry on match days. The following letter was sent to the Sussex CCC committee by the secretaries of five Brighton cricket clubs:

Feb 3, 1885

Gentlemen

You have thought fit to double the Subscription of the Clubs playing on the County Ground. The effect of this rise will be the breaking up of the following Clubs:

　Brighton Brunswick CC
　Brighton Early Risers CC
　Brighton District Teachers CC

Stanford CC

West Hove CC

as the members of these Clubs are not in a position to pay more than they have heretofore.

Thus instead of doing all that can be done to get more men to practise cricket and develop talent, the comparatively few who now play will be debarred, the funds of the Club will suffer and the future of Sussex Cricket will look more dismal than before.

The 10/- per annum that we have always paid (some of us for 15 years) used to admit to the ground on match days. This privilege was taken from us two years ago. Now, in addition to this, the subscription is doubled.

Great indignation is felt in the town in Cricket Circles at this action and men who were actively engaged in collecting for the 'Ground Purchase Fund' have ceased to support the cause, so that already the disastrous effect of this ill-judged measure is being felt.

Trusting that you will see your way to reconsider the matter and favour us with an early reply.

G. Lionel King, Honorary Secretary of the more influential Brighton Cricket Club wrote to Sussex CCC lending his support to the increased charges. For his part Lord Sheffield was not going to compromise and he wrote the following to the *Sussex Daily News* to confound the petitioners:

THE COUNTY CRICKET GROUND

SIR in consequence of the course taken by several of the local Clubs at Brighton, by which the estimated increase of the income of the County Cricket Club will probably be much reduced, I regret to say that I must postpone my promised subscription of £600 towards the purchase of the County Ground until another £1,000 has been added to the present sum of £4,400.

Yours etc

Sheffield Park

February 26th, 1885

Lord Sheffield's threat to withdraw his £600 was a blow to the Club's ambitions but before the next committee meeting he forwarded a telegram to show that his promised contribution was still likely:

> I shall be only too glad to hear that the income which was in danger through the threatened secession of the clubs is again secured and replace my subscription on the old footing.

F. W. Clements (Brighton Brunswick CC) then requested that a deputation of the disaffected clubs should meet the Sussex CCC committee and the petitioners succeeded in reducing the charge for club tickets from £1 to 15s each – 'providing this proposed arrangement meets with the approval of Lord Sheffield'.

W. H. Campion and W. G. Ashby were then requested by the Sussex CCC committee to visit Lord Sheffield for ratification and on this occasion the committee's proposal met with his approval. Lord Sheffield wrote enthusiastically to the secretary of Sussex CCC and his letter was published in the *Sussex Daily News*:

> Sheffield Park
> March 9th, 1885
>
> Dear Mr Goldsmith – The difficulties between the Committee and the Brighton Clubs which had completely altered the circumstances and conditions under which I had promised my subscription to the 'Purchase Fund', being satisfactorily arranged, I shall have much pleasure in contributing the amount originally promised whenever the sum specified of £4,400 is obtained.
>
> Believe me,
Yours truly,
SHEFFIELD

The compromise was agreed, the county club acquired its freehold and Lord Sheffield emerged from the dispute with much credit.

Cuckfield Cricket Club

A year later Lord Sheffield was appointed patron of Cuckfield Cricket Club and through his generosity a new motor mower (with shed) was purchased and the club's Ockenden cricket ground was enclosed by an iron chain fence with 40 posts. In 1888, however, the club decided not to hire any professionals or play against clubs with professional assistance and this resulted in Lord Sheffield's withdrawal from the club. Although the club rules were later modified in an attempt to appease the wealthy patron, there is no record of any further involvement.

The Maryon-Wilsons

Sheffield Park dominated the parish of Fletching in every sense but there was another sizeable estate about a mile away with a magnificent house, gardens and cricket ground. This impressive property was 'Searles' and during Lord Sheffield's time it was occupied by the Maryon-Wilsons. There are stories of great rivalry between the two houses but it should be remembered that at Lord Sheffield's coming of age in 1853 it was Sir Thomas Maryon-Wilson who proposed the health of Viscount Pevensey.

The most colourful story concerning the Maryon-Wilsons and Lord Sheffield involves Sir Spencer Maryon-Wilson (10th bart, 1830–1897) being banned from Sheffield Park, probably in the months before the celebrated visit of the Prince of Wales and the Australian cricketers in 1896. The adjacent Fletching watermill, since demolished, happened to belong to the Maryon-Wilsons and Sir Spencer retaliated by extending the wooden tower in order to be able to watch the cricket. This took the form of a four-storey wooden extension, square in shape, that towered above the original mill with a flat roof.

Lord Sheffield is supposed to have hit back by ordering a number of tall young trees to be placed on the edge of the cricket ground to block the view. An old man at Danehill once recalled that Sir Spencer then reacted by firing cannon balls from the mill's tower on to the pitch and is said to have produced a cannon ball as evidence!

Sir Spencer's second son was George Maryon-Wilson (1861–1941),

George Maryon-Wilson J. P.

and he inherited 'Searles'. George proved to be an even greater head-
ache for Lord Sheffield.

George, like Lord Sheffield, was an old Etonian and he was also a
great cricket enthusiast. Since at least 1877 'Searles' had boasted its
own cricket ground and team, and in the early 1900s G. M.
Maryon-Wilson's XI regularly entertained the Sussex Martlets, an
influential team of amateurs based on the county club.

George Maryon-Wilson also presented the present Fletching
recreation ground to the village and prize bats to deserving players.

In June 1901 George Maryon-Wilson's XI entertained Fletching
CC at 'Searles' when 'some hundreds of people attended including
the farmers of the district'. The Chailey Industrial School Band was
in attendance and there was an excellent luncheon in a prettily
decorated marquee on the ground. The teams were photographed
and there was dancing in the evening; all of this was of course
reminiscent of the cricket at Sheffield Park.

However, before it is suggested that these commendable activities
would have met with Lord Sheffield's approval, it must be disclosed
that the match was played at the conclusion of a bitter row between
the two landowners. In the spring of 1901 George, in his role as JP

for Sussex and member of the County Licensing Committee, had refused to grant a liquor licence for events at Sheffield Park that would permit the sale of alcohol before noon. This angered Lord Sheffield and his position was summed up by an unknown writer to the *Times*:

Cricket at Sheffield Park seems likely to be definitely stopped by the extraordinary refusal of the Magistrates in the Uckfield Petty Sessional Division in Sussex, both last year and this year, to grant Lord Sheffield licences for his celebrated ground at Sheffield Park for any hours before 12 o'clock. As cricket matches begin, as a rule, between 10 and 11 o'clock, and as many of the players come by early trains and require refreshments, such a refusal causes the greatest inconvenience. Lord Sheffield has therefore decided under these peculiar circumstances to discontinue cricket on his ground. This remarkably harsh treatment of Lord Sheffield and his historic ground has created much astonishment and discussion in the cricketing community of Sussex, and has been very strongly criticised and condemned on all sides. What makes the refusal the more inexplicable and personally offensive is that Lord Sheffield has been in the habit of having licences for his ground invariably, for hours before noon, ever since licences came into existence some 30 or 40 years ago. The reason given by the Magistrates for refusing the licences is that a resolution has been passed by the Uckfield Bench, in consequence of some police representations, to the effect that no licences were to be granted before noon. To say the least of it, it seems exceedingly harsh and unjust to apply a resolution, obviously intended for places of public resort where the police find it difficult to maintain order, to such a place as Sheffield Park. It is to be hoped that the Magistrates may see their way to reconsider their decision, which certainly seems unjustifiable and difficult to understand.

On 23 March the *Sussex Agricultural Express* published the correspondence between Lord Sheffield and George Maryon-Wilson. In a covering letter Lord Sheffield added that 'it will explain to cricketers why there is no cricket again this year at Sheffield Park'. The following letter from Maryon-Wilson was final:

Searles, Fletching March 4th, 1901
Sir,

In reply to your letter of the 2nd inst. I regret that I cannot now promise an occasional licence for your cricket ground for any particular hour during the coming cricket season, but must consider each application on its merits when made. As I must decline further correspondence on this subject, I may point out that there are other magistrates in the district to whom these applications can be made should you be dissatisfied with my decision in the matter.

I am, yours faithfully,
GEORGE M. MARYON-WILSON

Lord Sheffield was indignant and he realised that redirecting his applications to either Mr Corbett or Mr Hardy (the other licensing magistrates) would be useless. His response to the above letter was lengthy and typically vitriolic:

Brighton, 129 Marine Parade
March 16th, 1901
Sir,

I regret your decision. Of course, under the circumstances which I described in my last note, your refusal compels me to abandon all hope of having cricket again on my ground this year. I protest strongly and firmly against your decision as being unjust and unfair, because there is no possible reason why you should not consider the application now 'on its merits' as well as at any future time in the summer. . . You will, no doubt, be able at the proper time, to give some adequate reason for a decision which inflicts so much injury on me personally, as well as on the district in which we both live, and without any apparent justification or necessity . . . Some of our players come very long distances by early trains, arriving often before nine o'clock. It is absolutely necessary that they should be allowed to obtain refreshments on their arrival – certainly before mid-day. Surely there was a reasonable and legitimate ground for asking for hours earlier than noon. To refuse to allow this reasonable request when you have full power to grant it, is an extraordinary harsh and unfair exercise of magisterial power, which will not be allowed to pass without some further notice. I make one more appeal to you to grant a licence for the hours we ask for on the occasion of what was intended to be our opening match on May 2nd; and for refusing which you have no just reason whatever.

I am, yours faithfully

SHEFFIELD

In May the Uckfield Bench rather surprisingly relented and Lord Sheffield was granted his licences in time for the cricket season at Sheffield Park to start, slightly late, on 16 May.

Triumphantly Lord Sheffield wrote to the local newspaper on 6 June from Brighton:

> After a long period of dispute our local magistrate at Fletching has, as the public are aware, waived his objections to granting licences for hours before noon.

He was concerned, however, that the situation could recur while the police resolutions existed and 'we are liable at any moment to be the victims again at the caprice of some resident magistrate'. He urged that the resolutions should be rescinded so that 'we may be allowed to have our licences in peace without having these resolutions hanging *in terrorem* over our heads'.

Lord Sheffield had won the day after much anxiety. There had been much support and sympathy for his position although letters were published wondering whether 'good cricket greatly depends on a dose of alcohol administered before play begins' and observing that 'it is hardly edifying to see a nobleman attempting through a long course of nagging to 'bluff' the lawful authorities'.

14

Travels with Lord Sheffield

We have already seen that as a young man in his late teens and early twenties, Lord Sheffield spent several years abroad. He saw army service in India and diplomatic service in Constantinople and Copenhagen. In later life his passion for travelling returned and between 1888 and 1895 he took annual trips to places near and far. His tour of Australia and Tasmania with the England team in 1891–92 was the highlight of all those trips. On occasions he sailed his yacht, the *Heloise,* to his chosen destination.

To carry out many of the arrangements Lord Sheffield had the valuable support of Alfred Shaw and William Moore. Shaw had visited Australia on four previous occasions so he was particularly helpful to his lordship on the 1891–92 tour.

Some of the lesser journeys were highly eventful and in 1901 Lord Sheffield wrote to Shaw:

> It is by no means the lot of every cricketer to have bowled on the deck of a 'liner' a few dozen of passengers (I was one of the victims) under the broad daylight of the sun at midnight on the Ice Fiord at Spitzbergen. It is not every cricketer who has shot woodcocks on the ruins of Jericho, or has eaten his Christmas pudding at Assouan, on the confines of Nubia, or has sat in the sandbag battery at Inkerman or has been taken for a spy by the Russians at Sebastopol (as we all were).

Many of Lord Sheffield's trips abroad were recorded by Alfred Shaw and his well observed comments have survived.

Holland 1888

Alfred Shaw recalled a pleasing incident after Lord Sheffield's team had played at The Hague:

> Lord Sheffield took his party to Haarlem, to see the wonderful bulb-growing districts, a sight, by the way, that once seen cannot be forgotten. On the way we had to walk some distance, and we crossed a field in which a school team were practising at cricket. His Lordship said to me, 'Go and bowl a few overs to them.' I took my coat off, and did so, the scholars being very glad to have a grown-up stranger from across the sea to assist them. They appeared rather astonished at my bowling, and after we had had a good half-hour's cricket, Lord Sheffield told them who I was. To my surprise, they knew me by name, and they expressed themselves as much delighted at my having practised with them. I know I was very pleased at the genuine warmth of my reception when my identity was known. Nor did the incident end there, for some of these enthusiasts caused a report of it to appear in some of the Holland papers, while I several times had letters subsequently from scholars to whom I had bowled in the rough field on the way to the bulbs of Haarlem.

Isle of Wight and Torquay 1889

At a time when Sheffield Park was closed to the public because of the threats to Lord Sheffield, a cricket tour was arranged by the noble earl which involved travelling by his yacht, the *Heloise*, to Torquay and back, calling at Ryde.

The team which included both amateurs and professionals was made up as follows:

Rev. F. F. J. Greenfield, A. Harcourt, R. M. Curteis, E. J. Golding, G. Lynn, J. Gilbert, F. W. Marlow, F. Gibb, A. Lavender, J. Charlwood, H. Budgen, G. F. Quaife, Stubberfield (umpire) and Taylor (scorer). They assembled at the Star and Garter Hotel, Brighton on Saturday, 25 May and played a match on the County Ground at Hove – Lord Sheffield's XI against a strong team got together by F. Clements – in which Lynn scored 70 and Marlow 44.

At 8.00 a.m. on the Sunday morning three landaus took the team to Southwick where they met up with Lord Sheffield, Harcourt, Rev. Greenfield, Curteis, Dr Fenn and Captain Haden and crew. The *Heloise* started in fog but the journey was enlivened by meals and hymn singing with Budgen playing the accordion. It took 23½ hours sailing to reach Ryde Pier.

Alfred Shaw allocated rooms in the Esplanade Hotel and after breakfast the team left for the cricket ground where the match played was lost.

The next day the team received a friendly 'good morning' and hand shake from his lordship before the yacht took them past the Needles on its way to Portland. After a wet journey they arrived at the Royal Breakwater Hotel at 4.10 p.m.

Some of the team visited Weymouth by train the following afternoon and witnessed the Yeomanry Sports on the Sands and when they returned to Portland further sports were in evidence involving the boys from TS *Boscawen*.

Re-boarding the *Heloise* on Thursday morning the team sailed for Torquay where they landed at 4 p.m. and went directly to quarters at the Queen's Hotel for refreshment. They drove to the cricket ground at 9.15 am on Friday morning. It was described as very pretty with an antique pavilion – rustic woodwork with thatched roof and a verandah covered with roses, honeysuckle and ivy; and mounds of rock work, geraniums and verbenas made a beautiful addition to the scenery of the ground. Lord Sheffield's XI lost the match but the team enjoyed a Saturday sightseeing and taking refreshment at the Globe Hotel, Newton Abbott before returning to Torquay via Kingkerswell, several large potteries and Torre Station.

Billy Marlow was allowed to leave the party at this point, courtesy of Lord Sheffield, to play for Staffordshire. The team then re-boarded the *Heloise* for the return trip, amused themselves with quoits on deck – marked out by Alfred Shaw on Lord Sheffield's instructions. The journey from Torquay to Ryde Pier took 23 hours and then some of the team travelled in a brake and pair for Carisbrooke Castle and Newport.

The team visited Portsmouth Harbour on a steamboat, the *Duchess of Connaught* and showed great interest in the ships, taking in a tour of the *Victory*. Returning to Ryde on the *Albert Edward*, they met up with Fred Tate who had arrived to replace Marlow for the forthcoming match against Ryde when Lord Sheffield's team, after conceding a first-innings lead, won by 65 runs.

Some of the team boarded the *Heloise* by 6.30 the next morning to sail back to Newhaven whilst Lord Sheffield allowed Shaw, Quaife, Lynn, Lavender, Charlwood and Gibb to travel by train to play in the Sussex Colts match at Hove.

Boulogne, July 1890
Before leaving for Boulogne for a short cricket tour, Lord Sheffield's team played a match at Newhaven on 22 July, having also played the inaugural match on this new ground only two months previously. Lord Sheffield's team was: J. Charlwood, R. M. Curteis, G. Lynn, E. J. Golding, E. Bailey, H. Phillips, A. Harcourt, J. Watson, W. T. Moore, A. Osborne and J. Gilbert, and they won the match on the first innings. Some of the team later played golf on a new course laid out by Lord Sheffield and then retired to the Ship Hotel.

In the morning an early start was made on the *Heloise* to catch the tide and Lord Sheffield came on deck at 9.00 a.m. to give the team a hearty 'good morning'. The team arrived at Boulogne at 5.20 p.m. and proceeded to Hotel Meurice where rooms were allotted by Alfred Shaw and W. T. Moore.

A walk to the cricket ground the next day for practice found Lord Sheffield already present with his yachting friends. The evening was spent by some of the team at the theatre but they were all present on the ground the next day by 10.15 a.m. Lord Sheffield himself won the toss, elected to bat and his team beat Boulogne, a team made up of Englishmen, by 65 runs. (Sheffield Park XI 96 and 79-5 dec; Boulogne 40 and 70).

A return match was played the next day but the Boulogne team was weaker and had to borrow two of Lord Sheffield's men, including the colourful Harry Stubberfield who took an early wicket for the French team. Sheffield Park declared at lunchtime at 174 for 2 (J. Charlwood 81*, G. Lynn 52) before bowling out the hosts for 107 and 25.

After a great deal of sight-seeing the team returned to Folkestone on the *Albert Victor*, Lord Sheffield having already left on the *Heloise*.

Egypt 1892
Shaw described a cruise up the Nile as far as the first cataract:

Lord Sheffield's party left Tilbury on 4 November. At Naples an incident occurred that showed that foreigners were not free from insult even in that popular Italian touring ground. We were returning from Pompeii to Naples, and I was sitting with my face very close to the carriage window, when a brick, thrown by some miscreant, crashed through the window and hit a fellow traveller who was sitting on the other side of the vehicle. My face was so close to the glass that the brick went under my chin and over my shoulder. I was covered with broken glass but not cut in the slightest. The fact that my face was so close to the glass must, I think, have saved me from very serious injury.

Up the Nile in a private dahabieh, we found that we had to be very wary of the natives, as well as of the dogs by which the banks are infested. We were not allowed to leave the barge without a guide and it seemed to me rather ludicrous to be escorted by a native sailor, armed with a tin lantern and a long stick.

Only those who have been in the interior of Egypt and have strolled among the mud villages on the Nile littoral, can have any conception of the indescribable filthiness of the native population and their surroundings.

It had been in contemplation by Lord Sheffield to push on as far as Wady Halfa, but we learned that there had been an engagement between the camel corps and the dervishes, so it was decided to retrace our steps to Cairo. Before leaving Assouan, through the generosity of Lord Sheffield, sports were arranged on a scale that had probably not been forgotten by the natives who took part in them to this day. There must have been six or eight thousand persons present, made up of Arabs, Soudanese and kindred castes, and perhaps about twenty English.

The camel race, with its fifty gigantic competitors, was one of the most inspiriting contests I ever saw. The long sweeping strides of fifty of these great beasts enabled one to realise what ships of the desert they

Lord Sheffield is by the banks of the Nile on the *Isis* in 1892. (A. Collier)

really are, though there was a ludicrous side to the picture, that of the howling and gesticulating natives, hanging on to the dorsal humps, and flogging the brutes with sticks for all they were worth. Genuinely amusing was the donkey race. Fifty of these self-willed quadrupeds were started in this competition but most of them set off at a tangent into the desert. The winner of the race was an Arab who rode bare-backed and without bridle. He kept his mount straight by vigorous use of a thick stick on either side of the brute's head, as the necessity demanded.

The greatest fun was in what was called the Forlorn Race. For this there were about one hundred and fifty entrants. They had to race up to the fort on the hill, about a mile away, where one of the English party stood armed with a brush and whitewash. Each runner had to receive a dab on his ebony pate, and anyone returning without the order of the whitewash on his coaly cranium was disqualified. Apparently some of the coloured sprinters were of the opinion that this whitewashing was the hall-mark of athletic success. They presented their lime-bedaubed Nubian locks with pride for a prize, but as we could only give prizes to ten, the rest had to go disappointed.

These sports were the first ever held on such a scale at this part of the Nile. The natives assembled from villages miles around, and I make bold to say that the name of Lord Sheffield is remembered with pleasure by many of these sons of Nubia to this day.

Holy Land 1893

A year after the trip up the Nile, Lord Sheffield's party were on their travels again. Alfred Shaw takes up the story:

On Friday, October 20th, 1893, the Earl of Sheffield and party commenced a tour to the Holy Land, the arrangements for which were in a large measure entrusted to myself. We reached Jerusalem on November 5th and the average visitor to the Holy Land must, I suppose, have some of his cherished notions rudely disturbed on reaching it for the first time. The axiom that cleanliness is next to godliness has evidently been forgotten, supposing it was ever learned, by the present occupants of the Promised Land . . . I cannot associate things holy with the filth and the noisome smells of the modern Jerusalem.

Lord Sheffield arranged for a camping-out expedition in the Valley of Jordan. It was a formidable cavalcade that set out from Jerusalem. In addition to his Lordship's party of ten, there were twenty-five muleteers and men with palanquins, six mounted Bedouins as guards, six foot guards, a cook and three waiters. The mules, horses and other beasts of burden numbered fifty-one, including one camel. There were eight sleeping tents and two saloon tents. We resembled a big convoy on the march.

Our tent was pitched just close to the river where Christ was baptised. I fished there for a while, but it was too hot for the fish to bite. It is always too hot, or too much wind, when you cannot catch fish. At last I caught one with a bit of bread, and it was a small chub about 12oz. We had a wash at this place, which we found much more refreshing than fishing. After washing at the same place where Christ was baptised we ought to be good, which I believe we are.

Before the start of the 1894 cricket season Lord Sheffield spent a month in Naples.

Alfred Shaw's bowling by the light of the midnight sun
was too much for the passengers of the *Lusitania*.
(Mrs H. Rawlings)

Spitzbergen & Norway 1894
Alfred Shaw describes the next trip:

Another of the pleasant excursions in which I was able to join,
through the kindness of the Earl of Sheffield, took place in August,
1894. The tour was to Norway and Spitzbergen, by the Orient liner,
the *Lusitania*. We were away from August 1st to September 3rd.
While at Tromso we took the opportunity of sailing across the fiord
to a Laplanders' camp. We arrived at the camp at about two o'clock,
and found about one hundred men, women and children, and 150
reindeer, the latter driven into a sort of stock yard. The Laplanders
are a very small lot, and look very dirty. They were selling horns,
skins and tobacco pouches, all made from the reindeer. They wear
nothing but what comes from the deer, as their coats, caps, trousers
and the women's and children's clothes are all made out of the skins.

From what I saw, the skins are not well cured, and they smell bad. The houses, or huts, are built of peat, or turf, made wide at the bottom, and tapered off to a point like a bell tent. There is a door at the side, and we had a peep in, but we soon shut the door again, as there is not a bit of furniture, and the people never wash.

One of the most interesting experiences of my life took place at midnight, on the eleventh day out. This was the playing of a cricket match on the ship's deck – the *Lusitania* – by the light of the midnight sun. The scene of this novel match was the anchorage in the Ice Fiord at Spitzbergen, about forty miles up the fiord. We were nestling in the bosom of a peaceful ice fiord at mid-night, with the arctic sun at its lowest point lighting up the snow-clad mountains and the magnificent glaciers around us. The light was equal to noonday at an English cricket match; indeed, it was much superior to the average light at one or two famous cricket grounds in the north of England.

It was Lord Sheffield who suggested a cricket match at this weird hour and amongst these eerie surroundings. The idea was promptly taken up by all on board. Wickets were pitched, a ball improvised, and at a quarter to twelve on the night of August 12th, 1894, this strange game commenced. Of course I had to bowl, and Lord Sheffield opened the batting. Between a quarter to twelve and half past twelve I had bowled out practically all the gentlemen passengers and officers, certainly forty persons all told. It will be seen that it must have been pretty quick work from the bowler's point of view. The novelty of the thing pleased everyone, and I dare say there are a few good people to-day who think with pleasure of that night in the Ice Fiord, when they had a few balls from Alf. Shaw on the deck of the *Lusitania*, under the rays of the midnight sun.

Crimea 1895

Lord Sheffield's next journey was to the Crimea. As Viscount Pevensey and barely twenty years of age he had acted as a private secretary at the British Embassy at Constantinople, and now, over forty years later, he had arranged a return visit. It was not a success and Alfred Shaw described some of the difficulties:

A trip to the Crimea that will never be forgotten by those who took part in it was arranged and carried out by Lord Sheffield in 1895. Unlike all the other visits abroad this one remains memorable for its unpleasantness rather than for its enjoyment. His Lordship's party left London on October 20th, 1895, and the tour lasted until the end of November of the same year. The outward journey from London to Brindisi by the P & O was enjoyable enough. It was at Brindisi that the trouble began.

We had to change into a French boat for Constantinople. To start with we found that his Lordship's cabin had been let to other persons. I had, therefore, to get them turned out, which was done after some trouble. Then it was discovered that no cabin had been reserved for me, and for the attendants attached to his Lordship's party. Lord Sheffield did all he could to induce the captain to make some better arrangements for our section of the party, but that officer either could not or would not interfere, so we endured the smells and hardships for ten days.

At Constantinople I had to make arrangements for getting to Sebastopol. I found that a boat only sailed once a week, on Wednesdays, and as we had landed in the Turkish capital on a Sunday we should, ordinarily, have had three days to wait. Wishing to avoid this I inspected a cattle boat named the *Olga* that had arrived that morning with a full cargo of beasts and a few passengers. The condition of the boat I need not describe, but we arranged to sail by it the next morning for the Crimea. Guessing that the Customs would not be easily negotiated – our party numbered nine, and there were eighty-nine pieces of baggage – I was up betimes on Monday morning. Early though it was I soon had occasion to think it was much too late to give me time to move the phlegmatic Turk who had charge of the Custom-house. What was everyone's business was no one's business; not the slightest attention could I obtain.

All this came of my simple mindedness. In other words, I did not know the ropes. Suddenly I bethought me of 'Backsheesh.' I produced half a sovereign. Its effect was electrical. The baggage passed through the Custom-house at express speed.

On reaching the cattle boat we found that some attempt had been made to sweep the decks, but it was only to make way for another cargo of unsavoury livestock. The cabin accommodation was again very limited, and I, Lord Sheffield's valet, and a lady's maid, had to herd in the fo'c'sle with a motley collection of unwashed Turks and Russians. Our 'berths' were laid on the floor of one large compartment dignified by the name of second saloon, the only partitions being drawn curtains. The foetid atmosphere, the repulsive food, and generally disgusting surroundings made this passage from Constantinople to Sebastopol one that I am not likely to forget.

But our troubles were by no means confined to ship-board. When we reached Sebastopol we found that our arrival had been anticipated by the authorities in a most unpleasant and surprising way. Before being allowed to land the head of the Customs came especially to examine us. We had to march on deck, answer to our names, and submit to be searched as if we were suspected persons – which we soon discovered we really were. We were led into the Custom-house, every particle of baggage was minutely searched, and we were virtually under lock and key for two hours. When we were allowed to depart, the officials retained our guns and cameras, as if they were of the belief they had detected and unarmed a company of English spies. We had just reached our hotel, and the baggage had been placed in our bedrooms, when the English Consul brought us the astounding intelligence that we could not be allowed to stay in Sebastopol. The reason assigned was that the authorities believed we were English officers, and were visiting the Crimea as spies. Protests were of no avail. We must go, and go at once.

The luncheon we had ordered we were only able to see. Our luggage was sent to another ship, and we were literally packed off bag and baggage to Yalta. A few Russian officers were on the ship, and they never let us out of their sight.

The disgraceful treatment to which Lord Sheffield and his party were thus subjected was the cause of much telegraphing between the noble Earl and the British and Russian authorities. The affair got into the English newspapers, and an attempt was made to minimise the extent of the discourtesy shown towards an English nobleman and his suite on pleasure bent in the Crimea. Lord Sheffield, on arriving later at Marseilles, scotched these attempts to whitewash the Russian officials by publishing the facts.

Having recovered our freedom at last we had carriages for four days, and visited all the historic Crimean battlefields around Sebastopol, taking a good many photographs that would have been as interesting to Lord Sheffield and his friends as they would have been harmless to the Russian authorities. But, alas ! our bona fides had not even now been fully established. We were leaving on the Sunday morning at eight o'clock and at ten o'clock the previous night the Commandant and Chief of Police came to our hotel and demanded every photograph that we had taken. The demand was made in a manner that brooked no resistance, so every plate had to be given up, and we were made to feel fortunate that we were not all put in durance vile together. As it was we had to pass through the police station on our way to the ship and sign our names in the police book. Our noble patron was, naturally, highly indignant at the mistrust and discourtesy displayed towards himself and his friends. My own feeling was one of delight at getting safely away. I have never been fired with ambition to again visit the shores of the Crimea.

Subsequently we stayed for about ten days in Constantinople and here we narrowly escaped having to witness, if not take part in, serious trouble. We left on a Thursday morning, and before the day closed the serious outbreak between the Mohammedans and Christians began. Some people were killed close to the hotel in which we had been staying.

Our voyage from Constantinople to Marseilles was as discomforting as portions of the outward journey had been. We were delayed three days at Smyrna, where the ship was so loaded with bags of currants for Marseilles that no room was left for the passengers to walk about. The day after passing the Straits of Messina we encountered a hurricane. The seas broke over the ship, and she was such an old tub that we were in serious doubt if she could hold together. At one time she did not make a mile an hour, so fierce was the hurricane. The spectacle in the clear moonlight, when the sea resembled a vast expanse of heaving white mountains, was grand and awe-inspiring. It was also horribly trying to the nerves. Fortunately the day before we reached Marseilles the seas subsided and we were able to enjoy the passage. The sea water had burst innumerable bags of currants, and the contents were so much scattered about the deck that we actually had to walk about to our knees in currants.

After the 1895 adventure to the Crimea later travels were less ambitious and William Moore's diary records short visits to Belgium and the Isle of Wight in 1896 when Lord Sheffield was accompanied by Miss Attenborough.

Lord Sheffield's later winters were spent abroad as his health deteriorated. In 1901 he was at Mentone on the Riviera and he was again abroad in the spring of 1902 when the Australian team arrived in England.

At the end of 1908 Lord Sheffield, who was now an invalid, removed to the south of France where he remained until his passing on 21 April 1909 at Beaulieu-sur-Mer near Nice.

15

Trials in the Park
1880–1891

Soon after Lord Sheffield began his second term as Sussex CCC president in 1879 he implemented his plan to encourage Sussex-born young cricketers by starting each season at Sheffield Park with a series of trial matches. The best of the young hopefuls were selected to play with established members of the Sussex XI in testing early season conditions. All expenses were paid by the earl and it appears that the county club had little direct involvement in staging these matches as similar arrangements were made at Hove.

The trial matches at Sheffield Park were usually held under the watchful guidance of two successful northern cricket professionals employed specifically by Lord Sheffield, William Mycroft and Alfred Shaw. Although Shaw later claimed that the quality of the young players was mediocre, there is no doubt that a good number of Sussex first-class cricketers were discovered. These trials were first held in 1880 and continued until 1891 with three fallow years from 1887 when the park was generally closed.

Lord Sheffield's two hard working professionals brought a wealth of experience with them as we can see.

William Mycroft (1841–1894)
William Mycroft was a left-arm round-arm bowler who had greatly distinguished himself for his native Derbyshire. He and Joe Flint had bowled out Nottinghamshire for 14 in 1873 and three years later he took 17 Hampshire wickets at Southampton.

The cricket historian Arthur Haygarth described him as a popular man, a thorough worker, good humoured, honest, civil and an obliging

William Mycroft, seated, was employed by Lord Sheffield at different times between 1880 and 1890 to coach aspiring young cricketers. His companions, Harry Stubberfield (centre) and Alfred Shaw, were also employed by Lord Sheffield. (MCC)

cricketer. In 1880 he resigned his place on the MCC ground staff to accept Lord Sheffield's private engagement although he returned to Lord's the following year. His work was impressive throughout and he was regularly engaged at Sheffield Park during April to coach the rising cricketing talent in Sussex. When Mycroft's benefit match took place at Derby in 1883 (Lancashire & Yorkshire v England), Lord Sheffield contributed £50.

Alfred Shaw (1842–1907)

Lord Sheffield was satisfied with Mycroft's engagement but his great desire for the improvement of Sussex cricket later led him to employ one of the great professionals of the day, the celebrated Alfred Shaw. Shaw's vast experience included cricket tours to Australia and North America, a spell as England's Test captain (1881–2) and captaincy of Nottinghamshire for four successive Championship-winning seasons (1883–6) when he was also employed at Sheffield Park.

Alfred Shaw worked tirelessly to develop young
Sussex cricketers for Lord Sheffield.

After a dispute with Nottinghamshire he came out of retirement
in 1894 to play for Sussex at the advanced age of 51. Lord Sheffield
was quick to give his permission for the appointment. That season
Shaw had the satisfaction of helping Sussex defeat his native
Nottinghamshire for the first time in 20 years and to finish at the top
of the Sussex bowling averages. Shaw was employed at Sheffield Park
every season from 1883 to 1895 and became not only a cricket coach
to Lord Sheffield but his organiser, adviser, travelling companion
and friend. In a letter in 1896 Shaw confided that 'his Lordship is a
very good fellow but he takes a lot of understanding.'

Alfred Shaw described his role in searching out and developing
young cricketers for Lord Sheffield in his autobiography, published
in 1902:

My appointment was made known all over the county, and my
services were placed for coaching purposes at the disposal of the

Sussex County Committee whenever they felt fit to call upon me. Young players were recommended from various parts of the county, and their expenses etc, for the time they were being coached, even to the payment for loss of time, were generously defrayed by the noble Earl. Wickets were prepared for the use of my pupils at his Lordship's park, at the county ground at Brighton, and at Hastings, Eastbourne and elsewhere. I used to divide the practice days between these places, and I met, say, four young players each time on the respective grounds. It was astounding what a class of cricketer I sometimes had recommended to me for trial. In the course of my career as Lord Sheffield's cricket instructor I was able to realise the meaning of the saying about so-and-so's swans being merely geese. Lads and young men who mayhap could bowl and bat fairly well on their native village wickets – which sometimes were as rough as common land – were sent up to me enthusiastically recommended as fit for an England eleven.

Yet it is no exaggeration to say that of all the candidates brought to me for trial not more than one in a hundred had any conception of first-class cricket. I am sorry to say it but my time was often literally wasted in trying to impart a reasonable amount of cricket education to most unreceptive candidates. Yet it had to be done, because the candidates were 'highly recommended.' The results were unsatisfactory alike to Lord Sheffield and myself. At the end of each year we had a barren list of players, and much disappointment, he for all his generosity and outlay, I for constant and painstaking endeavour.

The expense to which Lord Sheffield went in his efforts to raise the quality and quantity of native Sussex cricket talent may be judged from the following. Three or four trial matches were arranged yearly at Sheffield Park before the regular county season opened, the sides being selected from the official county team with an infusion of the best of the young players. These matches would not cost his Lordship less than £50 each. All through the summer we had matches in different places in the county, as many in fact as forty in the season, and most of these games would cost his Lordship £20 apiece. Then there was the cost of keeping some of the young players for practice purposes. My own salary was, I considered, a good one. . . how extremely anxious I was that there should be a good cricket return for Lord Sheffield's enterprise and generosity.

Shaw went on to name some well-known Sussex cricketers for whom Lord Sheffield's investment did a great deal to bring into prominence. They included W. Blackman, W. Newham, George Brann, C. Aubrey Smith, G. H. A. Arlington, F. M. Lucas, J. W. Juniper, W. A. Tester, F. Parris, F. Tate, H. Butt, F. W. Marlow, George and Joe Bean, E. H. Killick and C. F. Butcher.

Students of Sussex cricket history will recognise the quality of these names – five played for England – but it is indicative of Sussex's poor fortunes at this time that four of them died as young men with much still to offer: William Blackman (22), John Juniper (23), F. Murray Lucas (27) and Billy Tester (33).

Two other young cricketers benefited from Lord Sheffield's coaching programme but are strangely missing from the above list. They are the brothers Walter and William Quaife from Newhaven – the younger one being another future England player – but perhaps because of the consternation they caused Lord Sheffield (explained in chapter 13) Shaw diplomatically omitted them.

Shaw and Mycroft were well known in the county and always found time to offer advice to players of all abilities. They were also newsworthy, particularly for the local press, and when the pair visited Eastbourne in May 1885 the following article appeared in the *Eastbourne Chronicle*:

The well-known professional cricketers, Shaw and Mycroft, paid a visit to Eastbourne this week and were taken over Saffron Field (the new ground of the Eastbourne and Devonshire Park Cricket Club). Both were alike astonished and gratified by the appearance of the ground, which they spoke of as magnificent for the purpose to which it is to be appropriated. They afterwards went to South Fields and engaged in some bowling practice, the brothers Jesse and Arthur Hide assisting them as batsmen.

This was all in a day's work for Shaw. He had only recently returned from Australia where he managed England's tour including five Test matches. He had also played in three early season trial matches for Sussex, retained the captaincy of county champions Nottinghamshire still found time to visit the newly developed Saffrons and indulge in some practice with Sussex's Hide brothers.

The opening match at the Saffrons was played a year later in May 1886 when Lord Sheffield sent a team to play Eastbourne (see chapter 18). Shaw was of course present and the Hide brothers opened the batting for the home team.

Sheffield Park Trial Matches 1880

When the first trial match was played at Sheffield Park in 1880 there was no local railway station and Lord Sheffield's pavilion and the ladies' pavilion had not then been built. Nevertheless the report of the match tells us that some well-known Sussex county cricketers played and provided details of building activity.

30 April, 1 May	16 Colts of Sussex v Sheffield Park
Sussex Colts	314 (A. Payne 80*, W. H. Millard 69, W. Mycroft 9-139)
Sheffield Park	20-9 (A. Sclater 4-12, J. Juniper 3-8)

With regard to the ground little has been done since we saw it last year. The new dressing and retiring-rooms in the rear of the pavilion have, however, been finished, and are found to be a great convenience. Lord Sheffield, however, contemplates further improvements, which will make this one of the best, as it is also the prettiest, theatres of cricket in England. Everybody on arrival at Sheffield Park on Friday was delighted to see that his lordship has so far recovered from his recent attack of indisposition as to be enabled to be present. Accompanied by his brother, the Hon. Douglas Holroyd, the earl reached the ground at an early hour, took a thorough interest in the play, presided at the mid-day luncheon, and remained till the stumps were drawn, in the evening.

Sussex Colts had the assistance of James Lillywhite (junior), England's first Test match captain, and there were good performances from Alfred Payne, shortly to make his Sussex debut, and Arthur Sclater, an amateur from Newick who tragically died in 1882.

8 May	13 Colts of Sussex v Sheffield Park
Sussex Colts	121 (A. Sclater 52, W. Mycroft 7-50)
&	66-5 (A. Sclater 27)
Sheffield Park	145 (A. H. Wood 59, W. E. Pedley 30, J. Juniper 7-41)

A. Sclater hit Mr Hardy for four and made the hit of the day by driving the same bowler grandly to long on for seven by the pavilion towards the lake.

The unfortunate Mr Hardy above was Herbert Carey Hardy of Danehurst, Danehill who was a Sussex CCC committee member as well as being a Sussex JP. His wife Louisa was a great niece of Jane Austen. James Lillywhite (junior) again appeared for Sussex Colts.

12 May	14 Colts of Sussex v Sheffield Park
Sussex Colts	91 (A. Payne 25, W. Mycroft 7-37)
&	95-8 (E. J. McCormick 36)
Sheffield Park	88 (W. Payne 20, A. Sclater 5 wickets)

The brothers Alfred and William Payne were professionals from East Grinstead. James Lillywhite (junior) played for the Sussex Colts and the Sheffield Park innings was opened by Rev. Walter Summers, Vicar of Danehill.

4 June	14 of Sussex v Sheffield Park
Sussex	333 (R. T. Ellis 75, A. Payne 50, E. J. McCormick 62, F. G Turnbull 56, W. Mycroft 8-113)
Sheffield Park	39-2 (A. H. Wood 22*)

Robert Ellis was captain and manager of Sussex in 1880. Arthur Wood was a former Hampshire captain who had moved to Sussex.

1881

29 April	15 of Sussex v Sheffield Park
Sussex	124 (J. Phillips 37, W. Mycroft 10-47)
&	130-5 (J. Phillips 60, E. J. McCormick 49*)
Sheffield Park	121 (G. Humphreys 33, J. Juniper 4-47)

The ground, which has been still further improved during the winter, was in magnificent order, and did credit both to his lordship's liberality in promoting the national pastime, and to the care taken by the ground keeper.

The two Hastings batsmen James Phillips and Edward McCormick added 109 for the third wicket in the second innings.

5 May	14 of Sussex v Sheffield Park
Sussex	150 (J. Lillywhite (jun) 50, W. Millard 39, W. Mycroft 9-51)
Sheffield Park	134 (C. A. Smith 29, J. Gilbert 27, Rev. W. Summers 26, J. Seneschal 10-52)

Since last year the mansion has been renovated and improved, and, as it meets the eye immediately on entering the park through a vista in the trees, adorning the slope above the lake, is now a graceful accessory to a pleasing picture.

The future Sussex and England captain C. Aubrey Smith was seventeen years old. The 'evergreen' John Gilbert was over 50. John Seneschal, from Rutland, took ten of the eleven Sheffield Park wickets.

10 May	15 of Sussex v Sheffield Park
Sussex	73 (W. Mycroft 8-29, Rev F. Greenfield 6-38) and 82-4 (E. J. McCormick 40, W. Tester 32*)
Sheffield Park	142 (W. Humphreys 30, W. Payne 28, Burtenshaw 6-26)

At two o'clock an excellent and substantial luncheon was served by Mrs Comber in the pavilion, at which his lordship himself presided and about fifty sat down . . . three fresh young players appeared, namely Wells (the son of a well-known Sussex cricketer Tiny Wells), Cuthbert of Eastbourne and Coleman of Brighton. We understand that Messrs C. J. and M. P. Lucas had written to Lord Sheffield expressing regret at inability to play.

Rev. Greenfield was captain of Sussex in 1881; Walter Humphreys was a famous 'lob' bowler and William Tester is one of cricket's many suicides.

1883

25 April Sussex v Sheffield Park

Sheffield Park	54 (W. Humphreys 19, A. Shaw 6-15)
&	17 (J. Juniper 7-6, J. Skinner 4-9)
Sussex	172 (G. Brann 52, W. Newham 48, A. Hide 6-45)

Only the two young amateurs from Ardingly School, Brann and Newham, excelled with the bat. Brann, aged 18, made his Sussex debut later in the season. William Newham, a future Test player, was 22. The left-arm fast bowler Jack Juniper, from Southwick, achieved a remarkable analysis against a strong team.

1884

25 April A.Shaw's Team v Rev. F. Greenfield's Team

Shaw's Team	126 (W. Newham 23, A. Hide 5-19)
Greenfield's Team	64 (W. Blackman 24, J. Hide 5-39)
&	105 (W. Blackman 51, W. Tester 4-18)

Two members of the Australian touring team, George Alexander and Harry Boyle, turned out in this 13-a-side match. Two fine innings were played by another Ardingly boy, William Blackman, aged 21. He died of consumption the following year.

During the recess an army of workmen have been employed on the ground combining art with nature – some tons of rock have been added to the cascade – one of if not the largest artificial falls in the country. The ground generally has been well cared for by Mr Moore.

28 April A. Shaw's Team v Rev. F. Greenfield's Team
Greenfield's Team 117 (W. Humphreys 45*, A. Hide 37, A. Shaw
                          6-32)
&   17-0
Shaw's Team   161 (J. Hide 49, A. Payne 42, J. Juniper 7-50)

Greenfield's team included Hockheimer, later described as a former professional to Lord Sheffield. He became groundsman at Wanstead but when umpiring for that club against Essex Club and Ground in 1909 he had the misfortune to be struck by the ball and died in hospital several days later.

1885

22 April A. Shaw's Team v Rev. F. Greenfield's Team
Greenfield's Team   207 (J. Phillips 40, J. Juniper 6-85)
Shaw's Team   52 (W. Mycroft 4-15)
and   38-2 (J.Hide 20*)

29 April A. Shaw's Team v R. T. Ellis's Team
Ellis's Team   108 (R. T. Ellis 40, A. Shaw 8 wickets) and 67-5
Shaw's Team   88 (F. Tate 5-21)

Fred Tate was only 17 years old in this match and still two years away from making his Sussex debut. Both teams played thirteen men.

1886

30 April Rev. F. Greenfield's Team v W. Newham's Team
Greenfield's Team   16 (G. Bean 9-4)
&   81
Newham's Team   72 (W. Mycroft 7-31, J. Hide 6-26)
&   26-1

The 22-year-old George Bean resided at Sheffield Park while qualifying for Sussex and he made his Sussex debut soon after this Trial Match. He completely demolished Rev. Greenfield's team of 13 men with figures of 12.1-9-4-9: 'The only batsman who made any stand being Harry Budgen of St Peter's (Brighton).' In the second innings the ill-fated Hockheimer was described as a capital partner for Walter Humphreys and 'he opened his shoulders very freely and showed some good hitting powers'. The match was finished when Bean hit Wells' first ball for six and scored a two and a four in the same over.

1890

28 April A. Shaw's Team v W. Newham's Team

Shaw's Team	22 (G. Bean 7 wickets)
&	32 (F. Gibb 8 wickets)
Newham's Team	147 (G. Bean 52, F. W. Marlow 50, J. Hide 6 wickets)

After a lapse of three seasons when no trial matches were held at Sheffield Park, George Bean again displayed his formidable all-round powers. Frank Gibb was a left-arm fast bowler from Wadhurst who played ten first-class matches for Sussex in 1890.

1 May A. Shaw's Team v W. Newham's Team

Newham's Team	68 (W. Newham 39, J. Hide 9 wickets)
&	169 (F. W. Marlow 100*)
Shaw's Team	89 (F. Worger 22)

William Marlow from Staffordshire, aged 22, was qualifying for Sussex by residence. He made his debut for the county the following year and enjoyed a successful professional career with a reputation as a brilliant fielder. 'The match was played on May Day in glorious weather. The Industrial School band from Chailey played some capital music during the day.'

Four young cricketers who played with success for Sussex featured in Lord Sheffield's Trial Matches: Arthur Sclater (1859–1882) (Tony Turk), John Juniper (1862–1885) (*Sussex County Magazine*) George Bean (1864-1923) (R. Packham), Edward McCormick (1862–1941) (R. Packham).

1891

24 April W. L. Murdoch's Team v A. Shaw's Team
Murdoch's Team   54 (A. Shaw 5 wickets)
&   73-2 (W. L. Murdoch 30*)
Shaw's Team   253 (W. G. Quaife 62*, G. Bean 45
                         W. Humphreys 5 wickets)

W. L. Murdoch's had last appeared at Sheffield Park twelve months earlier when he was captain of the Australians against Lord Sheffield's XI and was photographed with W. G. Grace. The top scorer in this Trial Match was the 5ft 4ins William Quaife, aged 19 from Newhaven. He played for Sussex v Hampshire later in 1891 but later moved to Warwickshire where he played in the county team for 35 years. He was always ready to acknowledge his indebtedness to Alfred Shaw for the coaching he received at Sheffield Park.

29 April W. L. Murdoch's Team v A. Shaw's Team
A. Shaw's Team   123 (W. G. Quaife 30, R. Hilton 6-70)
&   140-4 (F. W. Marlow 93*)
Murdoch's Team   89 (G. Bean 32, A. Shaw 7-34)

'Marlow's brilliant hitting encourages the hope that he may play some fine innings for Sussex County this season.' W. L. Murdoch was dismissed for a duck by Richard Lowe who was qualifying for Sussex and who made his first-class debut this year for Lord Sheffield's XI. Robert Hilton was a 6ft 7ins tall bowler who was on the Sussex CCC ground staff but never played a first-class match. Alfred Shaw was now 48 years old and three years away from making his Sussex debut.

16

Club Cricket at Sheffield Park 1845–1909

Sheffield Park's place in cricket history owes much to the celebrated first class fixtures played there in the years from 1884 to 1896 when Lord Sheffield's 'Select' XI took on the Australian Test sides on five separate occasions as well as touring sides from South Africa and the Parsees from Bombay.

In addition to these grand matches, Lord Sheffield staged trial matches for young players with aspirations to play for Sussex. These trial matches were supervised by William Mycroft and Alfred Shaw and produced some good individual performances with both bat and ball. Some of the fixtures were very one-sided so were of little value as trials.

But most cricket matches played in the Park were club games at first involving Fletching Cricket Club (founded in 1840) and then, at the time of the first ground reconstruction in 1855, Sheffield Park Cricket Club was formed. From that date the young lord and his brother Douglas turned in some good performances. At the height of the club's activity there were two home fixtures each week with only occasional away fixtures. When the brothers were in the Sheffield Park side the press showed an interest as in the following report from 1858:

Haywards Heath v Sheffield Park

The first public day of our new cricket club came off on Tuesday last in Mr Davey's meadow at Bulltrough. There was a large assembly present and the fact that the noble lord, member for the county, and his brother were engaged in the match caused a good deal of excitement.

In the 1860s Sheffield Park played against several local teams including East Grinstead, East Hoathly, Haywards Heath & Cuckfield, Hurstpierpoint, Lewes, Maresfield, Warbleton and Uckfield and until the major reconstruction of the ground in 1877-78 the matches appear to have been well contested. From that point the Sheffield Park team, augmented by Lord Sheffield's purse, became exceptionally strong with regular appearances by well-known Sussex cricketers, some of whom were being nurtured for the county team. It is surprising that the fixture list was not correspondingly strengthened.

There are few records available that relate to Sheffield Park Cricket Club but a keen researcher would find sufficient material in local newspapers to compile an interesting history for the cricket enthusiast. One such enthusiast was Alfred Gaston who wrote extensively on Sussex cricket in the Sussex press and was on friendly terms with Lord Sheffield. In his column in *The Argus* for 16 July 1906 Gaston noted some of the huge totals made at Sheffield Park and these are listed at Appendix G.

The totals made ranged between 665 and 405 and in each case it was the home team, Sheffield Park, that amassed these scores. Clearly Lord Sheffield liked to see his team do well even though the opponents were usually village teams or clubs from the Brighton parks.

The minnow teams were usually 'devoured' by the Sheffield Park club but Lord Sheffield's customary hospitality helped to make amends for a long day in the field. In addition the bands from Chailey, Newick and East Grinstead were regularly in attendance.

Gaston's research also unearthed some remarkable individual performances which indicate how one-sided some of the fixtures must have been. The following are three examples:

In 1890 the Sheffield Park professional, Osborne, took all ten Horsted Keynes wickets for just four runs.

In 1897 there were 419 runs scored before lunch in the match between Sheffield Park and Nutley. The Sussex CCC amateur George Arlington went on to score 309, an innings that included one hit for seven, 12 hits for five and 24 hits for four. Even the 64 year-old R.W. Kellow scored 92.

In 1904 Sussex CCC's Australian Ben Dwyer took nine Portslade wickets for 10 runs.

There are countless other examples to be discovered but very few where a member of a visiting team achieved a performance of note. So it is was a relief to find the following:

Playing for St Peter's, Brighton against Sheffield Park on Saturday 20 June 1891, Ernest Newman made a leg-hit for 12 runs from the bowling of Alfred Payne, the ball travelling past the refreshment bar and down the hill as far as the ornamental wooden bridge.

Further evidence of visiting teams being offered as lambs to the slaughter is shown in Gaston's table of individual innings in excess of 200 runs. All the scores were made by Sheffield Park batsmen against local opposition.

Score	Batsman	Against	Year
309	G. H. Arlington	Nutley	1897
285	A. Payne	Barcombe	1891
255	W. A. Tester	Stanford	1882
255	G. H. Arlington	Preston Stragglers	1895
250*	J. Gilbert	Newick	1884
239	W. Humphreys	Birch Grove	1885
230*	G. H. Arlington	Stragglers	1896
213	A. Blackman	Isfield	1894
207*	G. H. Arlington	Framfield	1896

Despite the one-sided fixtures many famous, interesting and exceedingly accomplished cricketers played in the Sheffield Park teams and three players merit special mention:

John Gilbert (1830–96) was 53 years old when he made his highest score for Sheffield Park of 250 not out against Newick in 1884: 'During the afternoon he ran 450 runs and as the only boundary was the pavilion, as a mere matter of staying power, it was a

A tiny silver plaque presented by Lord Sheffield to John Gilbert on a new bat for his impressive score of 250 not out. (T. Turk)

remarkable performance for a man of his years.' Lord Sheffield marked Gilbert's achievement with a silver plaque and a new bat.

Seven years after John Gilbert's great innings *Cricket* informed its readers that:

> For nearly half a century John Gilbert has been a familiar personality in Sussex cricket and the veteran's hand does not seem even now to have lost its ancient cunning. Playing for Sheffield Park against Barcombe (in 1891) he did an excellent bowling performance taking three wickets with his first three balls, and altogether five wickets in fifteen balls for six runs.

When he died at Cob's Nest, Newick in 1896 the press noted that he had been one of the first to join Sheffield Park Cricket Club when it started and had been a regular playing member of the club for about 50 years. Lord Sheffield sent a magnificent wreath for the funeral and his card read: 'In memory of a valued friend, and of a sincere friendship of fifty years, Sheffield.' John Gilbert's only first-class match was for Lord Sheffield's XI against Alfred Shaw's XI in 1881 when he was 50 years old.

Henry Stubberfield (1835-1918) (N. J. G. Sharp)

George Arlington (1871–1940) was a powerful, dashing batsman whose four enormous scores for Sheffield Park dominate Gaston's table of double centurions. His career for Sussex (1894–8) of 29 first-class matches was disappointing but in club cricket he scored over a hundred centuries. These included 224* for Lewes Priory v. Seaford in 1898; 162* for Hastings v. Brighton Brunswick in 1898 and 156* and 102 for Stratford-on-Avon v. G. F. Jackson's XI at the Saffrons, Eastbourne in 1903. Sadly in 1940 he brought about his own demise when he walked off into the Queensland bush.

Henry Stubberfield (1835–1918) had been a useful bowler in the Sussex eleven between 1857 and 1874 representing his county in 57 first-class matches. He was later employed by Lord Sheffield at Sheffield Park where he became something of an institution. He accompanied other professionals like Alfred Shaw and John Gilbert on some of Lord Sheffield's overseas excursions. He was at different times a carpenter, tobacconist and publican as well as a professional cricketer in New York. 'Old Stubber' appears in many team

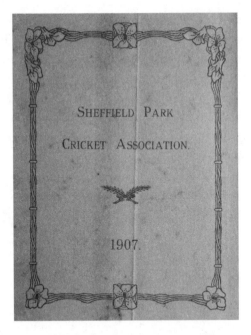

Sheffield Park Cricket Association Fixtures
and Rules 1907. (Mrs H.Rawlings)

photographs as an umpire at Sheffield Park and elsewhere and he
umpired the match at Hove in 1864 when W. G. Grace scored 170
not out as a 15-year-old. In 1893 while attending the match at
Sheffield Park between Lord Sheffield's XI and the Australians, he
slipped on a stone and broke his leg at the ankle.

The fortunes of Sheffield Park Cricket Club were directed,
naturally, by Lord Sheffield and there were seasons when there was
little or no cricket. The Park was closed in 1887–89 and 1900–03
while Lord Sheffield sought to discover the perpetrators of anonymous letters and obtain a drinks licence for his matches. In 1895 the
season ended prematurely when Lord Sheffield departed for
the Crimea.

There was a marked decline in Sheffield Park cricket in the
seasons preceding the earl's death in 1909 and in 1905 the club only
played five matches. However, in 1907 Lord Sheffield agreed to
support a desire for league cricket:

SHEFFIELD PARK CRICKET ASSOCIATION
In response to the suggestion on the part of the new Committee of
the Sussex County C.C. that Associations should be formed in all
parts of the county in order to foster latent talent, Lord Sheffield has
organised the above League. Six clubs are affiliated this year viz.:
Sheffield Park, Maresfield, Isfield, Ringmer, Nutley and Uckfield.
Lord Sheffield will present a Cup with thirteen sovereigns in it to the
winning team each year.

The heady days, though, were over and Sheffield Park CC lost all its
matches to teams they had once soundly beaten. The final table read:

	P	W	L	D	Pts
Maresfield	5	5	0	0	20
Uckfield	5	4	1	0	16
Ringmer	5	3	2	0	12
Isfield	5	2	3	0	8
Nutley	5	1	4	0	4
Sheffield Park	5	0	5	0	0

Sheffield Park Centurions

During the existence of Sheffield Park Cricket Club scores in local
club and village cricket were usually very modest but at Sheffield
Park the home batsmen were quite likely to make large scores.
William Moore's pitches were the best prepared of any outside the
first-class game. Before the reconstruction of the ground in 1876, it
is on record that Charles Payne's century, when he was bowled out
by Lord Sheffield, was the only one scored at that point. From 1877
to 1907 there were at least 98 centuries scored, (see Appendix G)
which is evidence of both the groundsman's skill and the inadequacy
of some visiting bowlers. Most of the centuries, which include nine
scores over 200, were scored by batsmen of some note though
remarkably none were scored in the first-class matches played there.

* * *

Lord Sheffield's desire to promote cricket in Sussex was not confined to the county club or to the first class and club matches played at Sheffield Park. He maintained an involvement with many local clubs and at different times he was president or patron of Brighton Brunswick, Cuckfield, Eastbourne, Lindfield, Newhaven, Newick, Preston (just outside Brighton), Preston Stragglers, Rye and Sheffield Park in addition to his three terms of presidency and one as patron of the county club. There is no doubt that these clubs, and there were probably others, received considerable financial support and prestige from his involvement.

His encouragement of local cricket also extended to the creation and support of new cricket grounds in the county and he contributed to the establishment of The Saffrons ground at Eastbourne, Preston Park and a new cricket ground at Newhaven.

Eastbourne
Eastbourne v Lord Sheffield's XI
5 May 1886
A report of the opening match at the Saffrons appeared in the *Eastbourne Chronicle* for 8 May :

CRICKET AT SAFFRONS FIELD OPENING MATCH
Saffrons Field was the scene on Wednesday of the inaugural cricket match, and circumstances combined to render the day's proceedings in every respect an unqualified success. The match took place between a representative eleven of the Eastbourne Club and Lord Sheffield's Eleven and both sides exhibited some capital play, a very interesting game being the result. Prior to the match Mr C. Jackson (an ardent devotee to cricket) presented the Eastbourne Club, on behalf of the Misses Jackson, with a handsome new flag, and on tendering the gift expressed a hope that the match that day would be the precursor of many successful matches on that admirable ground. There was only a small attendance when play commenced, but as the match proceeded the number of spectators increased, and it is computed that during the afternoon the match was witnessed by fully a thousand onlookers. The

Lord Sheffield's XI for the opening match at the Saffrons, Eastbourne 1886: Back row: ? , Taylor (Scorer), Rev. W. Summers, H. Stubberfield, G. Bean, A. Shaw, W. T. Moore. Seated: W. Payne, R. T. Ellis, F. F. J. Greenfield, J. Gilbert, E. McCormick, A. Huggett. In front: W. Humphreys, A. Payne, H. Phillips (N.J.G.Sharp)

performances of the Militia Band lent an additional charm to the proceedings.

The game commenced about 11.30. The Eastbourne captain won the toss and elected to take first innings, sending in the brothers Hide. The bowling was entrusted to Bean and Huggett. The score was steadily raised to 24 when Jesse had to retire being bowled by Bean for an excellent 14. The Rev. von Scott did not stop long and at 35 Arthur Hide was dismissed. Whitfeld, the two Jacksons and Hurst were soon disposed of but L. Jeffery and R. S. Hart gave the bowlers some trouble. At 79 a separation was, however, effected, Hart playing on to Huggett. A determined stand was made by the last two men, W. A. Cardwell and L. Jeffery, bringing on two bowling changes. At 153, however, Cardwell fell to McCormick for a useful 20. Jeffery played a good not out innings of 41. The players then adjourned for luncheon.

After luncheon Sheffield Park lost two wickets for 10 runs. Humphreys, however, played excellently but was dismissed by a good catch. Ellis and McCormick fell to good catches. Half the wickets were down for 35 runs but Greenfield and Bean on being partnered took the score to 67 when the professional retired.

Ten runs later Greenfield was clean bowled by Jesse Hide for a useful 12 and then W. Payne and Huggett were together. The two East Grinstead players showed first-class cricket although a faulty stroke was made now and again, and, in spite of three bowling changes, passed their opponents' score. At 174, however, a separation was effected, Huggett foolishly running himself out in attempting a short run. The retiring batsman had displayed good cricket and among his figures were one four, seven threes and eight twos. During their long partnership 107 runs had been registered. J.Gilbert joined Payne and the two batsmen played out time. Sheffield Park was thus left victorious by 40 runs on the first innings and had two wickets to spare. Messrs Lavis of Terminus-road photographed both teams separately and also together, and some copies are now exhibited in their windows.

EASTBOURNE		LORD SHEFFIELD'S XI	
Jesse Hide b Bean	14	H. Phillips run out	0
A. Hide c W. Payne b Bean	12	A.Payne b A.Hide	2
Rev. Von. H. Scott b Bean	6	Humphreys c Hurst b J. Hide	20
T.M. Bergg c & b W. Payne	13	Rev F.J. Greenfield b J. Hide	12
S. Whitfield c Greenfield b Bean	0	R.T. Ellis c J. Hide b A. Hide	1
J.R. Jackson b Bean	5	McCormick c J. Hide b A. Hide	5
.F. Jackson b Huggett	8	G. Bean b J. Hide	16
A.S. Hurst b Huggett	5	W. Payne not out	58
L. Jeffery not out	41	Huggett run out	58
Hart b Huggett	17	J. Gilbert not out	9
W.A. Cardwell b McCormick	20	Rev. W. Summers did not bat	
Extras	12	Extras	12
Total	153	Total	193

Preston Park
Brighton Brunswick v Sheffield Park
12 May 1887
The cricket ground at Preston Park, to the north of Brighton, was laid out in 1887 on the International Gun Polo Club grounds. It was

opened by the Mayor of Brighton, Edward Reeves, and although the extent of Lord Sheffield's involvement in the new ground is not specified in the following report, it is clear that he made a significant contribution. Lord Sheffield's team graced the occasion as they had at the opening of the Saffrons twelve months earlier and on this occasion the earl's team included seven Sussex county players, Montague Turner (Middlesex), his nephew Aubrey Harcourt, the veteran John Gilbert and Herbert Hardy of Danehurst, J.P., who was to die the following year leaving a widow, Louisa (née Knight). She was a great niece of Jane Austen and her father had played county cricket for Kent and Hampshire.

The Preston Park ground also had a cycle track and it attracted thousands of spectators to meetings after World War II. It also has a cricket war memorial in the pavilion.

The opening of the ground was recorded in the *Sussex Express*:

OPENING MATCH ON THE PRESTON PARK
CRICKET GROUND – LORD SHEFFIELD'S
ELEVEN v BRIGHTON BRUNSWICK

The opening match on the new cricket ground in Preston Park was played on Thursday between Lord Sheffield's team and a team representing the Brighton Brunswick Club. The ground is regarded as a decided acquisition to the attractions of the town and general admiration was expressed by both cricketers and the public at the manner in which the shrubs and trees have been utilised and displayed by the Recreation Grounds Committee and its officers, and it was predicted that but a comparatively short time was required to make the turf, which measures about 200 yards by 170 yards, perfect. An admirable feature in the arrangement was the number of seats ranged in tiers along the raised eastern boundary of the ground, providing accommodation for two thousand spectators, sheltered from cold winds and having the full beauty of the landscape before them. Bands played during the day and upwards of seven thousand people witnessed the match, the weather being very favourable.

At two o'clock a very imposing luncheon party assembled within

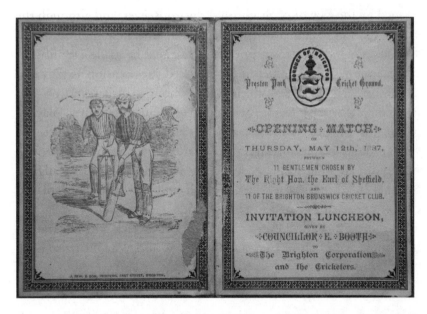

Menu and Toast List for the opening match at Preston Park, near Brighton 12 May, 1887. (N. J. G. Sharp)

a grand marquee at the invitation of Councillor Booth, president of the Brighton Brunswick Club. Councillor BOOTH presided and was supported by the Mayor (Alderman Reeves), Colonel Tester, Colonel Verrall, Colonel Wood, Aldermen Abbey, Brigden, Davey and Lamb, the Rev. J.J. Hannah, the Rev. Dr Hamilton, the Town Clerk (Mr Tillstone), Councillor Saunders (chairman of the Recreation Grounds Committee), Alderman Martin and Alderman Manwaring. Letters of apology for absence were received from the Earl of Sheffield, Mr W.T.Marriott, Q.C., M.P., Dr Tindall Robertson, M.P., Ven. Archdeacon Hannah etc.

During the course of the after-dinner proceedings, Alderman BRIGDEN proposed 'Health, happiness and long life to the Earl of Sheffield' and remarked that all were aware that this nobleman had associated his name with cricket for many years and that no individual nobleman or gentleman had made such munificent gifts, or shown such hospitality to those of the cricketing fraternity as the Earl of Sheffield (applause). Certainly he deserved their highest thanks (hear, hear). All were pleased that the noble earl had got a team to come to Brighton to assist them in a formal opening of the ground, and that they esteemed it a great favour (applause). Whilst recently things had transpired which had been of an annoying and irritating character to his lordship, he could assure him that the Mayor and Corporation of Brighton, and the town generally, were of opinion that there was no gentleman who was so kind and liberal towards Brighton and Sussex generally as the Earl of Sheffield (applause). He was associated with many of the philanthropic institutions of the town and it was the desire of the earl to do all he could for his fellow men (loud applause). The match was of a very one-sided character, Sheffield Park winning easily by 187 runs.

BRIGHTON BRUNSWICK		SHEFFIELD PARK	
G. Humphreys b. J. Hide	0	Mr F. J. Greenfield b. F. Clements	94
B. J. Saunders c. Hide b. Bean	24	A.Payne b. Blackman	1
F. T. Pearson c. Hide b. Bean	1	Tester c. Stevens b. F. Clements	39
A. Blackman b. Bean	10	W. Payne b. Stevens	5
W. Dudney c. Harcourt b. Bean	1	J. Hide b. Blackman	30
H. Stevens c. Greenfield b. Hide	9	Bean c.Humphreys b. Blackman	22
W. Clements c. Tester b. Bean	6	Mr A. Harcourt b. Blackman	4
F. Clements run out	0	Mr M. Turner c and b. F. Clements	6
F. Bailey b. Bean	3	Mr R. M. Curteis not out	15
A. G. E. Godden not out	1	J. Gilbert b. F. Clements	2
G. Goldsmith b. Bean	1	Mr H. C. Hardy b. Blackman	6
Extras	2	Extras	21
	58		245

Bowling					Bowling				
J. Hide	21	4	40	2	Mr Goldsmith	16	4	40	0
Bean	22.2	14	16	7	Mr A. Blackman	28	5	72	5
					Mr F. Clements	23	3	57	4
					Mr F. Bailey	2	0	8	0
					Mr E. H. Stevens	5	1	13	1
					Mr F. T. Pearson	7	2	24	0
					Mr W. Clements	2	1	10	0

Newhaven
Newhaven v Lord Sheffield's XI
26 May 1890

LORD SHEFFIELD AND NEWHAVEN
OPENING OF THE NEW CRICKET GROUND

Lord Sheffield's practical endeavours for the improvement of Newhaven and its surroundings was marked yesterday by an important step towards their realisation in the opening of the magnificent cricket ground, which his lordship has laid out at very considerable expense. As will doubtless be known, this cricket ground forms a section of his lordship's grand scheme for improving and beautifying a hitherto barren and swampy locality. The cricket ground is situated on the western side of the river in a valley bounded by the Pier road on the east, the coast line of cliffs (on the summit of which is Newhaven fort) on the south, and in a northerly and westerly direction by a spur of the South Downs. Those unacquainted with this spot in its former aspect can hardly conceive the great transformation which has converted it from the marshland that it was into a fine terrain of over five acres in extent, with a surface as level as a billiard table. This has been brought about by the judicious distribution of more than 9,000 tons of chalk filling, taken from the chalk quarries adjoining, faced with a two-foot layer of mould and covered with Down turf. All obstructing ponds and ditches have been filled in and an efficient system of land drainage has been substituted. The work has been carried out under the immediate supervision of Mr Moore (his lordship's landscape gardener and ground manager at Sheffield Park) and throughout the past winter, in accordance with his lordship's considerate desire, exclusively Newhaven labour has been employed thereon.

The approach to the site is by way of the Fort road, which has been completely transformed during the last ten weeks. The road has been widened (by additional land given by Lord Sheffield), curbed and channelled with stone, and on the side adjoining Lord Sheffield's land a substantial brick footpath has been laid.

This improvement will be a great boon to the Newhaven

Opening match at the new ground for Newhaven Cricket Club 26 May, 1890 (Sussex CCC)

community and will still further tend to attract a residential population to this picturesque spot, which is now ripe for building purposes. It is the earl's intention to ultimately further extend the cricket ground itself and to lay out a recreation ground. The difficulty his lordship experienced in securing the tenancy of that portion of the ground belonging to the War Department was, indeed, great and was only secured by his determination to, if possible, carry out his scheme.

He proposed that the time for completing the work should extend over two years so as to afford the certainty of employment to a large amount of labour during two consecutive winters. As the works would cost £4,000 the larger portion of which would be spent in labour, he had the satisfaction of feeling that he was contributing to the well-being of the poorer classes in the town by giving them the means of procuring continuous employment during the trying winter months for two years.

Lord Sheffield has not been unmindful of the numerous juvenile population of the town, to whom the intended recreation ground will come as a great boon, and who, but for the generous indulgence of Mr Hobbs in allowing them the run of his field for years past, would practically have been without a playground.

It is not anticipated that the ground opened yesterday will be used on many occasions this year but will be allowed to mature undisturbed, Lord Sheffield having made arrangements for the Newhaven club to retain their present ground for this season.

Not only have the supporters of cricket reason to be grateful to Lord Sheffield but his general interest in all recreations has been fully manifested, as besides being president of the Newhaven Harbour regatta and of the cricket and cycling clubs, he is also patron of the rowing and golf clubs, each and all of which institutions he has liberally supported. The material comforts of the poor during the past three or four winters have been liberally provided for by his lordship by the distribution of food and clothing, thus showing his sympathetic kindness in his capacity of Lord of the Manor.

During the past month the site of the new cricket ground has been the scene of active operations in preparation for the grand opening day, and towards the latter end of the week the iron fencing, with wire netting, which now encircles the ground, was completed, and numerous marquees and tents erected.

On Sunday the arrival of Lord Sheffield in his yacht (the *Heloise*) was witnessed by over a thousand people who had assembled on the western pier promenade. Punctually to the arranged time the *Heloise* was taken in tow by the harbour tug. Hearty indeed was the welcome that greeted her appearance. A shot was fired from the harbour gun and rounds of cheers were given by the large assembly, which were acknowledged by his lordship and party bowing their recognition, the crew responding with cheers, to the applause of those on shore. Never before in the history of Newhaven was such an enthusiastic gathering assembled with so pleasing and gratifying an object.

The eventful day for Newhaven opened grandly, and the towns-people were very early in the day busily engaged decorating the town, numbers of lines of streamers were placed across the streets from the house tops, and all the ships in the harbour and the many flagstaffs on shore were decorated in a most elaborate manner, and gave proof of the unanimity of appreciation of the noble earl's desire to provide for Newhaven a pleasant and successful day.

The ground and its surroundings presented a most animated and healthful appearance. The row of dwellings on the hillside had during the past few days received a white coating, as also had the surrounding buildings, fences etc and the general appearance of freshness was marked. Flagstaffs with varied coloured streamers surrounded the ground, at the entrance to which was erected a triumphal archway, artistically decorated with flags, evergreens, azaleas, rhododendrons, laburnum, lilac, thorn blossoms, and foliage surmounted by an earl's coronet. Wickets, bats, balls, pads and gloves were introduced into the decoration which was completed in good time.

The earl was met at the entrance by the Chairman and members of the Local Board, also the representatives of the various societies and institutions in the town. The cyclist club were strongly represented by a number of the members with their cycles, they taking up their position inside the archway, thus forming a picturesque avenue.

The arrival of Lord Sheffield was the signal for a most hearty outburst of cheering and enthusiastic expressions. The teams took to the field punctually to time, Mr Aubrey Harcourt captaining his lordship's eleven, whilst Mr H. Woolgar, the captain of the Newhaven Cricket Club, officiated similarly for the Newhaven team.

The scores in the match were:

NEWHAVEN

First innings		Second innings	
W. G. Quaife b. Parris	39	c. Menzies b. Parris	13
A. Banks c. Greenfield b. Hobden	6	b. Lynn	4
H. Woolgar c. and b. Turner	8	b. Greenfield	8
H. R. Budgen b. Parris	0	c. Lynn b. Greenfield	24
H. A. Chambers c. Curteis b. Lynn	19	lbw b. Parris	6
J. Percy b. Parris	0	st. Somerset b. Greenfield	0
F. W. Tate not out	2	b. Parris	0
J. Coppard c. Malcolmson b. Parris	0	b. Parris	5
E. Minter b. Parris	0	lbw b. Greenfield	0
E. A. Bailey lbw b. Lynn	0	b. Parris	0
G. C. Weller b. Lynn	2	not out	6
Extras	12	Extras	0
	88		66

Bowling

First innings					Second innings			
Harcourt	4	0	10	0				
Hobden	9	2	25	1				
Turner	7	4	10	1				
Lynn	4.1	0	9	3	9	1	25	1
Parris	12	3	22	5	13	6	23	5
Greenfield					5	0	18	4

LORD SHEFFIELD'S XI

First innings		Second innings	
Rev. F.Greenfield c. Banks b. Minter	16	not out	21
A. Somerset b. Minter	13	c. and b. Tate	19
W. Hobden c. Tate b. Minter	9	b. Quaife	18
G. H. Lynn b. Minter	7	c. Percy b. Tate	6
R. M. Curteis b. Tate	5	c. Tate b. Bailey	16
Capt. Menzies b. Tate	3	run out	0
Gen.Malcolmson st. Coppard b. Minter	3		
F. Parris not out	5	not out	1
A. Harcourt b. Minter	1		
W. Turner b. Minter	0		
J. Gilbert b. Tate	4		
Extras	4	Extras	4
	70		85

Bowling

First innings					Second innings			
Percy	5	1	15	0	3	1	8	0
Minter	14	4	31	7	4	1	9	0
Tate	9	3	19	3	14	3	34	2
Bailey					14	4	26	1
Quaife					4	1	4	1

17

Soldiers in the Park

Lord Sheffield's main preoccupations in his eventful life were the estate and gardens at Sheffield Park, cricket, yachting and travel and the Volunteer movement.

From 1889 there were annual gatherings of vast numbers of volunteers at Sheffield Park and the meetings were faithfully described in the local newspapers. Some of these grand occasions took place on the cricket ground and Lord Sheffield engaged the Brighton photographer E. Hawkins & Co. to record some impressive scenes. In an obituary notice these events were summarised:

> For several years Lord Sheffield marked his interest in the Sussex Volunteer Force by organising Field Days at Sheffield Park and paying the entire expenses of conveying officers and men from all parts of the county and entertaining them for the day. In the organisation of these gatherings he was greatly assisted by the late Colonel Hugh Verrall, who, besides being commanding officer of the 1st Vol. Batt. Royal Sussex Regiment, also acted in legal matters for his lordship.

Lord Sheffield was aware of his grandfather's military prowess. The first earl had commanded a troop of Light Horse in Germany under the Marquis of Granby in 1760 and on the outbreak of war in 1778 he accepted a commission in the Sussex Militia which he subsequently commanded. In the following year he raised a regiment of Light Dragoons without expense to the public.

In 1853 the third earl had given a remarkable speech to the Sheffield Park tenantry on the occasion of his twenty-first birthday at the Sheffield Arms. He was still Viscount Pevensey and his impressive speech, delivered at great length, contains the following:

Without being an alarmist, or a prophet, I tell you the peril of war is imminent. The nation most in proximity to our shore, already satiated with the butchery of their own citizens, and the bloodless excitement of maniac victory, naturally turn their eyes to the nation which defeated their armies, and destroyed the ancestor of their imperial despot and attempted to destroy the lineal claims of his descendants . . .

France owes us a heavy repayment for the cannon balls of Waterloo and she is now willing to liquidate that debt at an excessively high rate of interest, perhaps of 1000 per cent, if her purse of human carcases will permit . . .

Now, gentlemen, I maintain there is not only a likelihood but a necessity for a war; and whether that struggle be commenced at a distance on the continent or by a descent on our coast, it is equally our duty to be prepared for the last emergency. Let the whole of the French army come, and I will venture to say that I do not believe that one individual would ever return to tell of their defeat . . .

Why then does Sussex hang back ? Is it because her sons, cradled in the lap of thirty-eight years peace, are reluctant to face the horrors of war ? I tell you, gentlemen, that as you value the blessings of peace, and wish for its maintenance, so must you be prepared for war !

It is easy to dismiss the strong opinions of a 21-year-old but there is no doubt that the young viscount was aware of the privileges of high birth and was anxious to fulfil its obligations. His 'manly and patriotic address' to the tenants had the desired result for a week later it was announced that Fletching had 18 volunteers to the Sussex Militia compared to only two before the speech: 'Sussex is not wanting in its military ardour, it only requires direction.'

Nearly half a century later Lord Sheffield demonstrated that his interest in military matters was thoroughly practical when, in May 1900, a national appeal was made for the formation of rifle clubs. Lord Sheffield's response was to issue the following circular letter:

The Prime Minister of England, the Marquis of Salisbury, having appealed to the patriotism of the English people to prepare themselves by the formation of local 'Rifle Clubs' throughout the

An undated photograph of the march past in front of Lord Sheffield's pavilion. (N. J. G. Sharp)

country to meet the danger of an invasion, which the English Minister seems to foresee in the not very distant future, I propose to offer facilities to the residents in the parishes of Fletching, Danehill, Newick and Chailey, to practise rifle shooting and to become acquainted with the use of the rifle. I will provide a rifle range in my Park, of 600 yards -free of all expense to those who use it. All arms and ammunition will be provided either by myself or the government. I will provide all the targets, butts, shelters and other necessaries for the shooters free of all cost. An efficient Musketry Instructor will be provided and I will offer prizes of considerable value for the best shots. Further details will be announced as soon as completed. Anyone between the ages of thirteen and sixty-five years (if physically capable) wishing to take advantage of this opportunity of learning to use the rifle will kindly place his signature here (space for name and address). Anyone resident in the above-mentioned parishes and willing to join can obtain this form on application to THE EARL OF SHEFFIELD, SHEFFIELD PARK.

However, Lord Sheffield's greatest contribution to military affairs was undoubtedly the spectacular events for the Sussex Volunteer movement that were staged annually at Sheffield Park. These grand occasions consisted of mock battles between volunteers involving neighbouring parishes, an impressive march past at the cricket ground and of course Lord Sheffield's splendid hospitality.

Perhaps the most brilliant of all the Volunteer functions held in the Park was the great Review on 25 July 1903 when a 'mighty multitude' of visitors witnessed a sham fight and march past of the military forces of the County:

> Practically all the Volunteers of Sussex took part, together with the 2nd Battalion of the Royal Sussex Regiment and two squadrons of the 18th Hussars. Characteristic kindness and thoughtfulness were shown by Lord Sheffield in the facilities given to the public for enjoying themselves, and from a military standpoint the proceedings were a brilliant success which thoroughly repaid his Lordship for the great expense incurred in an undertaking that was prompted primarily by high patriotic feeling. Although he was unable to attend the Review, Lord Roberts conveyed his appreciation of the support Lord Sheffield had always given to the Volunteer movement, and of the keen interest he had always taken in its progress.

A Photograph for the Royal Engineers

Lord Sheffield was a great supporter of the 1st Sussex Royal Engineer Volunteer Battalion and on occasions placed his grounds at their disposal for camping and military operations: the camp of 1900 extended over four weeks. As the Hon. Colonel of the Regiment he presented silver rose bowls to the men of the battalion who served in South Africa.

On one occasion Lord Sheffield enquired whether a military bridge could be built over a lake. The quartermaster was G. F. Chambers, an Eastbourne historian, and he replied that he only had bridging materials for a length of 50ft whereas the breadth of the lake was 180ft. Lord Sheffield then instructed Thomas Colgate, his agent, to scour the country and collect as many oil casks and planks as possible. This was successful, the bridge was built and Lord Sheffield was so delighted that he allowed himself to be photographed standing alone on the bridge as if 'monarch of all he surveyed'. Mr Colgate told Chambers that he had never known the notoriously shy earl to give his consent under any circumstances to be photographed.

Manoeuvres

The first of Lord Sheffield's Grand Volunteer Reviews took place on 6 July 1889 and was described as one of the prettiest sights imaginable. Special trains were chartered from Brighton, Lewes, Hastings and Rye to convey the volunteers to Sheffield Park and all expenses were paid by Lord Sheffield. After dinner an attacking force consisting of about a thousand men with five guns and 34 horses carried out a mock battle against a defending force of about 600 men. The battle terminated when three companies which had been sent round the northern boundary of the park suddenly appeared from the woods to the north-east of the cricket ground and took the guns placed there to command the road leading to the bridge over the lower lake. After an evening meal the volunteers engaged in sports and there was a tug-of-war between a team of men employed on the Sheffield Park estate and the crew of Lord Sheffield's yacht, *Heloise*.

Finally the flag signallers of the 1st Sussex conveyed the following message from the officers to Lord Sheffield:

> Colonel Wood, Colonel Tamplin and Major Cafe desire to offer their sincere thanks to the Earl of Sheffield for a most pleasant day which their men have thoroughly enjoyed.

Lord Sheffield replied through the flag signallers placed at the top of his cricket pavilion:

> Lord Sheffield thanks Colonel Wood, Colonel Tamplin and Major Cafe for their most kind message. He congratulates them upon the splendid spectacle they have afforded and wishes the Sussex Volunteers prosperity and success.

Volunteer Review at Sheffield Park 18 July 1891. (N. J. G. Sharp)

Sad Fatality

The reviews were an important part of the Sheffield Park calendar and increased in size annually. Lord Sheffield's arrangements were meticulous and generous and in 1891 he had castigated the London press for ignoring his reports of the reviews. Sadly in 1898 there was a freak accident:

A VOLUNTEER'S SHOCKING END

Inspection day marred by shocking accident on 3 June. Part of the programme was to blow up an oak tree in the park and this having been bored, gun cotton was applied and during the course of the morning the fuse was lighted. Sgt Samuel Tingley, aged 35, who was standing 175 yards away from the tree, appears to have been hit by a small piece of the tree and instantly fell. The portion of wood hit him in the head and when his comrades rushed to his assistance they were horrified to find that death had been instantaneous. Mr R. Gravely, a local medical officer, was sent for but could only pronounce life to be extinct. The body was conveyed to the Griffin.

Newick Station Surprise

The manoeuvres were not confined to the immediate area around Sheffield Park and in 1890 a force of volunteers had surprised and captured the staff at Newick & Chailey railway station. Nine men were dressed in railway uniforms – superintendents, ticket collectors and porters – and overpowered the station master and staff who were then forced to assist in the disembarkment of the troops. Passengers alighting at the station were unaware of the alteration to the personnel and it was remarked that the pseudo railway men performed their work as if it was their everyday occupation.

Haldane and Kitchener

In July 1894 a special siding was constructed south of Sheffield Park station to house an armoured train. Lord Haldane, Secretary for War, and Lord Kitchener, then CinC in India were among many notables present and Lord Sheffield had invited every volunteer corps in Sussex and detachments from neighbouring counties. Six special military trains brought 2,000 officers and men with their horses and guns to Newick & Chailey station to form one army while four more specials brought a similar number to Sheffield Park. A battle between the Northern and Southern Forces followed and the Southern army took a battering when the armoured train moved into the cutting beyond Lane End bridge, midway between Sheffield Park and Newick & Chailey, 'blowing the bridge down'.

The March Past

Lord Sheffield's grand reviews always featured a March Past on the cricket ground after the completion of the manoeuvres. These were often photographed and the following is a colourful description from July 1890:

The March Past

The closing ceremony was the March Past which took place on the cricket ground which was suitably roped off. The regiments entered at the extreme end facing his lordship's pavilion while the saluting flag was fixed immediately beneath the same ornate structure. The bands were massed and played facing the pavilion from the gallery of which Lord Sheffield was discerned, surrounded by a number of fashionable ladies and local magnates.

First came the commanding officers of the attacking and defending forces. The Carabineers came next and their handsome uniforms made a pretty sight. Then came Col. Cardwell and the guns of the 2nd Sussex (Eastbourne) Artillery, followed by two strong batteries.

The gun wagons created sad havoc with the beautiful cut turf but of course this was unavoidable. The first of the Eastbourne batteries marched past in a splendid line and they were loudly applauded. The 1st Sussex (Brighton) Rifles made an excellent show. Headed by their pioneers, men of seemingly herculean proportions, they were followed by six strong companies whose regular marching received more than one mark of public approbation. The troupe of cyclists brought up the rear and these were also loudly applauded.The 2nd Sussex Rifles came next, Colonel Campion and the Duke of Norfolk leading the way. The Cadet Corps (formed of students of Hurstpierpoint College) brought up the rear of the defending force. The Brighton Naval Artillery as usual came in for hearty cheering and their famous gun appeared to attract considerable attention.

The Hastings bluejackets, who were distinguished by straw hats in contrast to the white-covered caps of the Brighton men, also marched past exceedingly well. Following came the Brighton Yeomanry and guns and six batteries of Brighton Artillery.

All the batteries with one exception marched in good order and with military precision and their popularity was denoted by the hearty applause which greeted them from the spectators. The Cinque Port Rifles, somewhat appropriately, came last. There were six companies in all but they were not nearly so strong as the Brighton and West Sussex Corps. They looked very smart in their neat grey, and their marching, with the exception of two companies, was compact and steady.

The troops passed out of the cricket ground and were re-formed behind the Pavilion. They then re-entered the ground and marched past in reverse order in quarter column at the trail, acquitting themselves this time with even greater success.

Entertainment

Following the military activity and the March Past, Lord Sheffield ensured that the volunteers were suitably refreshed and the following report also refers to the 1890 review:

LORD SHEFFIELD'S HOSPITALITY

Immediately after the march past Lord Sheffield entertained the officers and a numerous party of friends in the marquee near his pavilion. The repast was described as a tea, but it approached more nearly the character of a banquet. [Guest List included the Duke of Norfolk, Duke of Richmond, Earl and Countess De La Warr, Lord Leconfield, Viscount Gage, Lord Monk Bretton and Sir Anchitel Ashburnham].

The non-commissioned officers and men were marched to their respective canteens and owing to the excellent arrangements of Mr Welfare every man was served with bread and cheese and ale in less than 20 minutes. As the evening closed the battalions left the grounds one after another for their railway stations and bade adieu to the noble earl with rounds of hearty cheering.

Military Funeral

The reviews played an important part in the history of Sheffield Park from 1889 until Lord Sheffield's death in 1909. Extensive coverage appeared in the *Sussex Agricultural Express* where there were often eye-catching headlines such as those from August 1895:

GRAND VOLUNTEER REVIEW AT SHEFFIELD PARK
LORD SHEFFIELD'S MUNIFICENCE
THE BATTLE OF CHAILEY CLUMP
A BRILLIANT SUCCESS

When Lord Sheffield died his position as Hon. Colonel of the Home Counties Royal Engineers entitled him to full military honours. Over 200 members of the regiment attended the funeral with firing party and band and the coffin was conveyed on a gun carriage drawn by six horses with postillions.

18

Death of Lord Sheffield

Lord Sheffield's health had been a concern for many years and although he was able to take on the Sussex CCC presidency in 1904 and entertain 240 of the Chichester Regiment of the Church Lads' Brigade at Sheffield Park that year, he slowly became quite poorly and often spent winters abroad.

In 1907 Lord Sheffield decided to form a Sheffield Park Cricket Association for league matches to be played between Sheffield Park (Fletching residents only), Chailey, Horsted Keynes, Maresfield, Nutley, Isfield and Uckfield.

A sign of his decline came at the end of the same year when he decided to dispose of a valuable part of his library. Nearly 400 rare books and scarce tracts – many of them relating to America – were taken to the sale room 'and their value was attested by the remarkable prices paid by collectors for these treasures'. Several of the tracts were purchased at sums running into three figures. Earlier in the same year many extremely valuable engravings from Sheffield Park had also been sold.

In the early part of 1908 Lord Sheffield stayed at Brighton for some time but scarcely ever went out and on returning to Sheffield Park there was no improvement. For a considerable period he had suffered from a heart condition and during the winter of 1908–1909 he was seldom able to get about except in a bath chair.

His health gradually declined further and he lost his old, keen interest in public affairs 'a pathetic melancholy falling upon him'. There were some brighter intervals and everything possible was done for him. At the end of 1908 his removal to the south of France inspired for a while further hope of a recovery but there was a relapse. He passed away at Beaulieu-sur-Mer, near Nice, in the

The funeral procession at Sheffield Park 4 May 1909. (R. Packham)

afternoon of Wednesday, 21 April 1909. He had been due to return to Sheffield Park the following week.

The *Argus* added that:

> the public have heard from time to time of late that his lordship has been unwell but only his intimate friends knew how serious his illness was. The death of his lordship has caused much regret among the English community in the neighbourhood (Beaulieu) and many expressions of sympathy have been tendered to Miss Attenborough, his lordship's adopted daughter and her sister. The news yesterday of his lordship's death created surprise throughout the Sheffield Park district as well as in all other parts of Sussex.
>
> Yesterday there was a meeting of the Sussex County Cricket Club when a resolution was passed expressing regret at the death of one who had done so much for the Club and for the game.

On the day that members of the 1909 Australian cricket team arrived in London, A. J. Gaston wrote:

Lord Sheffield's coffin in Fletching High Street. (R. Packham)

The death of Lord Sheffield has cast quite a gloom upon thousands of cricket enthusiasts, especially in Sussex, the county which he loved so well, and his memory will for long be greatly cherished. No nobleman strived more zealously in the interests of the grand old game of cricket than Lord Sheffield. The money he spent on entertaining teams, especially the Australians and South Africans at his charming ground at Sheffield Park, when the whole of his grounds were thrown open to the public, will never be known, and the grand matches and illuminations will not readily be forgotten. His Lordship was exceedingly kind to me on many occasions, not only at the great cricket carnivals, but at other periods granting me the favour of reproducing for my cricket lectures in Sussex some of the most beautiful portraits from his Lordship's private collection of Sheffield House, the park, the lake and the picturesque cricket ground. The late Earl lived to see cricket pass through many changes. In all of these, his generosity, counsel and support in great matches and small, were freely given and beneficially used, and his efforts were deeply appreciated by young and old throughout the county of Sussex.

The funeral procession outside Fletching Church. (R. Packham)

The Funeral

Lord Sheffield's body was brought back to Sheffield Park and was placed in the hall of the mansion until the funeral. There is a photograph of a mourning room at Sheffield Park showing a rare portrait of Lord Sheffield on display. Nearly a fortnight after he died this complex, benevolent man was laid to rest at a military funeral at Fletching:

> In the family mausoleum, which adjoins the fine old village church at Fletching, the late Lord Sheffield was laid to rest on Tuesday afternoon, hundreds of men, women and children witnessing the last solemn rites. In view of the late Earl's position as Hon. Colonel of the Home Counties Royal Engineers, it was befitting that full military honours should be paid him. Between 200 and 300 members of the regiment attended the funeral, with firing party and band, and from the mansion in the Park to Fletching Church the coffin was conveyed on a gun carriage drawn by six horses with postillions. The engineers were draughted from Eastbourne, Brighton and Hastings.

Shortly after three o'clock, the body encased in a shell and handsomely carved coffin of olive wood with brass fittings, was removed from the hall at the mansion, where it had remained since its arrival from Beaulieu, on to the gun carriage, six officers of the regiment acting as bearers. The coffin was covered with the Union Jack, and on the top lay the late Colonel's helmet and sword, also two beautiful wreaths, one from his adopted daughter (Miss Attenborough), and the other from his niece, the Countess of Winchilsea. By way of the riding road, the mournful procession wended its way through the beautiful park to Fletching Church, which is opposite the lodge gate.

The firing party headed the cortege, followed by the other members of the regiment and the band. Next came the coffin and carriage bearing the floral tributes, following which were the mourners' carriages, household servants, estate employees, tenantry and general public. En route the band played appropriate burial music. The arrival of the procession at the village was awaited by crowds of people from the immediate neighbourhood, whilst a number of mourners had assembled from a distance. The pretty little village has probably never been so well filled for years.

At the church lych-gate the coffin was met by the choir and clergy, who preceded it to the church, the Vicar, Rev. E.P.Hood, reciting the opening verses. The church was crowded, the seating accommodation being practically utilised by the chief mourners, engineers and tenantry. The service opened with the singing of Psalm 39, after which Canon Gepp, chaplain at Beaulieu, where Lord Sheffield died, and Honorary Canon of Norwich, read the lesson. The brief but impressive service concluded with the hymn, 'And Thou, beloved Lord, Thy soul resigning.'

Leaving the church the cortege proceeded along the narrow path to the mausoleum, which is situated on the north side of the church. There the remainder of the burial service was conducted, and to the accompaniment of the band the hymn, 'Let Saints on earth in concert sing' was rendered. At the conclusion of the service a portion of the firing party fired volleys over the mausoleum, the band playing bars of the Dead March between. The solemn proceedings terminated with the sounding of the 'Last Post' by the trumpeters and drummers. So great was the crowd round the mausoleum that the whole of the firing party were unable to shoot. The chief mourners having taken a last glance at the coffin as it lay beside a dozen more, containing the remains of the deceased Lord's ancestors, the tenantry and general public were permitted to take a passing view. A coronet was to be seen resting on one of the old coffins. Twenty-three floral tributes were received and for inspection they were arranged in the churchyard. It was late in the evening when the village had recovered its normal state, and the funeral of Henry North Holroyd, 3rd Earl of Sheffield will ever remain in the memory of those who witnessed it.

On this memorable occasion the chief mourners were Miss May Attenborough (Lord Sheffield's adopted daughter for 14 years), her sister Hilda, Sir Arthur and Lady Paget and Lord Stanley. Local gentry were represented by Captain Sir John Shiffner, from Chailey, Colonel Dewe (Lewes), Robert Blencowe (of Bineham, Chailey) and Colonel Lynch-Staunton.

The employees of Sheffield Park were represented by Mr Weston (butler), Mrs Randell (housekeeper), Mr Greenfield (head gardener), Thomas Colgate (steward) and the principal tenantry.

Mourners from the cricket world included W. Newham and Coun. Godfree (both representing Sussex CCC), veteran Sussex professionals in Henry Stubberfield, Walter Humphreys and George Lynn; Robert Curteis from Windmill Hill, E. A. Bailey (Brighton) and of course A.J.Gaston, the well-known cricket historian, columnist, collector and friend of Lord Sheffield.

There were uniformed officers from the Uckfield Fire Brigade of which Lord Sheffield was principal subscriber and representatives from Newhaven and the Ashdown Forest Commoners' Protection Association.

Floral tributes were received from Lord Sheffield's niece, Edith, Countess of Winchilsea and Nottingham and from May Attenborough whose message read: 'In most loving memory of my guardian, from his adopted daughter, May. Eternal rest grant unto you.'

There were flowers from the Committee of Sussex CCC; Brighton, Hove & District Cricket Association; R. W. Kellow (Captain of the old St Mary's CC, Brighton) and the Brighton players in his Lordship's XI – E.A. Bailey, C. F. Butcher, A. Collins, P. Cartwright, L. V. Donne, J. Meaden and A.Wilton.

Tributes were also received from Miss Hilda Attenborough, Mr & Mrs William Moore (Lord Sheffield's groundsman), Fletching trade, Sheffield Park Estate tenants, Sussex County Rifle Association, Rev. E. P. Hood, Mr & Mrs Joseph Martin (Fletching Mill), Ashdown Forest Protection Association, Chailey Heritage Crafts School ('in memory of many kindnesses and happy visits to Sheffield Park') and the Sheffield Park household servants ('with deepest regret and in memory of a good and kind master from his sorrowing household servants').

The gross value of Lord Sheffield's estate was £126,994 but it was reported as being heavily mortgaged. Under the will Charles Greenfield (gardener), Shem Weston (butler) and William Moore (cricket groundman) each received £150 and Miss Attenborough and other members of her family were generously provided for.

With Lord Sheffield's death and there being no male heir of his grandfather (the first Earl), the earldom and the viscounty of Pevensey in the Peerage of Ireland and the barony of Sheffield in the Peerage of the United Kingdom, became extinct.

However, the barony of Sheffield of Roscommon passed to Lord Stanley of Alderley whose grandfather (the first Lord Stanley) had married Lady Maria Josepha Holroyd, daughter of the first Lord Sheffield. Through this line the present Lord Stanley of Alderley is the 8th Baron Sheffield and he kindly contributed a foreword to the programme for Lord Sheffield's XI v Old England at Fletching in 2006. His daughter is the wife of David Cameron, leader of the Conservative party.

19

Sheffield Park
1909–2009

Arthur Gilstrap Soames (1854–1934) appears to have had an arrangement with Lord Sheffield about having an option to purchase Sheffield Park in the event of the earl's death. Soames was another Etonian who made his money in brewing and malting in Lincolnshire and he had fallen in love with Sheffield Park while staying nearby in 1889. He was 54 years old when Lord Sheffield died and was one of the principal creditors finally purchasing the estate from the executors in 1910.

Soames was a very keen horticulturist but he also had to devote a considerable amount of time and money on the house. An article in the *Sussex County Magazine* in 1927 explains why :

> Mr Soames had to resuscitate the house entirely besides making many additions, for it was totally inadequate to present-day requirements. There was only one bathroom, no lighting and practically no heating. He made a new and very handsome dining room and the old dining room which was inconveniently situated is now a billiard room.

The signing of the Versailles peace treaty was celebrated in the Park and in 1919 Mr Soames surprised his friends by marrying the widow of Daniel van de Hegdt. She was Agnes Helen née Peel, a granddaughter of the great prime minister Sir Robert Peel and her aunt was Elizabeth, Duchess of Wellington who had married the son and successor of the Iron Duke. Helen brought with her many interesting pictures and engravings in connection with Wellington's career.

A.G.Soames (National Trust)

A glimpse of the cricket ground after World War I comes from the pen of Alfred Gaston, an old cricket friend of Lord Sheffield's who was invited to a garden party and 'county gathering' at Sheffield Park by Mr and Mrs Soames in May 1921:

> I had with others a delightful time among the lovely gardens at Sheffield Park last week. I went afterwards to view the cricket ground. It was a shock. All the past glories were absent and the once delightful pitch a thing of the past. One pleasing feature when we entered by the Park Lodge was to find the same trusted gamekeeper and his wife who were there when the Australian team visited Sheffield Park in 1884, 37 years ago.

The famous old cricket ground was fading away and there is a further reference to it in a report of another garden party in 1927:

> The guests could sit on the terrace that is entwined with yellow banksias, with graceful pendants of blue wisteria above their heads they will see the four great lakes in which pink, white and orange

water lilies grow. If they walked to the cricket ground the more ornamental of the two pavilions remains but the other has just been rebuilt by the owners as a refreshment stand for visitors when Sheffield Park is thrown open to the public for the benefit of the Royal Sussex County Hospital.

Arthur Soames, DL, JP, passed away at Sheffield Park on 22 July 1934, aged 80, leaving an estate of a gross value of £989,634 and he was buried in Fletching Church. 'As a young man he had been fond of hunting and shooting but in his later years he became an ardent horticulturist. He enlarged the gardens at Sheffield Park and succeeded in acclimatizing many rare trees and shrubs. The gardens are famous for these and for roses, rhododendrons and azaleas and they were among the first private gardens to be opened to the public in the cause of charity, notably the Royal Sussex County Hospital, of which Mr Soames was a generous benefactor, and the Queen's Institute of District Nursing.'

Queen Mary sent a telegram, to Mrs Soames:

> I am grieved to hear of your husband's death and send you my warmest sympathy in your sorrow – Mary R

The Queen visited the house in June 1932, May 1933 and October 1938 and liked to take tea in the Orangery. Her son, King George VI, signed the visitors' book on 13 September 1942. After her husband's death Mrs Soames remained at Sheffield Park and there is a memory that cricket was still occasionally played there by Fletching in the years before World War II.

World War II

Sheffield Park was requisitioned by the War Office during World War II and had nearly 400 huts erected. It was used as the headquarters of a Canadian Army Division before D-Day and then as a prisoner of war camp but Mrs Soames remained in residence.

After the departure of New Zealand troops from Sheffield Park,

Fletching received its first contingent of Canadian troops in October 1941, Le Regiment de la Chaudiere – a French speaking Infantry Division raised in Quebec – and its camp was laid out in Sheffield Park.

An adjacent camp was located from January 1942 at the eastern (Fletching) end of Sheffield Park when the 4th and 105th Anti-Tank Batteries of the 3rd Canadian Anti-Tank Regiment moved in. By April of that year Sheffield Park House had become the Royal Canadian Headquarters with a NAAFI canteen and YMCA recreations room. Le Regiment de la Chaudiere and the 3rd Anti-Tank Regiment were among the first to land on the D-Day Normandy beaches.

A bronze plaque in Fletching Church commemorates the presence of a later Canadian regiment in Sheffield Park and the park itself was machine gunned by enemy aircraft.

Post War

After the war Mrs Soames was faced with many repairs and in 1949 she handed over the property to her nephew, Captain Arthur Granville Soames, OBE, formerly of the Coldstream Guards and a veteran of World War I. In 1947 his eldest son Christopher Soames, also of the Coldstream Guards, married Mary, the youngest daughter of Sir Winston Churchill, and their son Nicholas is currently Member of Parliament for Mid-Sussex.

Captain Soames began the restoration of the garden but was obliged to sell up in 1953 thus ending the family's association with Sheffield Park.

The magnificent garden of 100 acres was purchased by the National Trust in 1954 with the encouragement of the Royal Horticultural Society and bequests, local authority grants and money raised by public appeal. The house was sold to Ashdale Estate Co. but in 1972 it was purchased by Mr and Mrs P.J.Radford and opened to the public. Regrettably, the house has now been divided into apartments and there are no open days. The imposing exterior, however, remains a splendid sight especially if viewed from across the lakes or from the cricket ground. It is very much as it was in Lord Sheffield's time.

Restoration of the Cricket Ground

On acquisition by the National Trust in 1954 the area of the Sheffield Park cricket ground was planted with forest trees and was largely untouched until 1977 when this side of the garden was opened up to visitors with the creation of The Queen's Walk to celebrate her Silver Jubilee.

The planting was devastated by the storms of 1987 and 1990 and so, in its centenary year of 1995 the National Trust decided to restore the cricket ground. Remaining trees were removed with help from forestry students from Plumpton Agricultural College and the money received from the timber was spent on removing tree stumps.

Newspapers and television became aware of the restoration project and on 20 June 1995 the *Mid-Sussex Citizen* reported:

> Will the campaign to save the old Sheffield Park cricket ground near Chailey be successful or will it be stumped? The matter will be considered in one of the programmes in the BBC2 series 'One Foot In The Past' which begins on July 13.
>
> A jumble of trees and long grass is all that remains today of the historic pitch. . .
>
> The programme could have the impact of a 'bouncer' in getting cricket back to Sheffield Park. Now, if they could get the current Prince of Wales involved, even as 12th man . . .

While the restoration project has moved steadily forward enthusiastic local cricketers have kept the memory alive of Lord Sheffield's great cricket matches by staging historic matches at nearby Fletching Cricket Club, complete with commemorative programmes.

These matches were:

9 Sep 1990 Old England v Australian High Commissioner's XI
13 Aug 2006 Old England v Lord Sheffield's XI
20 Jul 2008 Old England v Lord Sheffield's XI

The first of these matches was particularly memorable for the appearances of Colin Cowdrey and Bobby Simpson as rival captains.

The new pavilion on the restored ground at Sheffield Park, May 2009 (J.Hrk)

However, with the restored Sheffield Park ground near to completion future celebratory matches can be played on Lord Sheffield's original ground where Jim Parks's Old England XI will play Lord Sheffield's XI (with assistance from Australia House) on 28 June 2009. The National Trust is to be congratulated on the culmination of one of its most exciting projects.

Observant visitors to the ground can locate the sites of Lord Sheffield's pavilion and the Ladies' pavilion while they admire the newly-built pavilion on the eastern side of the ground. There are moves to acquire some historic articles and negotiations are in progress for the return of a spiral staircase from Forest Row Cricket Club that was originally in one of the Sheffield Park pavilions. Some of Messrs Hawkins' mounted photographs have been preserved in the tower of Fletching Church and it is hoped that they will grace the new pavilion. The great grand-daughter of Lord Sheffield's groundsman has a silk scarf, hat band and a 30 inch silk reel, all in Lord Sheffield's colours of gold, red and purple and they may, too, return to Sheffield Park. Additionally there is an old roller still in service on a farm in Fletching that might one day make a return journey to its original home.

Armadillos Cricket Club
A wandering club, the Armadillos, in search of a home ground, has signed a lease with the National Trust to play at Sheffield Park and considerable sums of money have been invested. The club's brochure states:

It's a tale for the romantics; a wandering cricket team in want of a home, and an illustrious but abandoned ground surrounded by acres of stunning woodland. What the Armadillos have stumbled upon here is an opportunity to create something beautiful, something tranquil; something pure for an impure world.

The founding members of the Armadillos had been regulars at Twickenham and felt the need to play cricket with family and friends. The inaugural fixture was at Ashdown Forest C.C. in August 1983 and from the 22 players appearing on that occasion 12 are still involved with the club which now has 50 to 60 members and actively recruiting. The club's name was chosen when Horsted Keynes C.C. required an entry for its fixture card and Kipling's description of an armadillo was thought to best describe most of the club's members:

Stickly-prickly, slow and steady, low to the ground
Gregarious and with a long tail

In the spring of 2009 after much hard work the old ground at Sheffield Park has reappeared and a new pavilion is being completed. Water has been laid on and the square and outfield are ready for the return of country house cricket. The ground is already an important visitor attraction and there are plans for detailed information panels to be placed by the entrance to the ground to present the glamorous story of Sheffield Park cricket to a new and admiring public.

The celebratory match on 28 June would undoubtedly have met with Lord Sheffield's approval in the centenary year of his death and he will surely be there in spirit when the band plays and the cricket and hospitality begin.

Chronology

1769	John Baker Holroyd (later 1st Lord Sheffield) acquired Sheffield Park
1825	George Holroyd (2nd Lord Sheffield) married Lady Harriet Lascelles
1832	Birth of Henry North Holroyd, Viscount Pevensey (later 3rd Lord Sheffield)
1845	First cricket match at Sheffield Park: Fletching v Chailey
1851-56	Viscount Pevensey served in diplomatic service (Crimea & Copenhagen)
1854	Viscount Pevensey played for Sussex at Lewes in first-class match
1855	New cricket ground constructed at Sheffield Park
1857-68	Viscount Pevensey elected president of Sussex CCC
1857-65	Viscount Pevensey elected MP for East Sussex
1876	Viscount Pevensey became 3rd Lord Sheffield on death of his father
1879-96	Lord Sheffield re-elected president of Sussex CCC
1879	Completion of enlarged and reconstructed cricket ground at Sheffield Park
1881	First first-class match at Sheffield Park: Lord Sheffield's XI v Alfred Shaw's XI
1882	Opening of Sheffield Park railway station. It is now southern point of Bluebell Railway
1884	First visit of Australians to Sheffield Park
1886	First visit of an Indian team to England (Parsees) Their first match was at Sheffield Park

1887-89	Lord Sheffield closes Sheffield Park due to threatening letters
1888	Visit of Maori rugby footballers to Sheffield Park
1891	17 January : Cricket played on ice at Upper Woman's Way Pond, Sheffield Park
1891-92	Lord Sheffield accompanied the England team to Australia
1893	Grand fireworks display at Sheffield Park to honour Australians
1893	Lord Sheffield donated £150 for Sheffield Shield in Australia
1894	First visit of a South African team to England. Their first match was at Sheffield Park
1894	Nottingham Forest FC played Sussex Martlets at football at Sheffield Park
1895	2 February: Second cricket match played on ice
1895	Lord Sheffield adopted Mabel Attenborough as his daughter
1896	11 May: Visit of HRH Prince of Wales to Sheffield Park: 25,000 people present on first day of Lord Sheffield's XI v Australians
1897	George Arlington scored 309 for Sheffield Park v Nutley – the highest score at Sheffield Park
1901	Lord Sheffield refused liquor licences for his matches
1904	Lord Sheffield re-elected president of Sussex CCC
1907	Sheffield Park Cricket Association founded by Lord Sheffield
1909	21 April: Death of Lord Sheffield at Beaulieu, France
1909	4 May: Funeral of Lord Sheffield at Fletching
1910-54	Sheffield Park owned by Soames Family
1954	Sheffield Park Garden acquired by National Trust
2009	28 June: Jim Parks's Old England XI match at Sheffield Park to celebrate restoration of the cricket ground

Appendix A

First Cricket Match at Sheffield Park

The first cricket match to be played at Sheffield Park was that between Fletching and Chailey on 28 August 1845. Viscount Pevensey (later 3rd Lord Sheffield), aged 13 was on holiday from Eton and made his cricketing debut.

FLETCHING

Viscount Pevensey	b. Martin	1	b. Friend	8
J. Comber	b. Oden	6	b. Martin	4
D. Gilbert	b. Oden	4	b. Martin	8
B. Verrall Esq	b. Oden	1	b. Martin	18
E. Blaker Esq	c. Oden	0	b. Oden	0
W. Kenward	c. Wilson	5	c. Peacock	13
A. Hale	b. Oden	5	b. Martin	2
E. Newnham	b. Martin	0	not out	0
J. Gilbert	b. Martin	10	b. Oden	0
J. Leney	b Martin	2	c. Friend	0
H. Awcock	not out	1	c. Friend	2
Byes		1	Byes	5
Wides		1	Wides	7
		37		67

In the second innings Viscount Pevensey batted at number 9.

CHAILEY

T. Oden	run out	7	b. D. Gilbert	15
S. Waters	b. Kenward	20	b. D. Gilbert	0
W. Peacock	c. Verrall	5	b. J. Gilbert	5
G. Norman	b. Kenward	4	b. J. Gilbert	0
H. Wilson	c. Awcock	0	c. Awcock	5
Vincent Esq.	b. Kenward	3	not out	8
Walker Esq.	c. Hale	2		
J. Martin	b. D. Gilbert	5		
R. Hobden	b. D. Gilbert	0		
E. Drawbridge	c. Vinall	0		
G. Friend	not out	0	not out	0
Byes		16	Byes	11
Wides		1	Wides	2
		63	(5 wkts)	46

The poster advertising the match indicates that both teams
included players from Newick.

Appendix B

Lord Sheffield: First-Class Cricketer

Lord Sheffield's biographies invariably omit the fact that he played in one first-class match for Sussex (as Viscount Pevensey) in 1854. The following is the score:

SIXTEEN OF SUSSEX v THE UNITED ENGLAND ELEVEN
Played in the Dripping Pan, Lewes, September 4, 5 and 6, 1854
The United won by eight wickets

SIXTEEN OF SUSSEX

1	W.Eager	run out	4	c Lockyer b Dean	0
2	G.Wells	c Grundy b Wisden	10	run out	1
3	James Challen jun.	b Grundy	7	c Wright b Dean	5
4	G.Picknell	b Grundy	0	c Wisden b Sherman	9
5	E.Napper, Esq	b Wisden	7	b Sherman	2
6	G.G.Brown	lbw b Wisden	15	b Grundy	12
7	H.L.Nicholson, Esq	b Dean	20	b Dean	34
8	J.H.Hale, Esq	c Sherman b Dean	1	c Dean b Wisden	4
9	H.M.Curteis, Esq	b Wisden	0	b Dean	3
10	A.Carpenter	st Lockyer b Wisden	1	b Grundy	14
11	W.Humphry, Esq	run out	5	b Grundy	0
12	W.Napper, Esq	c Wright b Dean	2	not out	6
13	Viscount Pevensey	b Dean	0	c Adams b Dean	0
14	T.A.Raynes, Esq	not out	6	b Dean	0
15	C.J.Hammond	b Dean	0	c Adams b Sherman	8
16	J.Hodson	lbw b Wisden	0	b Grundy	6
	Extras		0	b 1, lb 3	4
			78		108

THE UNITED ENGLAND ELEVEN

#					
1	J.Dean	c Wells b Hodson	14	c Carpenter b W.Napper	2
2	T.M.Adams	b W.Napper	8	c Nicholson b Brown	30
3	J.Grundy	c and b W.Napper	24	not out	17
4	F.P.Miller,Esq	b W.Napper	0		
5	G.H.Wright	b Hodson	9	not out	3
6	T.Lockyer	c E.Napper b Challen	38		
7	J.Wisden	b Hodson	0		
8	W.Mortlock	b Picknell	27		
9	S.Dakin	run out	2		
10	T.Sherman	not out	2		
11	Robert Cheesman	b Challen	0		
	Extras	b 1, lb 3, w 4	8	w 3	3
			132 (2 wkts)		55

THE UNITED ENGLAND ELEVEN BOWLING

	O	M	R	W	O	M	R	W
Grundy	19	6	33	2	24	15	24	4
Wisden	31.2	13	33	6	16	8	20	1
Dean	14	8	12	5	28	10	41	6
Sherman					20	10	19	3

SIXTEEN OF SUSSEX BOWLING

	O	M	R	W	O	M	R	W
Challen	14.2	10	6	2	9	6	7	0
Hodson	41	19	45	3	11	5	12	0
W.Napper	30	11	35	3	16	7	19	1
E.Napper	1	0	3	0				
Wells	2	0	6	0				
Brown	4	0	12	0	2	2	0	1
Carpenter	8	4	7	0	7	4	9	0
Picknell	14	8	10	1	4	1	5	0

Appendix C

Lord Sheffield's Eleven First-Class Matches

v	A.Shaw's XI	Sheffield Park	25-27	Aug	1881
v	W. G. Grace's XI	Sheffield Park	5-7	Jul	1883
v	Australians	Sheffield Park	12-13	May	1884
v	A.Shaw's Australian Team	Sheffield Park	21-23	May	1885
v	Australians	Sheffield Park	13-15	May	1886
v	Australians	Sheffield Park	8-10	May	1890
v	MCC	Sheffield Park	25-26	May	1891
v	South Australia	Adelaide	20-23	Nov	1891
v	Victoria	Melbourne	27-28	Nov	1891
v	New South Wales	Sydney	4-7	Dec	1891
v	AUSTRALIA (1st Test)	Melbourne	1-6	Jan	1892
v	AUSTRALIA (2nd Test)	Sydney	Jan 29-3	Feb	1892
v	New South Wales	Sydney	19-23	Feb	1892
v	Victoria	Melbourne	17-19	Mar	1892
v	AUSTRALIA (3rd Test)	Adelaide	24-28	Mar	1892
v	Rest of England	Nottingham	16-18	May	1892
v	Australians	Sheffield Park	8-10	May	1893
v	Australians	Sheffield Park	11-13	May	1896

The only first-class match in England not to be played at Sheffield Park was that at Trent Bridge, Nottingham against Rest of England on 16-18 May 1892. The match was played shortly after the team's return from Australia for Alfred Shaw's benefit but it was ruined by rain. The following is the score:

Lord Sheffield's Eleven , Rest Of England
Played On The Trent Bridge Ground, Nottingham. May 16, 17 and 18. 1892.
Match Drawn

Lord Sheffield's Eleven

1	*Dr W. G. Grace	c Sherwin b Hearne	2	b. Flowers	63
2	R.Abel	c Dixon b Ferris	10	c Martin b Ferris	17
3	JM Read	c Martin b Hearne	4	not out	14
4	Mr A.E.Stoddart	b Hearne	0	not out	21
5	R Peel	c Flowers b Martin	35		
6	G.A Lohmann	b Martin	11		
7	G.Bean	c O'Brien b Flowers	18		
8	J.Briggs	b Flowers	0		
9	Mr G.MacGregor	b Martin	4		
10	W.Attewell	b Martin	3		
11	J.W.Sharpe	not out	1		
	Extras	byes	1	no balls	2
	Total		89	(2 wickets)	117

Rest Of England

1	A.Shrewsbury	c Bean b Briggs	2
2	W.Chatterton	b Briggs	48
3	W.Gunn	c Attewell b Peel	37
4	Mr T.C.O'Brien	b Attewell	6
5	Mr J.A.Dixon	c Grace b Attewell	69
6	*Mr F Marchant	c Abel b Lohmann	5
7	W.Flowers	not out	30
8	Mr J.J.Ferris	b Attewell	3
9	J.T.Hearne	c Read b Briggs	6
10	F.Martin		
11	M Sherwin		
	Extras		8
	Total	(for 8 wkts dec)	214

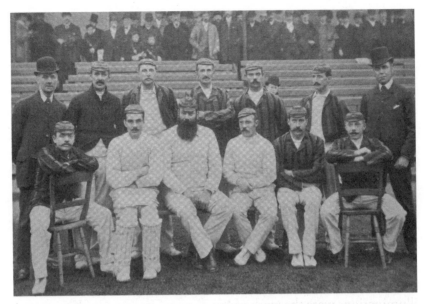

Lord Sheffield's XI at Trent Bridge shortly after returning from Australia, May 1892. Back row: R.Carpenter (Umpire), W. Attewell, G. Lohmann, J. M. Read, G. Bean, J. Sharpe, R. Thoms (Umpire). Seated J. Briggs, G. MacGregor, W. G. Grace, R. Peel, A. E. Stoddart, R. Abel (N. J. G. Sharp)

Rest of England Bowling

	O	M	R	W	O	M	R	W
Ferris	22	10	32	1	14	5	26	1
Hearne	31	13	29	3	16	4	48	0
Martin	17	7	14	4	9	3	29	0
Flowers	7	2	13	2	7	5	11	1
Chatterton					1	0	1	0

Lord Sheffield's Eleven Bowling

Lohmann	44	26	55	1
Briggs	44.1	19	55	3
Sharpe	9	3	17	0
Attewell	33	18	40	3
Peel	13	3	39	1

Umpires: R Thoms and R. Carpenter.

Appendix D

Welcome Home Illuminated Address

On 4 June, 1892 there was a special day (and cricket match) at Sheffield Park to celebrate Lord Sheffield's return from Australia. Two illuminated addresses were read and presented to Lord Sheffield from the tenants and the Fletching parishioners. During the afternoon the addresses were hung in the luncheon pavilion where they were inspected and admired by hundreds. Both the illuminations were the work of Mr Tanner Trangmar of Kensington Place, Brighton who was congratulated upon his success.

(a) Tenants

The address of the tenants was surmounted by Lord Sheffield's crest, surrounded by pansies and forget-me-nots – his favourite flowers. At each top corner were ploughs and other agricultural instruments and at the bottom were reaping hooks, prongs and harvest tools, while on each side in the centre of the border were crossed scythes etc. The whole was bordered by the colours of Lord Sheffield's eleven when they went to France about two years previously and appended to the address were the names of 40 tenants. The address was mounted on terra cotta plush and the whole enclosed in a frame of white and gold.

(b) Parishioners

The address from the parishioners of Fletching, other friends and neighbours and local cricket clubs was more elaborate and was written on vellum. In the centre of the top was an earl's coronet entwined with the letter S, surrounded with a cluster of forget-me-nots and pansies. On the left side were the arms of the noble earl in heraldic colours and on the right the arms of Australia with the motto 'Advance Australia'. In the middle of the left border was a small Australian scene. Opposite was an English water scene of similar size with a swan, and surrounding both these scenes were trophies of cricket stumps, crossed bats and wicket-keeper's gloves, surrounded by laurel leaves. At the bottom were displayed indiscriminately bats, balls, cricket bags, stumps, pads and other cricket accessories, and in the centre were the arms of Sussex with oak leaves and a ribbon underneath bearing the words 'Sussex Cricket.' Appended were about 300 names and the whole was surrounded by a border of violet, orange and crimson – Lord Sheffield's colours for the Australian tour. The address was mounted on a grey plush and enclosed in a gold frame.

Appendix E

SUSSEX CCC BAZAAR

CLARENCE ROOMS HOTEL METROPOLE BRIGHTON

4 – 6 DECEMBER 1894

ARTICLES FOR SALE

AND EXHIBITION ONLY

AT LORD SHEFFIELD'S STALL

CATALOGUE.
ARTICLES FOR SALE
Contributed BY
LORD SHEFFIELD.

1 POLAR BEAR SKIN from Tromsö.

1 BOTTLE OF WATER FROM THE JORDAN, from the spot where the Baptism took place (brought by LORD SHEFFIELD).

MUMMIED WHEAT, 4,000 years old (brought by LORD SHEFFIELD from Thebes).

2 EGYPTIAN WALL HANGINGS, with Arabic inscriptions, from Cairo.

1 LADIES' EGYPTIAN EMBROIDERED JACKET from Cairo.

1 HORSE'S HEAD GEAR (Dervishes') from the field of battle of Sarras, 1892.

1 DERVISH SPEAR-HEAD from battle of Toski, 1889.

2 CARVINGS in Mother of Pearl, from Bethlehem.

PIECES OF WOOD FROM THE VIRGIN'S TREE near; Heliopolis, under which the Holy Family rested in their flight.

IVORY CHURCH CARVED OUT OF A SINGLE WALRUS TUSK, from Bergen.

1 WHALEBONE CANE, from Tromsö.

EIDEEDUCK and EGG and NEST, from Tromsö.

4 CIGAR ASH TRAYS, from Cairo.

1 OIL PAINTING OF FIREWORKS.

PHOTOGRAPHS : —
    Golgotha (Jerusalem), Gordon's Site of the Crucifixion.
    1 Cricket Match between Australia and Lord Sheffield's Team at Sydney, 1891.
    A Camel Race at Assouan in Nubia.
    Inniskilling Dragoons Cheering LORD SHEFFIELD at Volunteer Beview, 1892.

Sheffield Park—The House.
    „   „ Cricket Ground.
Australian Matches in Sheffield Park, 1884, 1886, 1890, 1898.
Fireworks in the Park at Australian Match, 1898.
Large Photos of Volunteer Reviews at Sheffield Park.
BISHEREENS (Small and Large Photos).
Small Photos of Volunteer Reviews.
Large Photo of Pond and Cricket Ground from Upper Cascade.
Photos of the Cascades.
Photos of Alfred Shaw.
Photos of Alfred Shaw and A. Byford on Donkeys at Cairo.
Photos of Sussex Team of 1894.
Photos of Lord Sheffield's Team and the South Australian Team, taken in the Botanical Gardens at Adelaide, Australia, 1891.
LORD SHEFFIELD's Dahabeah on the Nile.
Royal Artillery Encamped in the Park.
Volunteers at the Park.
The "Isis" Dahabeah.
Photos of Two Mummies brought by LORD SHEFFIELD from Thebes, 1882.
Photos of Grace and Murdoch (taken together).
Photographed Fac-similes of Autographs of the Principal Personages in the Great War with Napoleon, with photographed fac-simile of Napoleon's Autograph. A Key to the Autographs with each copy.

ARTICLES
FOR EXHIBITION ONLY
BY
LORD SHEFFIELD.

PHOTOGRAPH OF TROPHY PRESENTED BY LORD SHEFFIELD for
  Competition between the Australian Colonies. The Photo
  was presented to Lord Sheffield by the Australasian Cricket
  Council.

A MINIATURE OF THE "EYE" OF THE PRINCESS CHARLOTTE OF
  WALES (married to PRINCE LEOPOLD), given by her to
  LADY GLENBERRIE.

AN AUTHORITY FROM PRINCE CHARLES (Son of CHARLES I.)
  to some person (name not stated) to raise a Regiment in
  Sussex in 1649.

BALL USED BY ALFRED SHAW TO BOWL OUT LORD SHEFFIELD
  AND HIS PARTY AT SPITSBERGEN at Midnight, under the
  Midnight Sun, August 12th, in Latitude 78.50.

CAPTAIN PARRY'S JOURNAL, with Pictures of Cricket
Match in Arctic Regions in 1821.

2 REINDEER HEADS, killed by COLONEL BROOKE and COLONEL
  WHITING, in Spitsbergen, August 18th, 1894.

2 POLAR BEAR SKINS.

RUSSIAN MUSKET, brought by LORD SHEFFIELD from the
  Redan at Sebastopoi.

1 MAHDI FLAG from Battle of Sarras, 1892.

PIECE of THE OBELISK OF "ON" (or HEUOPOLIS), which was of
  great antiquity when Moses was at school there.

1 EIDERDOWN RUG, made from 104 Ducks, from Tromso.

1 WOLF SKIN.

A RUG MADE OF 18 REINDEER SKINS.

1 ESQUIMAUX DRESS, Tromso.

W. G. GRACE'S BAT.

BALLS USED BY LORD SHEFFIELD'S TEAM AT MALTA,
  COLOMBO, AND IN AUSTRALIA, 1891-92.

1 LARGE PHOTO OF THE MATCH BETWEEN AUSTRALIA AND
  LORD SHEFFIELD'S TEAM AT SYDNEY, 1891.

1 PHOTO OF HOBART CRICKET GROUND (TASMANIA).
  THE "IBIS" DAHABEAH.

2 CARVINGS IN MOTHER OF PEARL, from Bethlehem.

PRESENT FROM MR. IRONSIDES TO LORD SHEFFIELD, to
  commemorate his Visit to Australia, 1891-2,

BAT OF MR. SLATER (Sussex Wicket Keeper), lent by his
  Grandson.

Appendix F

Poems In The Park

Albert Craig ('The Cricket Rhymester') and the poets of *Punch* were attracted to the cricket matches at Sheffield Park.

In Sheffield Park
MONDAY, MAY 8, 1893.
First Match of the Australian Cricketers against
Lord Sheffield's English Eleven.

In Sheffield Park, in budding May!
True English scene, true cricket day,
A generous host, and glorious play!
      A date to mark!
A well-fought match, the Cornstalks' first!
A summer sun, a noble thirst!
The Season's on us with a burst,
        In Sheffield Park!

The wondrous veteran W.G.,
At forty-five scores sixty-three!
(At sixty-three GRACE may we see
Score forty-five!)
Pleasant once more to have a peep
At those sharp eyes that never sleep,
Those bear's-paws that know how to keep
        The game alive!
Safe SHREWSBURY and giant GUNN,
"At it once more ! Oh Lords, what fun

To see them drive, and cut, and run!
  A May-day lark
For elderly and paunchy lads!
Ah, Time his annual inches adds.
We cannot buckle on the pads
  In Sheffield Park!

Yet genuine pleasure still 'twill yield
To sit and watch, with noses peeled,
CONINGHAM smite and GREGORY field.
  How's that, Sir ! Hark!
Thanks to GRACE, SHREWSBURY and GUNN,
LOCKWOOD and BRIGGS—what glorious fun ! —
The first big match we've neatly won
  In Sheffield Park!

Now for a wet after our roast!
Lords no, there is no call to boast!
But in Lord SHEFFIELD *what* a host
  Cricketers mark!
Who will forget that lovely day,
'Midst lovely scenery in mid-May,
Who had the luck to watch the play
  In Sheffield Park!

From Punch 20 May 1893

SHEFFIELD PARK.
PUNCH TO THE NEW AUSTRALIAN
ELEVEN.

Nine good bowlers and ten good bats,
Eleven fielders all active as cats,
Game everyone to catch anything catchable,
Two wicket-keepers both simply unmatchable
That is a team that should give us some trouble
And keep all our cricketing cracks at the double
Our home willow-wielders must play up like bricks
To collar that bowling, to tumble those sticks.
Well, welcome, boys anyhow ! You'll pull together.
Here's wishing you fortune, fair field, and fine weather.
We're looking for many a score-piling day.
And win, lose, or tie, not one wrangle I Hooray:– *Punch*

Earl Sheffield's hearty welcome
To the Australian XI, 1896.

To one of Nature's noblemen,
    We owe this kind reception ;
To "Cricket's" best and warmest friend
    The best without exception.
His Lordship's name and deathless fame
    All cricketers revere,
He gives all patrons of the game
    A cordial welcome here.
The annals of sport unmistakeably tell us,
The noble Colonials are brave-hearted fellows;
Made, like ouriads of the stuff we delight in,
If they die, they die hard, and like Britons – die
fighting.   A.C

ENGLAND v. AUSTRALIA.

At Lord Sheffied's Picturesque County Seat.

His Lordship, with his usual unbounded generosity, grants
Free Admission to the General Public.
MONDAY, MAY 8th, 1893.

The Opening Struggle.

MANY young friends, many elders
    Mingle in this happy throng,
Firm admirers of our Pastime
    Gather in their thousands strong.
Let us hope this opening struggle
    Will so entertain and please.
That you'll live to talk it over
    When you're seated at your ease.
Gains are intermix'd with losses,
    But ths bitter makes the sweet.
Stony roads make common carpets
    Seem like velvet to the feet.
If the lads of merrie England
    Fail to beat their friendly foe,
They will, like all true born Britons,
    Yearn to have another go.
There s a mighty work before you,
    Keen supporters urge you on,
May it grace the paje of hist'ry
    When the year has waned and gone.
Heroes of our dear old country
    Put your shoulders to the wheel
Make one grand united effort
    Victory will reward your zeal.
May old Father Time prove a jolly good sort,
By sparing all friends of our national sport,
May he prove a generous and kindly old man
By sparing our players as long as he can, A.C.

Appendix G

Largest Scores made at Sheffield Park
during Sixty Years of Cricket.

Score		For	Against	Date
665	(5 w)	Sheffield Park	Mr. Ellis's XI.	1884
580		Sheffield Park	Birchgrove	1885
536		Sheffield Park	Brighton Rangers	1884
544	(8 w)	Sheffield Park	Preston Stragglers	1896
530	(6 w)	Sheffield Park	Hove Goldstone	1893
524		Sheffield Park	Nutley	1897
519		Sheffield Park	Isfield	1894
513	(5 w)	Sheffield Park	Brighton Stanford	1884
495	(5 w)	Sheffield Park	Brighton Stanford	1882
491		Sheffield Park	Brighton Teachers	1883
473	(7 w)	Sheffield Park	Newick	1880
452	(6w)	Sheffield Park	Brighton St Mary's	1906
439		Sheffield Park	Brighton Clifton	1893
426		Sheffield Park	Brighton Teachers	1881
423		Sheffield Park	Preston Stragglers	1895
405	(2 w)	Sheffield Park	Framfield	1896

Centuries scored at Sheffield Park

These statistics have been collated from *Lillywhite's Companion, Lillywhite's Annual, Cricket, Sussex Cricket Annual* and the local newspapers and are not claimed to be comprehensive.

1877	G.H.Lynn	v	Brighton College	114*
	W.Francis	for	East Grinstead	122
	L.Jeffery	for	Southdown	124
1879	G.H.Lynn	v	Smithfield Rovers	129
	W.H.Millard	v	East Grinstead	124
1880	G.L.King	for	Rev. Greenfield's XI	102
	W.H.Millard	v	Brighton & District Teachers	102
	A.Payne	v	Brighton & District Teachers	156
	W.Tester	v	Brighton & District Teachers	146
1881	Rev. F.F.J.Greenfield	v	Cuckfield	154
	A.Payne	v	Brighton & District Teachers	141
1882	W.Tester	v	Stanford (Brighton)	255*
	W.A.Bettesworth	for	Ardingly College	100*
	J.Gilbert	v	Chailey	115
	J.Gilbert Lightweights	v	Heavyweights	165
	F.Turner Lightweights	v	Heavyweights	140
	H.Phillips	v	Alfred Shaw's XI	135
	T.Rogers	v	Brighton Working Men	122*
	W.Scotton	v	Alfred Shaw's XI	102
1883	A.Huggett	v	Stanford (Brighton)	159
	W.Payne	v	Mr Cornish's XI	125
	W.Payne	v	Uckfield	05
	W.Tester	v	Stanford (Brighton)	182
	W.Tester	v	Brighton Brunswick	118*
1884	Maynard	v	Ashdown Forest	137
	W.Humphreys	v	East Grinstead	103
	W.Humphreys	v	R.T. Ellis's XI	156
	A.Huggett	v	Brighton Rangers FC	155
	A.Huggett	v	R.T. Ellis's XI	124*
	J.Bean	v	Brighton & District Teachers	127
	J.Gilbert	v	Newick	250*

	R.T.Ellis	v	Brighton Rangers FC	105
	P.Higham-Hodge	v	Ashdown Forest	106*
	A.Payne	v	L. Weedon's XI	121*
	A.Payne	v	Brighton Rangers FC	108
	A.Payne	v	R.T. Ellis's XI	176
	W.Tester	v	East Grinstead	105
1885	W.Humphreys	v	Birchgrove	239*
	Rev. F. F. J.Greenfield	v	Birchgrove	112
1886	E.J.Golding	v	Hurstpierpoint College	118
	E.J.Golding for Rev			
	Greenfield's XI	v	Lord Sheffield's XI	109
	W. Knowles for			
	Lord Sheffield's XI	v	Mr Courthope's XI	135
	A. Payne	v	Brighton & District Teachers	133
	W.Payne	v	St Wilfrid's, Haywards Heath	108*
	W.Payne	v	Brighton Railway Traffic	112*
	W.Payne	v	Hastings Alexandra	103*
	W.Payne	v	St Peter's, Brighton	119
1887	F.Solbe for E.Solbe's XI	v	Lord Sheffield's XI	186
1889	J. Charlwood	v	Rev. Greenfield's XI	102
	F.W Marlow	for	H. Phillips' XI	157

Lord Sheffield presented Marlow with an inscribed bat for the above innings. It was sold by Sussex CCC in 1980 for £18.

1890	F.W.Marlow	v	Alfred Shaw's XI	100*
	F.W.Marlow	v	St Mary's, Brighton	122
	E.J.Golding	v	Preston Stragglers	100*
1891	A.Payne	v	Barcombe	285
	A.Payne	v	Horsted Keynes	100
	A.Payne	v	Ringmer	104*
	J.Charlwood	v	Brighton Greyhounds	114
1892	S.Hollands	v	Brighton Teachers	100*
	W.L.Murdoch	v	Mr Hope's XI	117*
	W.L.Murdoch	v	W.Clement's XI	159*
	A. Payne	v	Brighton Greyhounds	168*
1893	H.Budgen	v	Preston Stragglers	131*
	A.Blackman	v	Preston Stragglers	102
	B.Brooks	for	St Peter's, Brighton	107*
	J.A.Charlwood	v	Goldstone	122*

	A.Blackman	for	Brighton Teachers	149
	S.Hollands	v	Brighton Teachers	109
	J.Meaden	for	St Peter's, Brighton	103
	A.F.Somerset	v	Barcombe	174
	F.Worger	v	Goldstone	170
	F.Worger	v	Brighton Clifton	110
	J.Charlwood	v	Brighton Clifton	129
	J.Bean	v	Brighton St Nicholas	134*
	F.W.Marlow	for	Brighton Greyhounds	105*
	C.F.Butcher	v	Brighton Onward	126*
1894	C.F.Butcher	v	Barcombe	162
	A.Blackman	v	Isfield	213
1895	F.Worger	v	Newick	116*
	C.Coleman	v	Framfield	108*
	A.J.Jordan	v	Royal Irish Rifles	160
	G.H.Arlington	v	Preston Stragglers	255
	G.H.Arlington	v	Rye	139
1896	G.H.Arlington	v	Hastings	154*
	G.H.Arlington	v	Framfield	207*
	G.H.Arlington	v	Preston Stragglers	230*
1897	G.H.Arlington	v	Nutley	309
1899	E.Bailey	v	Newhaven	100*
1904	A.Blackman	v	Horsted Keynes	104
	P.Cartwright	v	Nutley	149
	P.Cartwright	v	St Mary's, Brighton	107
1905	P.Cartwright	v	?	149
	L.V.Donne for			
	Lord Sheffield's XI	v	B.B.de la Bere's XI	137
	S.Herbert for			
	Brighton Clifton	v	Lord Sheffield's XI	126
	J.E.Smith	v	?	38
1906	W.L.Berry for			
	Lord Sheffield's XI	v	Brighton St Mary's	110
	P.Cartwright for			
	Lord Sheffield's XI	v	Brighton St Mary's	107
	J.W.Fuller for			
	Lord Sheffield's XI1	v	Brighton StMary's	102*
1907	J.Dare	for	Maresfield	108

Appendix H

Photographs In The Park

The teams playing in the inaugural first-class match at Sheffield Park in 1881 were Lord Sheffield's XI and Alfred Shaw's XI and they were photographed by the Brighton photographers Hennah and Kent: Thomas Hennah had photographed the England cricketers on board the *Nova Scotia* in 1859.

Team photographs became an important part of Lord Sheffield's match days and when Hennah and Kent were taken over by Messrs. Hawkins, also of Brighton, the practice continued. After the 1881 match Lord Sheffield's ornate pavilion provided the background to the photographs which are today sought after by collectors.

In 2008 Nicholas Sharp conducted a survey of some leading cricket collectors and established the existence of a photograph for every team playing in a first-class match at Sheffield Park (1881-96) with the exception of the 1883 and 1885 teams and the MCC team of 1891. The existence of elusive team photographs for 1885 is confirmed by the following from *Cricket* 1885 p155:

> Messrs. Hawkins & Co., Kings Road, Brighton took photographs of Shaw's Australian Team and Lord Sheffield's Eleven during the course of the match at Sheffield Park last week.

Additionally there are team photographs of the Parsees (1886) and South Africans (1894), their opponents (Lord Sheffield's XI), the Maori and Middlesex rugby teams (1888) and the Nottingham Forest and Sussex Martlets Football teams (1894), although a copy of the Forest team has not been located. Hawkins also took photographs of minor cricket teams, cricket on the ice, skaters, children, volunteer meetings, the cascades and other events at Sheffield Park.

In 1884 Hawkins published a photograph of 'The Australians in the Field' taken from the top balcony of Lord Sheffield's pavilion and this is almost certainly the view included in Alfred Shaw's autobiography. There is a similar Hawkins view in *Cricket of To-Day* by Percy Cross Standing.

Posterity owes much to E. Hawkins & Co. especially for the panoramic view of a crowded Sheffield Park on match day and the iconic image of W. G. Grace and W. L. Murdoch by his Lordship's steps in 1890.

Bibliography

'A Sussex Peer', *Drifting Towards The Breakers!* (private) 1895

Argus (Brighton)

Batchelder, Alf., *Pavilions In The Park* – A *History of the Melbourne Cricket Club and Its Ground*, Australian Scholarly Publishing, 2005

Butcher, Michael, *Paraffin Lights* – *Water from the Well*, Knowles, 2000

Chambers, G.F., *Old Memories of Eastbourne*

Cricket: A Weekly Record of the Game

Cricket Field 1892-95

Danehill Parish Historical Society Magazine

Eastbourne Chronicle

East Sussex News

Gaston A.J., – extract from '*Cricket & Cricketers*' by Leather Hunter in *The Argus* 16.7.1906

Golding, E.J. (E.J.G. and W.M.), *A Trip in the Earl of Sheffield's Yacht* 'Heloise' (private) 1889

Harte, Chris., The History of the Sheffield Shield, Allen & Unwin, London 1987

Illustrated London News 1853

Lillywhite's Cricketers' Annual 1872-1900

Lillywhite's Cricketers' Companion 1865-85

Luckin, M.W., *The History of South African Cricket*, Hortor, 1915

Marx, Klaus, *An Illustrated History of the Lewes & East Grinstead Railway*, Oxford Publishing, 2000

Pullin, A.W., *Alfred Shaw Cricketer*, Cassell, 1902

Sheffield Park Garden, National Trust, 2004

Smith, Rick and Ron Williams, *W. G. Down Under*, Apple Books, 1994

Sussex Agricultural Express

Sussex County Cricket Club Minute Books 1880-86, 1886-90, 1890-96 (unpublished)

Sussex County Magazine, 1927

Sussex Cricket Annual, 1901-09

Sussex Daily News

Turk, Tony, *A Victorian Diary of Newick, Sussex* 1875-99 (private), 1999

Westcott, Chris., *The History of Cricket at the Saffrons, Eastbourne*, Omnipress, 2000

Williams, Marcus and Gordon Phillips, *Wisden Book of Cricket Memorabilia*, Lennard, 1990